VISUAL MUSIC
INSTRUMENT PATENTS

VISUAL MUSIC
INSTRUMENT PATENTS

VOLUME ONE: 1876 to 1950

edited by Michael Betancourt

Borgo Press

Copyright © 2004 by Michael Betancourt, all rights reserved.

Volume Two is available in a matching edition.

Borgo Press
an academic press
part of Wildside Press
www.wildsidepress.com

CONTENTS

Foreword 7

Bainbridge Bishop 9
Alexander Wallace Rimington. 13
James M. Loring. 27
Charles F. Wilcox 33
Henry Fitch Taylor 47
Alexander Burnett Hector 57
Mary Hallock-Greenewalt 91
Maude Maple Miles. 107
Arthur C. Vinageras. 113
Hazel H. Adler. 123
Alexander E. O. Munsell 131
Wilhelm Schmeer 137
Thomas Wilfred 141
Richard M. Craig. 167
Clinton W. Hough. 173
Ernest Nanfeldt 195
Cecil Stokes. 203
Oskar Fischinger. 209

Patent Number Chronology 213

FOREWORD

Visual Music, Color Music, Lumia, whatever name is used to describe this particular art of colored light (often accompanied by music), is defined by the technology that allows its existence. Many, if not most of the instruments that have been built for its performance, no longer exist; their only enduring records of them is their patent applications.

The fate that these instruments have suffered, to be lost to time except for the continued existence of the instructions for their creation, may be the fate of any art form so technologically dependent as the color organ. This may become an issue for motion pictures on film as digital technologies and video projection systems replace the mechanical technology that dominated moving image art in the twentieth century.

These documents are arranged by inventor and sequenced chronologically starting with the earliest available patent in the United States collection, Bainbridge Bishop's 1876 patent on a device meant to be added to an existing organ, which allows the simultaneous performance of music and "color music." The final patent in this volume is Oskar Fischinger's 1950 patent on a device for giving colored light performances. The period in between Bishop and Fischinger contains the work of sixteen other inventors, some of whom (like Munsell) are better known for work in other fields.

All these patents are primary documents of both the invention itself and the inventor's aesthetic system linking color and music. Because these machines are hardware, the specific configuration and design provides insight into both the kinds of visual music each instrument was capable of producing, and into some of the particular combinations of musical scale, illumination, and color each invention was created to present to an audience.

Of particular interest in this last regard are the various notation systems that accompany some of these designs, or that stand as works in themselves. Each system makes assumptions about what should be played, how to play it, and how the musical scale can be connected to the visible spectrum.

Since they are written in the unambiguous language of engineering instead of the poetic ambiguity of literature or rhetoric, the explanations provide a brief, but unwaveringly specific explanation of how the instruments work and how each device is unique. These designs describe the range of possibilities for making visual music: from the virtuoso performance to the automated device, all the contemporary approaches are already in evidence.

Michael Betancourt

BAINBRIDGE BISHOP

The Color Organ (1876)

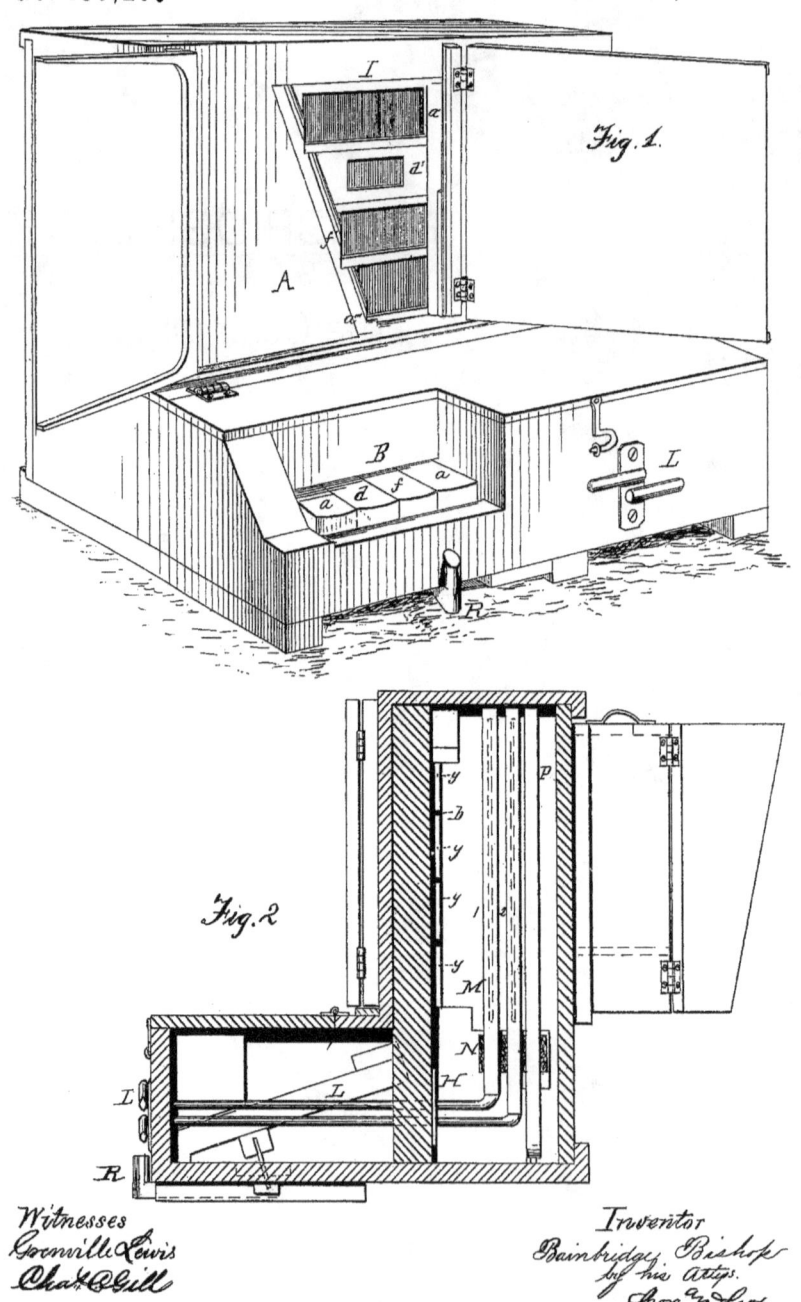

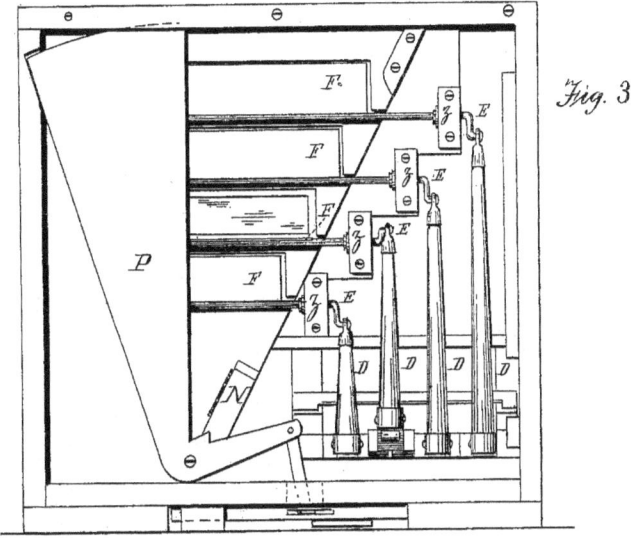

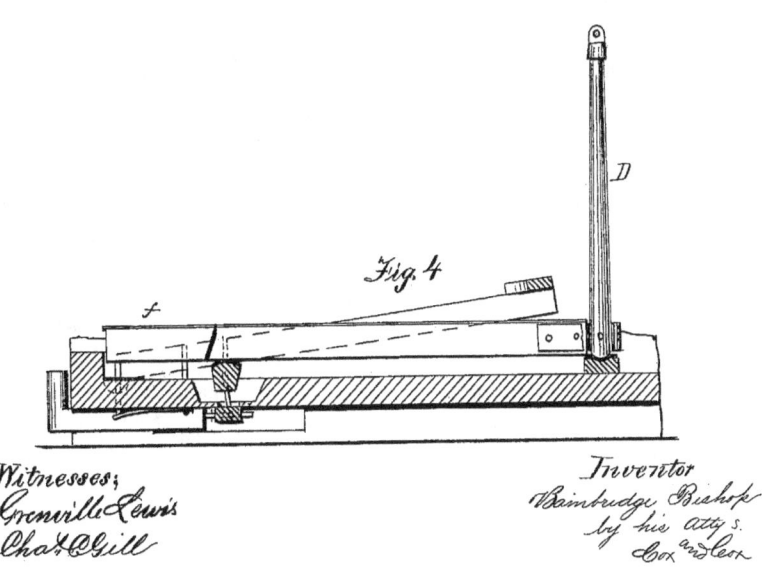

UNITED STATES PATENT OFFICE.

BAINBRIDGE BISHOP, OF NEW RUSSIA, NEW YORK.

IMPROVEMENT IN ATTACHMENTS FOR KEY-BOARD MUSICAL INSTRUMENTS.

Specification forming part of Letters Patent No. **186,298**, dated January 16, 1877; application filed June 7, 1876.

To all whom it may concern:

Be it known that I, BAINBRIDGE BISHOP, of New Russia, in the county of Essex and State of New York, have invented a new and useful Improvement in Instruments for Displaying Color, of which the following is a specification, reference being had to the accompanying drawings.

The invention relates to the art of typifying musical sounds by the display of colors, and, in the present instance, is exhibited in the device formed of elements hereinafter described.

It is well known that there are seven cardinal colors in the prism or spectrum, and also that there are seven cardinal sounds in the musical scale. Thus, the colors of the spectrum are as follows, in the order stated, to wit: violet, indigo, blue, green, yellow, orange, and red, while the sounds of the musical scale are as follows, in the order stated: do, re, mi, fa, sol, la, si, or, according to the literal scale, c, d, e, f, g, a, b. It is, therefore, clear that each cardinal note or sound may be represented by a color in the natural key in the order of colors shown in the spectrum; also, the sharp or flat of a note can be typified by blending the color it represents with, respectively, the next color on each side. Thus, if the natural note be represented by green, the sharp would be indicated by blue-green—the color produced by blending green, the typical color, with blue, the next color above; and the flat would be indicated by yellow-green—the color produced by blending green, the typical color, with yellow, the next color below.

Octaves may be indicated by deepening the tone of the color in the descending scale. Thus, the higher note being, for instance, represented by orange, the octave below would be a deeper orange.

I have discovered, and it is part of this invention, that the object I seek to attain will be very fully effected by adapting the colors to the key or scale of A minor, so that the different tones and semitones will be represented as follows: A, indigo; B, violet-red; C, red; D, orange; E, yellow; F-sharp, green; G-sharp, blue; A, indigo; B, violet-red; C, red.

Semitones: A, indigo; A-sharp, violet; B, violet-red; C, red; C-sharp, orange-red; D, orange; D-sharp, orange-yellow; E, yellow; F, yellow-green; F-sharp, green; G, green-blue; G-sharp, blue; A, indigo; A-sharp, violet; B, violet-red; C, red.

It is plain that the key of A minor is not the only one which permits of the adaptation described. Thus, the scale of color may be transposed and adapted to the key of C major and other keys, or the colors otherwise adapted so that the cardinal and modified colors will correspond with the tones and semitones, as specified, and the same intervals and order of arrangement be preserved.

The device in which the invention has been embodied is illustrated in the accompanying drawings, which represent, respectively, in Figure 1, a perspective view of a device embodying the elements of the invention; in Fig. 2, a sectional view of same, and in Fig. 3 a rear view of same with one of the screens F lowered. Fig. 4 is a sectional view, showing one of the keys and its connection with the pitman-rod.

In the accompanying drawings, A represents the case of a melodeon or organ, it being obvious, however, that the invention can be applied to a piano-forte or other analogous instrument. The front of the case, upon one side, is provided with the bank of keys B, representing the notes or letters a, d, f, a, of the musical scale, and so lettered, which extend rearward, and have attached at their inner extremities the lower ends of the pitman-rods D, extending upward, and having their upper ends pivoted upon the outer ends of the crank-shafts E, which are of graduated lengths, as desired, and extend through the block z, in which one side is journaled, the other end working in a bearing in the cleat b. To these crank-shafts E are rigidly secured the lower edges of the blinds F, which, with the adjacent parts of the shafts, fit snugly in the recesses y, provided for them in the partition H, which, directly opposite the blinds F, is provided with a series of panes, I, of stained glass of the various desired colors, and, in the present instance, lettered a', d', f', a'''. Thus, suppose the colors of the panes I shown in the present instance represent $a\ d\ f\ a$, the keys B being connected in any suitable manner with the reeds of an organ, when one of the keys is struck—for instance, *f*—the pitman-rod D is forced up, rotating the crank-shaft E, opening the corresponding blind, and thus, if a strong light be placed at the rear of the device, an indigo light, indicating *f*, is at once shown at the same time the reed of the key *f* speaks.

The arrangement of the colored panes is merely a matter of mechanical construction. Thus, panes of glass of the colors blue-green, representing *d*-sharp, and yellow-green, representing *d*-flat, could be readily inserted in proximity to the pane representing green, and operated by keys placed in the manner usual in piano key-boards.

Upon one side of the case A, in proper relation to the key-board, are provided the stops L, connected with the stop mechanism of the organ, and having their shafts extending through the case, and working in bearings in the front part thereof and the partition H, in the rear of which they are attached to the base of the triangular translucent screens M, of such dimensions that, when operated, they will shut off the light from the panes I.

Opposite the base of the screens is provided the inclined bumper N, to receive the screens when operated, and hold them in position. In the present instance these screens are colored yellow and red, and are numbered, respectively, 1 and 2, and represent, respectively, the key-notes, to wit, *c* and *a*. Thus, when the performer is playing in the key of *c* or *a*, the yellow screen 1, or the red screen 2, is respectively operated.

In a full-sized instrument there should be twelve of these screens, each of the color indicative of the key in which the performer is playing. The stops for operating the screens may readily be arranged in a manner analogous to that shown of the stops L.

In the rear of the screens is placed another screen, P, of semi-opaque material, and similar in shape to the screens M. This screen P is operated by means of any suitable attachment to the lever R, which works the swell of the organ, and thus the volume of light may be instantly increased with the increase of the volume of sound by simply moving the pedal.

It is obvious that the device may be used in conjunction with an organ, or any other instrument having a key-board, or it may be wholly detached therefrom, and provided with an independent series of keys.

In practice, the instrument is placed before a strong natural light, either direct or deflected, and the colors may be shown upon screens or other suitable surfaces.

What I claim as my invention, and desire to secure by Letters Patent, is—

1. The combination, with a musical instrument, of a device arranged to exhibit a series of colors corresponding with the notes played, substantially as specified.

2. An instrument having a series of movable colored plates combined with apparatus for producing musical sounds, and provided with a movable colored screen or screens, as set forth.

In testimony that I claim the foregoing improvement in instruments for displaying color, as above described, I have hereunto set my hand this 22d day of April, 1876.

BAINBRIDGE BISHOP.

Witnesses:
  BYRON POND,
  ALMON PORT.

ALEXANDER WALLACE RIMINGTON

The Color Organ (1894)

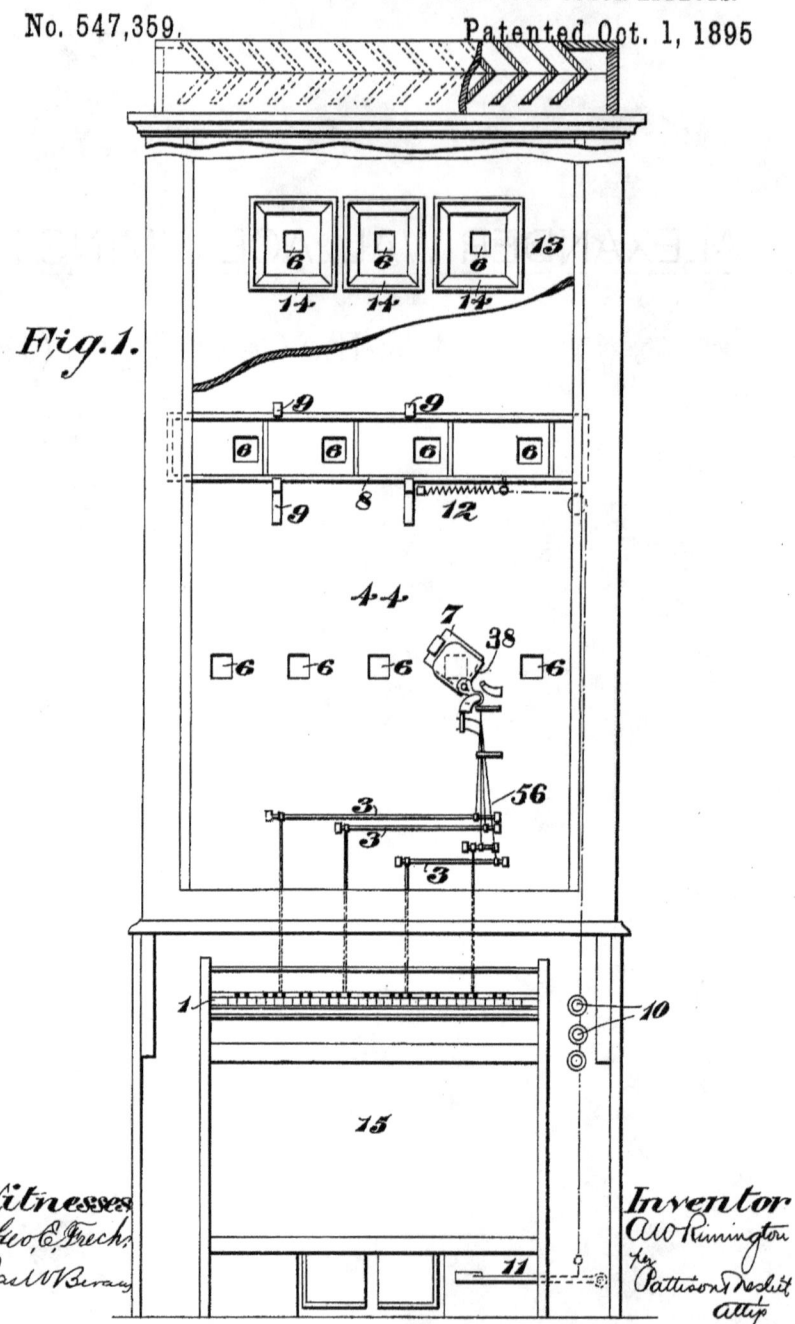

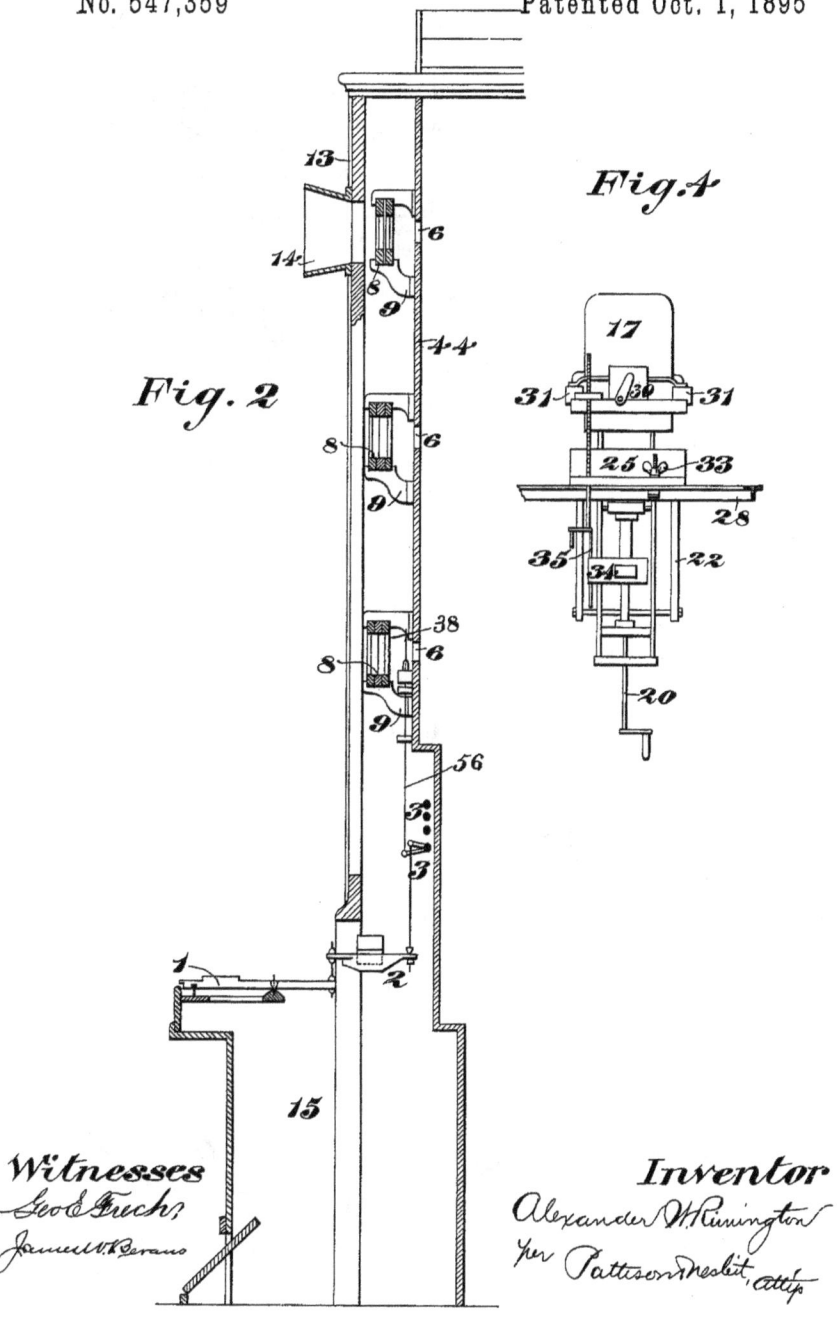

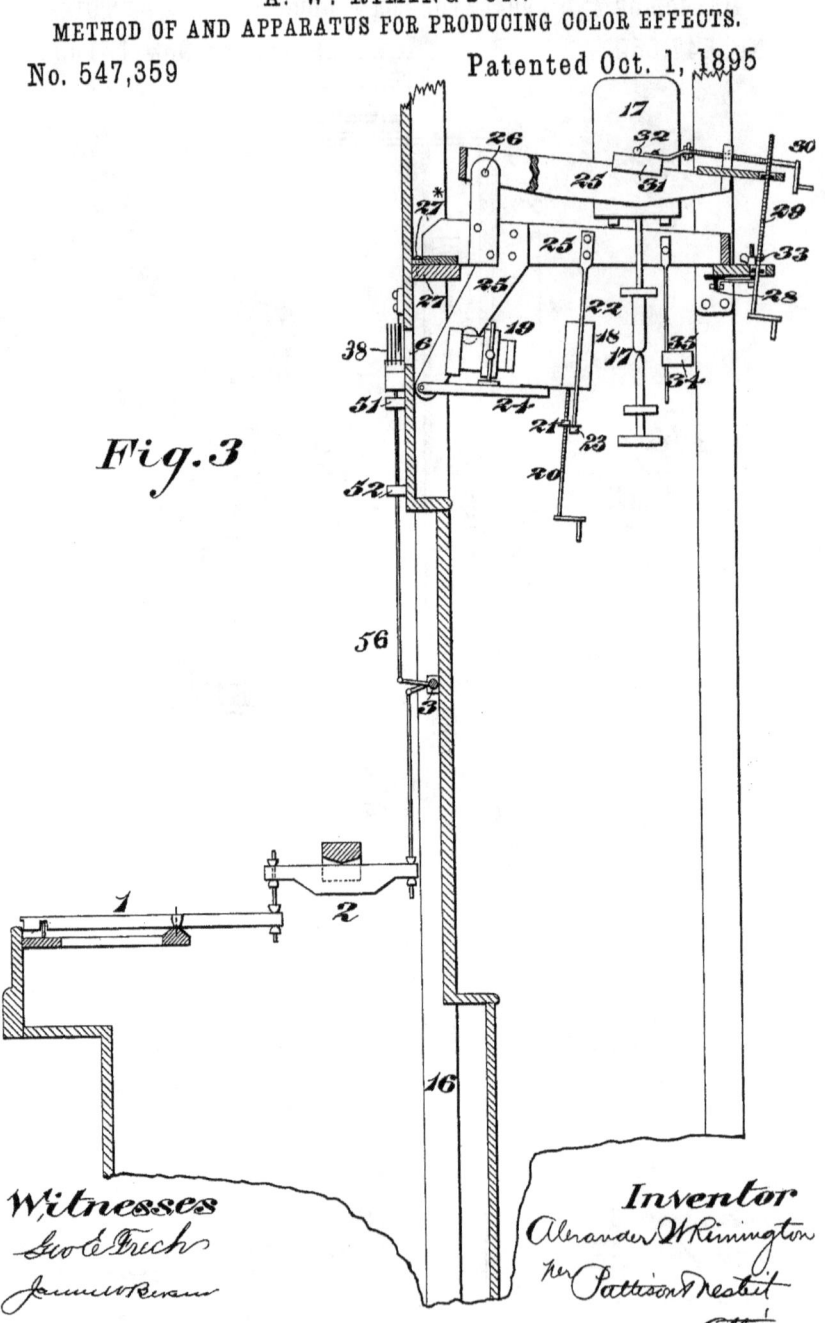

VISUAL MUSIC INSTRUMENT PATENTS (I)

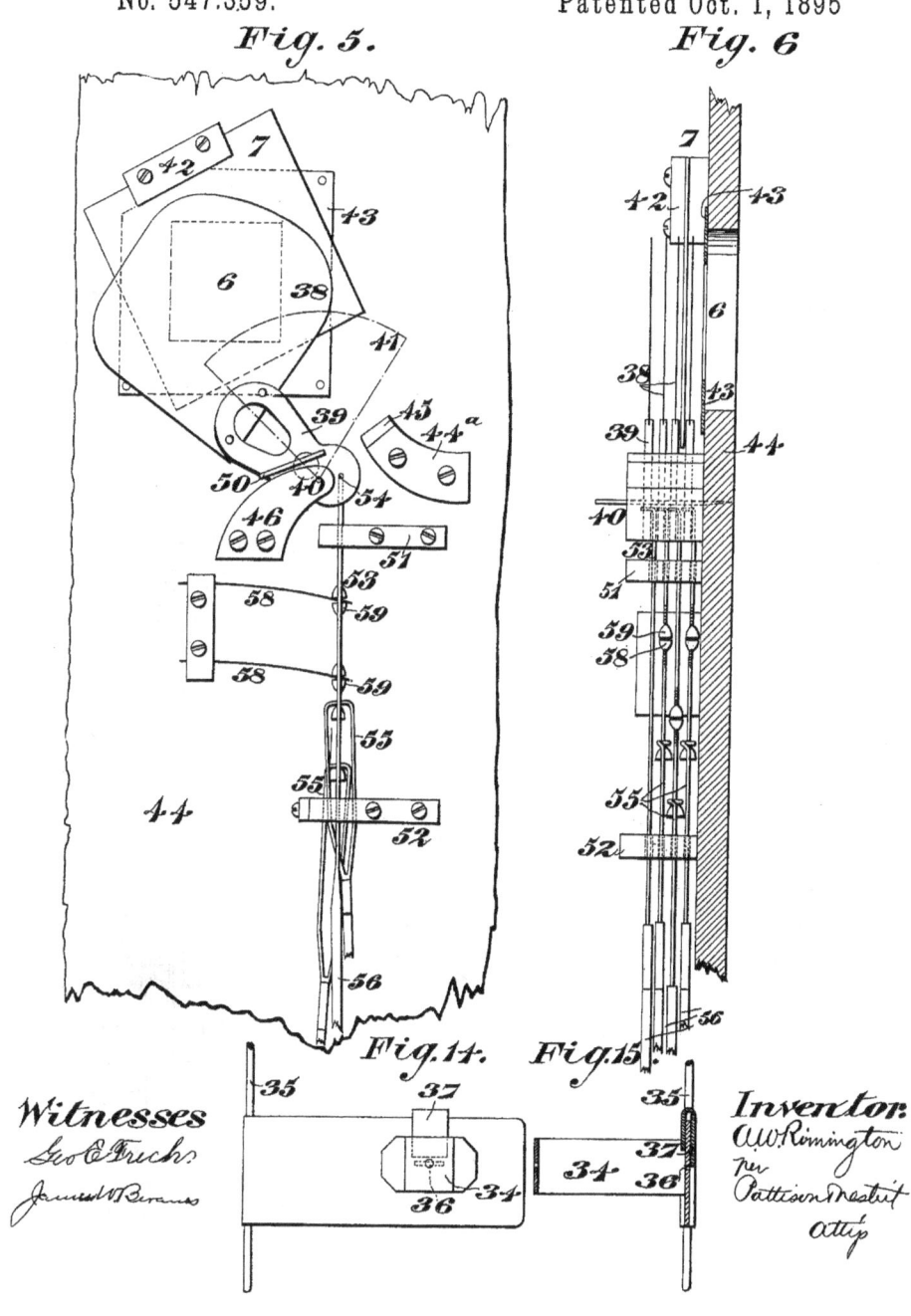

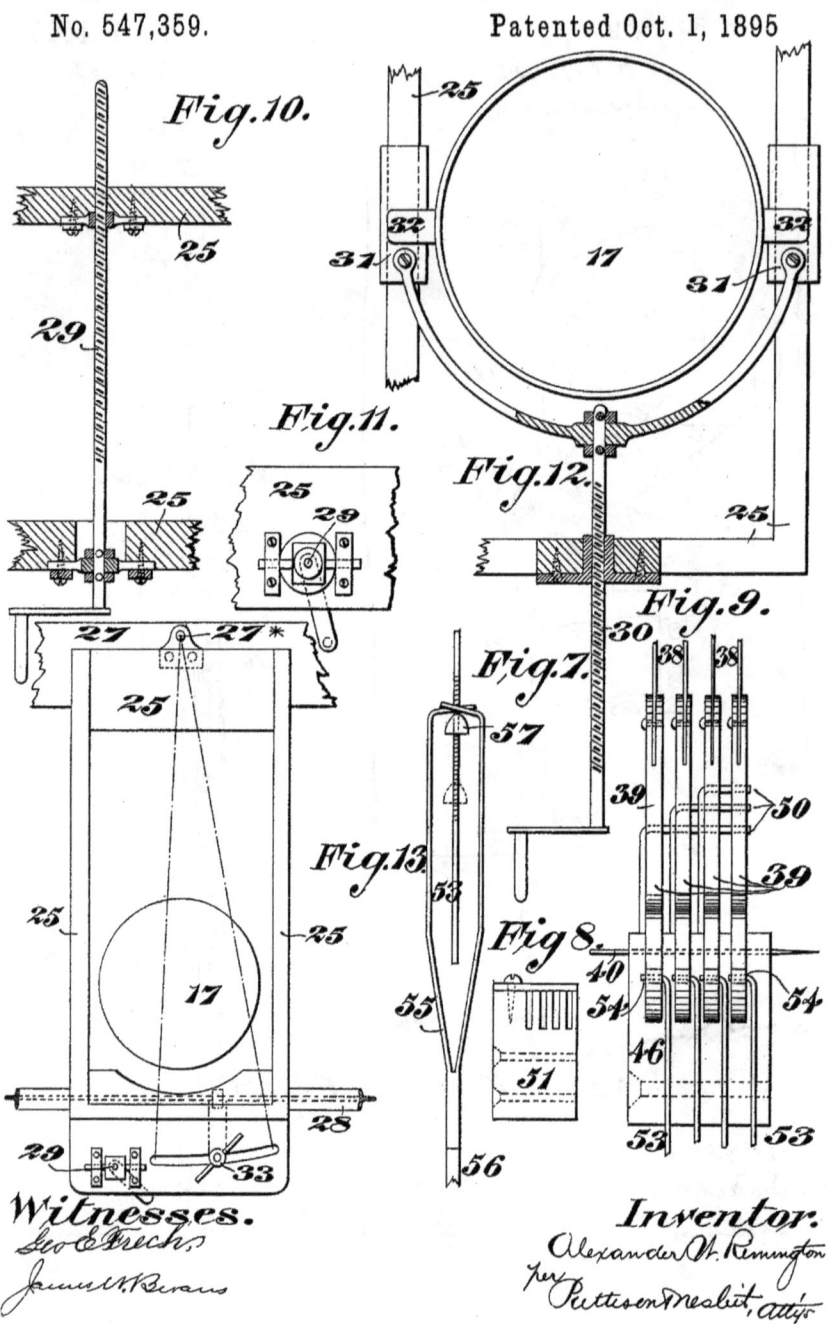

UNITED STATES PATENT OFFICE.

ALEXANDER WALLACE RIMINGTON, OF LONDON, ENGLAND.

METHOD OF AND APPARATUS FOR PRODUCING COLOR EFFECTS.

SPECIFICATION forming part of Letters Patent No. 547,359, dated October 1, 1895.

Application filed July 16, 1894. Serial No. 517,745. (No model.)

To all whom it may concern:

Be it known that I, ALEXANDER WALLACE RIMINGTON, a subject of the Queen of Great Britain and Ireland, residing at 26 Kensington Park Gardens, Bayswater, in the county of London, England, have invented a Method of and Apparatus for Producing Color Effects, of which the following is a specification.

According to this invention colored light is projected onto a screen or other suitable body or surface in such a manner as to give effects in color, bearing a more or less definite relationship to certain sound-vibrations. This may be effected in a variety of ways, such as by employing a keyboard with appropriate mechanism to control devices, such as diaphragms, adapted to arrest or permit rays of light to pass from any suitable source onto the screen or other object on which the color effects are to be produced, such rays of light being projected through suitable colored media onto the said screen or other object. Thus it will be understood that by this invention, *inter alia*, sound-music may, figuratively speaking, be translated into color-music. In order to throw colored light upon a screen or other suitable object according to the novel method set forth, apparatus variously constructed and arranged can, as already indicated, be employed. An arrangement for the purpose may comprise, for example, a keyboard arranged in any convenient manner—as, for instance, it may be similar to that of a pianoforte or organ, this keyboard being connected by a series of trackers or wires with a corresponding set of diaphragms, adjusted and balanced by weights or otherwise, arranged in front of a number of reflectors and lenses, and a set of colored glasses, films, or spectroscopic prisms, arranged in such a manner as to color the light reflected from the mirrors on passing through the lenses, there being in connection therewith special fittings with suitable sources of light, such as arc electric lamps or oxyhydrogen lamps. As an additional feature I in some cases also make provision for the introduction of the element of variable form and intensity into the rays of light passing through the corresponding color medium and the color space or image thus produced upon the screen.

Apparatus constructed and arranged in any convenient form to operate on the principle of this invention can be used, figuratively speaking, to translate sound-music into color-music by such adjustment of individual colors of the spectrum upon the said glass or other diaphragms in regard to the sound-vibrations to which they correspond as approximately to correspond also with the relative air-vibrations of the chromatic scale as such is understood in music. In other words, according to the just-indicated application of this invention, each note of the keyboard will be connected with a color whose place in the spectrum will correspond in a certain mathematical sense with the place occupied by a note upon the chromatic sound-scale of the musical instrument.

The invention is also applicable, by arranging the said colors and notes or keys of the keyboard to correspond with any other arbitrary scale which may be desired, for the purpose of producing other forms of color-music or carrying out color experiments.

By suitable modifications of certain features in carrying out the invention it can be adapted to meet the requirements of color measurement and notation for artistic and art industrial purposes. The mode of effecting this will be readily understood when it is remembered that the process admits of notation exactly as in the case of music.

In order to facilitate the use of the apparatus, the keys of the keyboard may be also colored to correspond with the respective colors projected upon the screen by lenses or reflectors.

The accompanying drawings illustrate, by way of example, a construction of apparatus for carrying my invention into effect.

In the drawings, Figure 1 shows a front elevation of the apparatus, partly in section. Fig. 2 shows parts of the apparatus in vertical section in a plane at right angles to Fig. 1. Fig. 3 is also a vertical section in a plane at right angles to Fig. 1, but is, like other views hereinafter referred to, drawn to a larger scale. This view shows one of the front apertures 6 and the arrangement with respect to it of the corresponding lamp 17, condenser 18, lens 19, and set of diaphragms 5, connected to the keyboard, as also the arrangements for supporting and adjusting the lamp, condenser, and lens. Fig. 4 is a detached view at right angles to Fig. 3, showing the means illustrated in that figure for supporting and adjusting the lamp and other parts. Fig. 5 shows, in front elevation, a set of diaphragms with their holders, actuating-wires, springs, buffer-stop, and other parts hereinafter described. Fig. 6 is a view, partly in section, at right angles to Fig. 5. Fig. 7 shows, to a larger scale, a wire loop 55 and a wire 53, which is connected, as hereinafter described, to a diaphragm-holder, and is furnished with an adjustable nut or button 57, so that downward movement of the loop 55 will, through the button 57 and wire 53, actuate the corresponding diaphragm-holder, and that the wire 53 can move downward without actuating the loop 55. Fig. 8 shows in plan the construction of the registers through which the wires 53 and loops 55, respectively, work. Fig. 9 shows, to a larger scale than Fig. 6, a series of diaphragm holders, together with attached, connected, and adjacent parts hereinafter more particularly referred to. Figs. 10 and 11 are detail views of the adjusting-screw arrangement shown to a smaller scale at 29 in Fig. 3. Fig. 12 is a detail view of the arrangement, shown to a smaller scale in Fig. 3, for adjusting the distance of the lamp from the front of the apparatus along the upper part of frame 25. Fig. 13 is a detail view of the arrangement, shown to a smaller scale in Fig. 3, for enabling the position of the lamp to be adjusted in a lateral sense. Figs. 14 and 15 are views, at right angles to one another, of the adjustable eyepiece employed to facilitate accurate adjustment of the lamp-arc, notwithstanding irregularities in the combustion of the carbons.

1 is a keyboard, similar to that of an ordinary organ, from which the movement of the keys is conveyed, by means of stickers and trackers and the back fall 2, to the rollers 3, which rollers transfer the movement, in the manner usual in an organ, to the trackers 56. These trackers actuate the diaphragms 38, of which there is a series opposite each front aperture 6, (see Figs. 1, 2, 3, 5, 6, and 9,) in such manner as to cause the said diaphragms to rise and fall or oscillate in front of the apertures 6, so that the respective diaphragms will be opposite to the corresponding apertures or not, according as the corresponding keys of the keyboard are for the time being elevated or depressed.

It is advisable to make the diaphragms 5 of some material that is strong, light, and capable of enduring high temperatures. I have obtained satisfactory results by using thin pieces of mica, and in order to obviate noise, which I found liable to occur when employing a single thickness, I construct each diaphragm of two layers or films secured in one and the same diaphragm-holder, so as to be held in contact with one another. The said diaphragms are colored with the respective colors referred to above, or tinted gray, or otherwise adapted to absorb a portion of the light sent through them, as hereinafter described, the object being to enable any given note or key to allow the given strength of a certain color to pass the corresponding aperture 6 and appear upon a screen or other suitable object placed in front of the instrument. That diaphragm of each series which is nearest to the corresponding aperture 6 is rendered non-transparent by being smoked and varnished, or may be made of a thin plate of metal or other suitable material. An arrangement is provided, as hereinafter explained, by which, on the depression of any given note of the octave, this non-transparent diaphragm is removed simultaneously with any other diaphragm or diaphragms of the series belonging to the same aperture 6, the object being that on the depression of any given key this non-transparent diaphragm shall invariably be moved from the front of its aperture 6, so as to allow the cone of light-rays from the corresponding lamp to pass through such aperture.

In addition to the movable diaphragms 5 there is a stationary diaphragm fixed immediately in front of the non-transparent diaphragm, and, whether the other movable diaphragm be colored or be tinted gray or otherwise rendered absorbent of light, this fixed diaphragm is invariably colored of the tint which corresponds to the given note upon the keyboard.

For the transparent colored diaphragms it is important to use transparent colors and varnishes capable of withstanding the high temperature and powerful light. As the result of numerous experiments, I have found it advantageous to use what is known as "Soehné's No. 3 varnish" and various colors of aniline origin, such as aurine, mixing the color and varnish in proportions depending upon the depth of color required, applying the varnish so colored to the mica or glass diaphragm in the same way that a photographer covers a photographic plate with collodion, and drying afterward by artificial heat. When I have failed to obtain the particular color desired, I have used, in lieu of juxtaposed colored films of mica, a piece of colored glass having, as nearly as possible, the color desired, and I have corrected the color by the use of a superimposed tint of colored varnish such as already described. In these cases the mica diaphragms, tinted gray or otherwise rendered partially non-transparent to light, have merely served to partially resist the passage of the light or to allow more or less of it to pass, for which reason such diaphragms may conveniently be called, for distinction, "absorption" diaphragms, the color being given by the one fixed plate of glass.

39 39 are the diaphragm-holders. They are made as light as possible. They may be of any suitable material. I have used mahogany with satisfactory results.

Referring to Figs. 5 to 9, the holders constituting a series are pivoted upon a rod or center 40, so as to be capable of oscillation in the direction indicated by the dotted lines 41.

7 is the fixed diaphragm. It is carried by the nipping-block 42.

43 is a perforated metal plate attached to the face of the diaphragm-board 44 and determining the effective area of the aperture 6, which may be of any desired shape.

44ᵃ is a buffer-block, to which is attached a piece of thick felt 45, which receives the impact of any diaphragm-holder 39 when thrown back by the depression of a note of the keyboard.

46 is a block or bracket accurately grooved to take the diaphragm-holders 39, which are mounted upon the steel center-pin 40, upon which they oscillate.

50 50 are arms formed of wire, (it may be brass wire,) each securely attached to a diaphragm-holder 39 and bent horizontally so as to extend across the back of the diaphragm or diaphragms at the inner side of that to which it is secured, the arrangement being such that upon the outermost diaphragm being moved it will carry the remaining three with it. Upon the second diaphragm being moved it will carry the two at its inner side, and so on.

51 and 52 are registers or guides constructed as shown in Fig. 8. Both these registers or guides are "clothed" to prevent noise and friction.

53 53 are wires each bent to a right angle at its upper part, so as to engage in a hole at 54 in the corresponding diaphragm-holder. Each of these wires is actuated by a wire loop 55 attached to a tracker 56. Upon each wire 53 there is a nut or button 57, so that when the tracker is actuated so as to pull down a wire loop 55 the corresponding wire 53 will be pulled down; but that upon any given diaphragm being moved the remaining wires, which are depressed by others of the diaphragm-holders simultaneously moved, may pass freely through their respective holes at the tops of the loops 55. The diaphragm-holders 39 and the wires 53 are held in position by springs 58, which are regulated by the nuts or buttons 59.

In order to overcome the slight disadvantage resulting from having to move a number of diaphragms and springs by the depression of one note in the upper octaves, and in order also to be able to increase the size of the diaphragms, if desired, without throwing undue stress on the notes of the keyboard, I may in some cases attach to the trackers a pneumatic arrangement such as is sometimes employed in organs. Behind the aperture 6 are placed the lamps or other suitable sources of light and the lenses whereby to project cones of light-rays through the apertures.

In the arrangement illustrated (see Fig. 3) 17 is a self-focusing electric-arc lamp, but there may be substituted an oxycalcium burner or other suitable source of illumination. 18 is a condenser and 19 a lens through which the light is carried to the aperture 6. 20 is a screw engaging in a nut 21, which is carried by the rods 22 and plate 23. The screw 20 is for the purpose of raising or lowering the table 24, which carries the condenser and lens. This table and the arc-lamp 17 are carried by the frame 25, which rests upon the wooden support 27 and is also supported by the T-shaped bar 28, forming part of the general framing of the instrument. The upper portion of the frame 25 is pivoted at 26 and can be raised or lowered by the screw 29, Figs. 10 and 11. This is to provide for the accurate adjustment of the carbon-points of the arc-lamp 17 opposite the condenser 18. Adjustment of the lamp in a direction from front to back of the apparatus is provided for by the screw 30, (see Fig. 12,) which is attached to the blocks 31, adapted to slide on the top of the frame and carry the lamp-pivots 32. Lateral adjustment is provided for by providing the frame 25, which is pivoted at 27*, with a slot and pinching-screw 33. (See Fig. 13.) The pivoted frame 25 slides upon the bar 28. In order to facilitate this lateral adjustment, to enable the carbon-arc to be accurately adjusted and kept in proper position, notwithstanding any irregularities in the combustion of the carbon-points, there is provided an eyepiece 34, Figs. 14 and 15. It can be raised and lowered upon the rod 35, and the small slit 36 is capable of being rendered as narrow as may be desired by the small metal slide 37, which is made to fit tightly upon the front plate of the eyepiece or gage.

It is to be understood that the various adjusting devices hereinbefore mentioned are provided in order that the cones or beams of light passing through the various openings 6 may be projected wholly or partially onto one and the same portion of a screen or other body, in order that the resultant color effect produced on such screen or body shall be that due to the combination of all the beams or cones of light projected at any given time.

Where it is desired to enable (a) glasses upon which forms produced by sound-vibrations or by photography, drawing, or painting, or (b) glasses of varying transparency to be shifted across the paths of the cones of light-rays, so as to increase or diminish the quantity of colored light projected upon the screen or other suitable object, the following arrangement may be conveniently employed.

Referring to Figs. 1 and 2, immediately in front of the diaphragms, or it may be in front of the lenses behind the apertures 6, I arrange a series of frames 8, which are carried upon brackets 9, or upon other suitable supports, and are adapted to be shifted from side to side by means of the stops 10 or pedal 11, and to return to a fixed position, by springs 12 or equivalent means, on the stop or stops being replaced or on the pedal being released. These frames 8 are each fitted with panes of glass, the number of which corresponds to that of the apertures 6 opposite which the frame is placed, the portion of each pane that is normally opposite an aperture being plain, so as to have no effect on a beam of light passing through it, while the remaining portion is of the nature mentioned under *a* or *b* and is brought opposite the opening by moving the frame to the right. In front of the frame 8 is an outer casing 13, which carries a series of projecting funnels 14, corresponding in position with the apertures 6, these funnels having for object to prevent any escape of light sidewise from behind the diaphragms. The space 15 is or may be occupied by an American organ or harmonium actuated by the same keyboard that actuates the diaphragms 5. In this way both light and sound music may conveniently be played at the same time and the color-organ will be enabled the better to be accompanied by other sound instruments or an orchestra, &c.

With regard to the form to be introduced by means of the sliding frames above referred to, I may mention that I have employed the kind of forms produced by sound known as the "Watts-Hughes voice pictures," photographs of cloud-forms, and other objects.

My invention is susceptible of various applications. One of these is the direct production, by means of the keyboard, from music written for an instrument such as the organ or pianoforte, of what I call "color-music," by which expression I desire to have it understood that I mean color effects produced upon a screen or other suitable object, and which are variable in point of combination, intensity, tint, and rapidity of change in the same way that in sound-music given notes are variable in point of combination, intensity, tone, and rapidity of change, at the will of the executive musician. In this connection it will be evident that by my invention I am enabled to associate time and rhythm with color and an almost infinite number of varying combinations of color in the same way that the almost infinite number of sound combinations may be obtained by means of known sound-instruments, such as the organ or piano; or color-music may be produced as a separate composition and independently of sound-music, though accompanied by it in some cases on other instruments or an orchestra.

My apparatus can also be constructed in such a manner as to express or take advantage of the remarkable analogy which exists between the prismatic spectrum of white light and the musical scale.

In the case of the spectrum, the lowest visible color in the red portion of the spectrum-band approximately corresponds to a rate of four hundred and fifty-one millions of millions of vibrations per second, and the highest visible color in the violet portion to a rate of seven hundred and eighty-five millions of millions of vibrations per second or, roughly, double that of the red portion.

Taking any tonic note—say, C—on the sound or musical scale, the corresponding note at the top of the octave has double the number of air-vibrations per second, and if we suppose the said tonic note to correspond with the extreme red of the spectrum and the seventh musical note, or note immediately below the upper tonic, to correspond to the extreme violet of the spectrum, we have the closest possible analogy, in point of ratio of vibration, between the color-octave of the spectrum and the sound-octave of the musical scale.

In one form of my instrument the intervals between the colors, taking them in point of position along the spectrum-band and their ratio of vibration, have been arranged upon the same chromatic and diatonic system as that of the notes of the musical scale, the octave being completed by the recurrence of the red, toward which the blue end of the spectrum would seem to tend, by the gradual conversion of the blue into violet, this upper red note thus recurring as the tonic recurs in the final note of the musical octave, and the relative ratio of vibration of the other notes being in an identical relationship on both the color-scale of this "color-organ," as it may be called, and any properly-tuned sound-organ or pianoforte. With this object in view, the color of the diaphragms used in my "color-organ," as I call it, are obtained, when it is used for this musical purpose, by calculating the approximate ratio of vibration at proper intervals along the whole length of the spectrum, projected upon a white screen and matching the color at the required points, corresponding in respect of the ratio of vibration to the notes of the musical scale. This is done by cutting off by a suitable slit, as understood in connection with the spectroscope, a narrow band of color at these respective points or intervals, and experimentally varying the color of the diaphragm by the use of various coloring agents, such as hereinbefore referred to, or by means of superimposed tinted glasses, until on passing a beam of white light through it a similar color band or indication is obtained or projected upon the spectrum-screen, corresponding in tint to that of the above-mentioned narrow band of color.

Another application of my invention is for the production of color effects entirely independently of sound-musical relationship, for stage and other purposes. It may also be used for experimenting upon and notation of combinations of colors for artistic, scientific, or manufacturing purposes.

What I claim is—

1. A method of producing color effects such as hereinabove referred to as "color music" which consists in causing separate and differently colored beams of light to be projected in a more or less intermittent and variable

manner upon a screen or other object so as to wholly or partly coincide thereon and produce color effects that are variable in point of combination, intensity, tint and rapidity of change.

2. A method of producing color effects such as hereinabove referred to as "color music," which consists in causing beams of light to pass through separate and differently colored media, varying the intensity of the colored beams of light thus obtained, and causing said colored beams of light to be projected in a more or less intermittent manner and in variable numbers at a time wholly or partly upon the same portion of a screen or other object so as to produce color effects thereon that are variable in point of combination, intensity, tint and rapidity of change, as set forth.

3. A method of producing color effects such as hereinabove referred to as "color music," consisting in causing one, two or more of a series of beams of light the colors of which correspond to numbers of light vibrations having approximately the same ratio to each other as that of the numbers of air vibrations corresponding to the notes upon the chromatic sound scale of a musical instrument, as herein set forth, to be projected in a more or less intermittent and variable manner upon a common portion of a screen or other object so as to thereby produce all the effects of rhythm or time as in sound music.

4. For producing color effects such as hereinabove referred to as "color music," apparatus comprising a source of light, appropriately colored media arranged in the paths of converging beams of light traveling from said source in a direction such that the several beams or portions of each will fall upon a portion of a screen or other object common to them, movable non-transparent diaphragms whereby the said beams of light or parts thereof can at will be arrested or allowed to travel from said source of light through said colored media in a regulated manner and be combined on said screen or other object and keys and connecting mechanism adapted to operate said non-transparent diaphragms, as set forth.

5. For producing color effects such as herein referred to as "color music," apparatus comprising means for converging beams of light or parts thereof onto a common portion of a screen or other object, appropriately colored media and absorption diaphragms arranged in the paths of said converging beams of light, opaque diaphragms whereby the said beams can be arrested or projected at will, and keys and connecting mechanism whereby said absorption and opaque diaphragms can be operated in any desired order substantially as herein described for the purposes specified.

6. For producing color effects such as hereinabove referred to as "color music," apparatus comprising a source of light, means for converging two or more beams of light or parts thereof from said source onto a common portion of a screen or other object, appropriately colored media arranged in the paths of said converging beams of light, opaque diaphragms whereby the said beams of light can at will be arrested, or projected in a regulated manner from said source of light through said colored media and wholly or in part combined on said screen or other object keys and connecting mechanism whereby said opaque diaphragms can be operated, variable effect diaphragms adapted to be interposed in the paths of said beams, and means for moving said variable effect diaphragms into and out of the paths of said beams, substantially as herein described for the purpose specified.

7. For producing color effects, apparatus comprising lamps, condensers and lenses whereby converging beams of light can be projected from said lamps onto a screen or other object so as to wholly or partially overlap each other thereon, colored and opaque diaphragms normally arranged in the paths of said beams, and keys and connecting mechanism whereby said opaque diaphragm can be operated in a systematic manner, substantially as herein described for the purpose specified.

8. For producing color effects, apparatus comprising lamps, condensers and lenses for projecting converging beams of light from said lamps onto a screen or other object so as wholly or partially to overlap one another thereon, colored and opaque diaphragms normally arranged in the paths of said beams, keys and connecting mechanism whereby said opaque diaphragms can be operated in a systematic manner, variable effect diaphragms adapted to be moved across the paths of said beams, and means for operating said variable effect diaphragms, substantially as herein described.

9. For producing color effects, apparatus comprising a casing formed with a number of apertures, lamps arranged behind said apertures, condensers and lenses arranged between said lamp and apertures, means for independently adjusting the position of each center of light and each combined condenser and lens, sets of diaphragms arranged opposite said apertures and each consisting of a fixed colored diaphragm, a set of movable absorption diaphragms, and a movable opaque diaphragm, a key board, and mechanism connecting each of the keys of said key-board with one of the movable absorption diaphragms, and the opaque diaphragm of the corresponding set of movable diaphragms substantially as herein described for the purposes specified.

10. For producing color effects, apparatus comprising a casing formed with a number of apertures, lamps arranged behind said apertures, condensers and lenses arranged between said lamp and apertures, means for in-

dependently adjusting the position of each center of light and each combined condenser and lens, sets of diaphragms arranged opposite said apertures and each consisting of a fixed colored diaphragm, a set of movable absorption diaphragms, and a movable opaque diaphragm, a key board, mechanism connecting each of the keys of said key-board with one of the movable absorption diaphragms and the opaque diaphragm of the corresponding set of movable diaphragms sliding frames carrying variable effect diaphragms, and means for bringing the latter diaphragms opposite said apertures substantially as herein described for the purposes specified.

In testimony whereof I have signed my name to this specification in the presence of two subscribing witnesses.

ALEXANDER WALLACE RIMINGTON.

Witnesses:
W. B. WILBERFORCE,
H. HEATHER.

JAMES M. LORING

Musical Chromoscope (1904)

No. 667,541 | Patented Feb. 5, 1901.

J. M. LORING.

MUSICAL CHROMOSCOPE

(Application filed May 12, 1900.)

(No Model.)

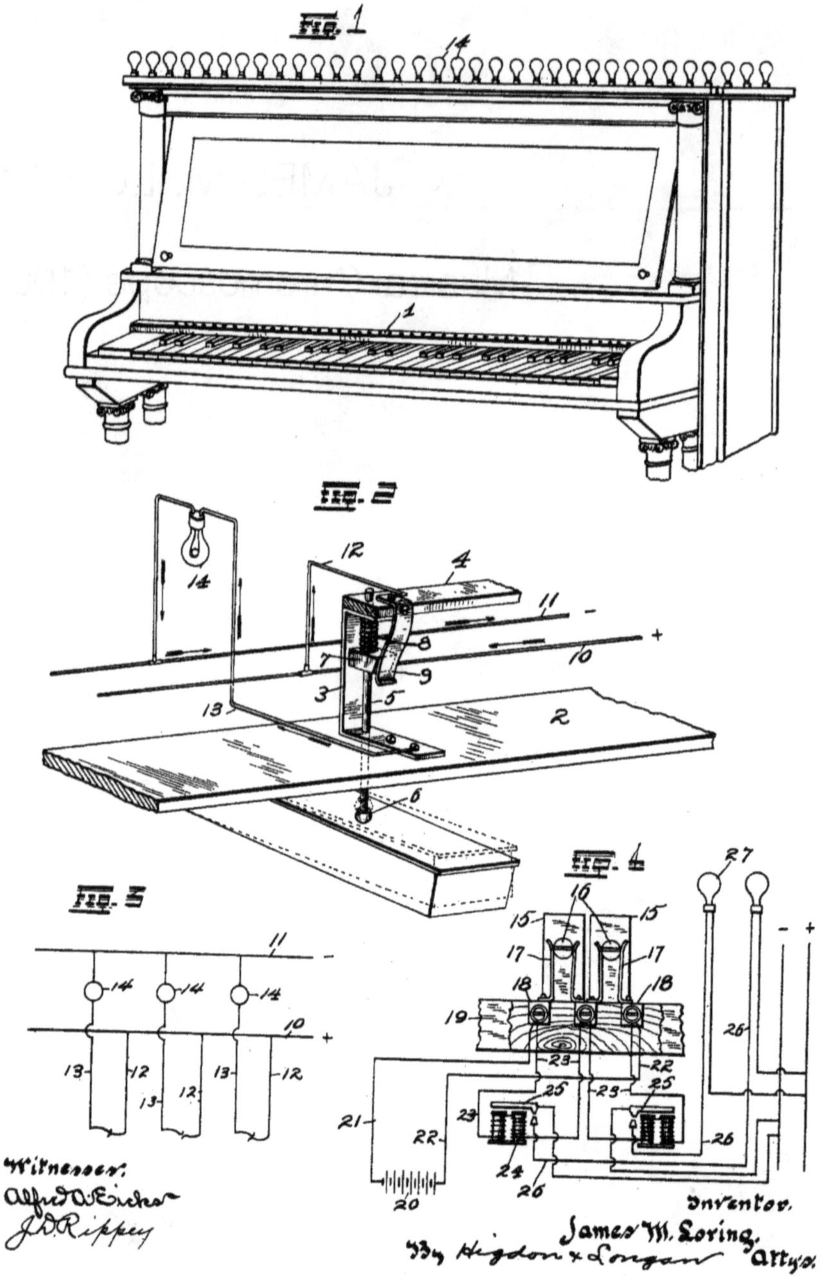

THE NORRIS PETERS CO., PHOTO-LITHO., WASHINGTON, D. C.

UNITED STATES PATENT OFFICE.

JAMES M. LORING, OF ST. LOUIS, MISSOURI.

MUSICAL CHROMOSCOPE

SPECIFICATION forming part of Letters Patent No. 667,541, dated February 5, 1901.

Application filed May 12, 1900. Serial No. 16,426. (No model.)

To all whom it may concern:

Be it known that I, JAMES M. LORING, of the city of St. Louis, in the State of Missouri, have invented certain new and useful Improve-
5 ments in Musical Chromoscopes, of which the following is a full, clear, and exact description, reference being had to the accompanying drawings, forming a part hereof.

This invention relates to chromoscopes;
10 and it consists of the novel construction, combination, and arrangement of parts hereinafter shown, described, and claimed.

Figure 1 is a perspective of a piano to which my invention is applied. Fig. 2 is a detail
15 diagrammatic view in perspective, illustrating the fittings of one key of the piano. Fig. 3 is a diagram of the circuit. Fig. 4 is a diagrammatic view of a modification.

The construction of this invention as shown
20 embodies an electrical circuit for each key of the piano, organ, or other instrument to which the invention is applied. As shown in the drawings the device is attached to an ordinary upright piano, and an explanation in
25 detail of the arrangement of the invention when in use on one instrument is sufficient to make clear its application to similar instruments.

In carrying out the invention as shown I
30 provide a box 1 of any preferred construction, which box is mounted above the rear ends of the instrument-keys in the manner shown in Fig. 1.

2 indicates the bottom of the box, which, as
35 shown, is at a suitable height above the instrument-keys, and to the said bottom on the inside of the box are secured guide-frames 3, there being one of the said frames for each of the instrument-keys. The upper ends of the
40 said guide-frames are secured to the top 4 of the box, and operating within each of the said guide-frames is a rod 5, the lower ends of the said rods projecting downwardly through the bottom 2 of the box and resting upon the
45 instrument-keys in the manner shown in Fig. 2. The lower ends of the said rods are preferably covered with a pad 6, by means of which the keys are protected from any injury which might otherwise be inflicted by the
50 rods. The upper ends of the rods project upwardly through the top 4 of the box.

Rigidly carried by each of the rods 5 a suitable distance below the top 4 of the box 1 is a contact-block 7, the function of which is to complete the circuit when the keys are oper- 55
ated in a manner yet to be described. The rods are actuated downwardly by means of suitable springs 8, the said springs being mounted around the rods between the contact-blocks 7 and the top of the box. 60

For each of the rods 5 I provide a contact-spring 9, which springs are carried by the top 4 of the box and project downwardly and rearwardly, terminating at a point to the rear of the forward ends of the contact-blocks 65
7, so that when the said contact-blocks are lowered by manipulating the instrument-keys, the block 7 and spring 9 will contact with each other and complete an electrical circuit, as hereinafter described. 70

Leading through the box 1 are suitable electrical conductors 10 11, the conductor 10 being connected to the contact-springs 9 by means of the connections 12. The conductor 11 is connected to the lower portion of the 75
metallic guide-frames 3 by similar connections 13, and at suitable intervals along the said connection may be placed bulbs 14 of various colors, if preferred. Thus a normally open circuit is provided which is only 80
closed when the instrument-keys are manipulated, allowing the block 7 and the spring 9 to contact with each other, which, as is readily apparent, will complete the circuit and allow the current to run through the 85
bulbs 14, thereby creating instantly one or more lights for each key which is manipulated. These bulbs are necessarily located exteriorly of the instrument and may be disposed over an entire room or building or 90
stage-proscenium, if desired, thereby giving a very pleasing effect when the instrument is played. A preferred manner of disposing the lights is to arrange those of the first octave at the left of dark colors, while those on the 95
right or treble are very brilliant and light, those between being of graduated arrangement. It is manifest that instead of using an electric lamp I may use any other common and well-known illuminating means which is 100
capable of electrical ignition—such, for example, as gas-lamps inclosed by colored glass, flash-lights, &c.

In Fig. 4 is shown a modified arrangement

of the different parts. To the rear end of each of the keys 15 is secured a metallic contact-pin 16, which in the normal position of the keys, as shown, rests between the upwardly-projecting ends of the contact-springs 17. The said contact-springs are secured to metallic blocks 18, which are supported to the rear of the keys by means of a supporting-strip 19. 20 indicates a system of constant-current batteries, leading from which is a conductor 21, the opposite end of the same being connected to one of the metallic blocks 18. When all the keys are down, the current passes through all the metallic blocks and contact-springs, which are supported to the rear of the instrument-keys, the pins 16 being the means by which the current passes from one opposite contact-spring to another, and from the metallic block 18 at the opposite end of the instrument the current passes through a conductor 22 back to the batteries. The instant, however, that the forward end of one of the keys is depressed the pin 16, carried by the rear end thereof, is removed out of contact with the springs 17 and the current will pass through a conductor 23, connected to the first metallic block 18 through which the current passes. Through the conductors 23, one of which is provided for each of the blocks 18, the current energizes the magnets 24, thereby operating the armatures 25, and completes a circuit through the conductor 26, which contacts with the armatures, and passes to the bulbs 27, disposed at suitable points about the room. This modified form is capable of as many uses as the one hereinbefore described and is fully as meritorious.

The herein-described chromoscope, comprising the electrical circuits herein described, can be attached to the piano, upright or grand, parlor or cabinet, or concert piano, or to the automatic piano, or melodeon or organ, or to any instrument with a simple keyboard without musical apparatus, or to any other suitable instrument, musical or otherwise.

The bulbs may be with parallel sides, known as the "candle" bulb, covered by a painted or stained cylinder, fitting easily over it, made of glass, isinglass, celluloid, or other transparent medium arranged in the order of the solar spectrum, preferably—as red, orange, yellow, green, blue, indigo, and violet—repeated in shades lighter as the treble is reached till all the keys are covered, known as the "chromatic scale;" or the bulbs can be arranged in any other pleasing manner. In the arrangement of the chromatic scale I provide for each C on the keyboard a red bulb; D, orange; E, yellow; F, green; G, blue; A, indigo; B, violet. However, different arrangements may be used, if preferred.

It is apparent that the mechanism may be fitted over the keyboard in front in connection with clamps or levers, by means of which the entire number of posts can be raised, so as not to come in contact with the piano-keys at all—in other words, that the attachment of electric bulbs or other illuminating means can be switched off or disconnected, permitting the musical instrument to be manipulated or played separate from the color lights, as before the attachment.

I may in some instances arrange a system of plain flat surface mirrors above or below the color bulbs at proper angles or inclination and may duplicate or triplicate them, so as to intensify the light effect, and thus increase the power of these varicolored lights. Also, if desired, similar mirrors can be placed at proper angles on either or both sides of the color bulbs, so as to further heighten the effect. In other instances I may place behind a bank of any of the series of seven colors a concave mirror, so as to gather the rays of light streaming from seven lighted-up bulbs by reflection on the concave mirror into a focus thrown upon a suitable screen so placed as to receive it, so that these seven colors may be blended into one upon the screen, place another concave mirror of proper size and shape to collect the rays of light from any six lighted-up bulbs, another from any five bulbs, or four or three or two bulbs, so that they shall be focused on a screen to the end that new tints and blends of colors may be produced, to be used by decorators, dyers, artists, and others.

The key mechanism is placed on sixty keys, each key connected with sixty cylinders, these cylinders comprising five banks of twelve each, and each bank containing seven whole notes and five sharps. The sharps are made by blending the two adjacent colors—C-sharp by blending red and orange, D-sharp by blending orange and yellow, (E has no sharp,) F-sharp by blending green and blue, G-sharp by blending blue and indigo, and A-sharp by blending indigo and violet. (B has no sharp.) These colors are thrown by incandescent electric lamps.

I claim—

1. The herein-described chromoscope, comprising a normally open electrical circuit arranged adjacent to the keys of musical device, suitable illuminating means disposed at intervals along said circuit, and means whereby said circuit is closed whenever the instrument-keys are operated, substantially as specified.

2. The herein-described chromoscope for musical instruments, comprising an electrical circuit which circuit is normally open and is adjacent to the keys of the musical instrument, connections leading from said circuit to the instrument-keys, and means whereby said circuit is closed whenever the instrument-keys are manipulated, substantially as specified.

3. A device of the class described comprising a suitable musical instrument having keys, a normally open electrical circuit adjacent to the keys of said instrument, rods rest-

ing upon said keys, means for operating said rods whenever the instrument-keys are depressed, and means whereby the circuit is closed when said rods are operated, substantially as specified.

4. A chromoscope, comprising a suitable musical instrument having keys, an electrical circuit which circuit is normally open, suitable illuminating-bulbs disposed at intervals along said circuit, a plurality of rods, means for operating said rods whenever the instrument-keys are depressed, and means whereby an illumination is effected when the said rods are operated, substantially as specified.

5. A chromoscope, comprising a normally open electrical circuit arranged within a musical instrument having keys, means whereby said circuit is closed by the depression of the instrument-keys, and means whereby an illumination is effected when the said keys are operated, substantially as specified.

6. An apparatus constructed to exhibit the primary colors and their blends twelve in number and known as the diachromatic scale, and the primary musical tones and their sharps twelve in number, known as the diatonic scale, connected by means of electrical conductors for the purpose described.

7. A musical instrument, having keys and suitable electrical connections whereby the primary colors may be exhibited synchronously with the operation of the primary keys, substantially as specified.

8. A musical instrument, having keys and means for exhibiting the diachromatic scale whenever the keys are operated to produce music, the members of the diachromatic scale being arranged in sequence according to their waves or undulations and being connected to the corresponding key of the diatonic scale, substantially as specified.

In testimony whereof I affix my signature in presence of witnesses.

JAMES M. LORING.

Witnesses:
H. T. LORING,
CHAS. O. MCINTYRE,
JOHN C. HIGDON.

CHARLES F. WILCOX

Method of Composition (1916)

VISUAL MUSIC INSTRUMENT PATENTS (I)

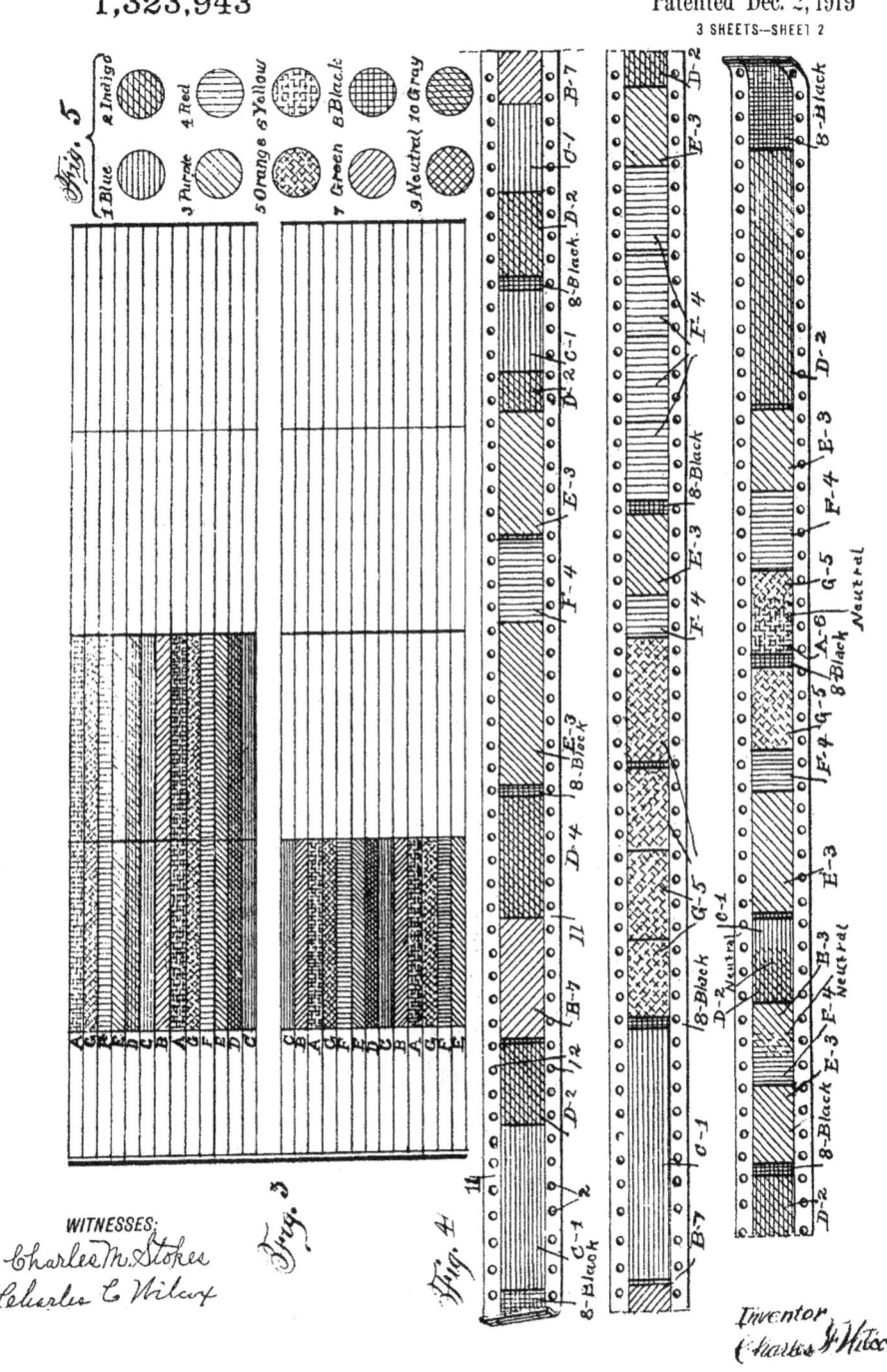

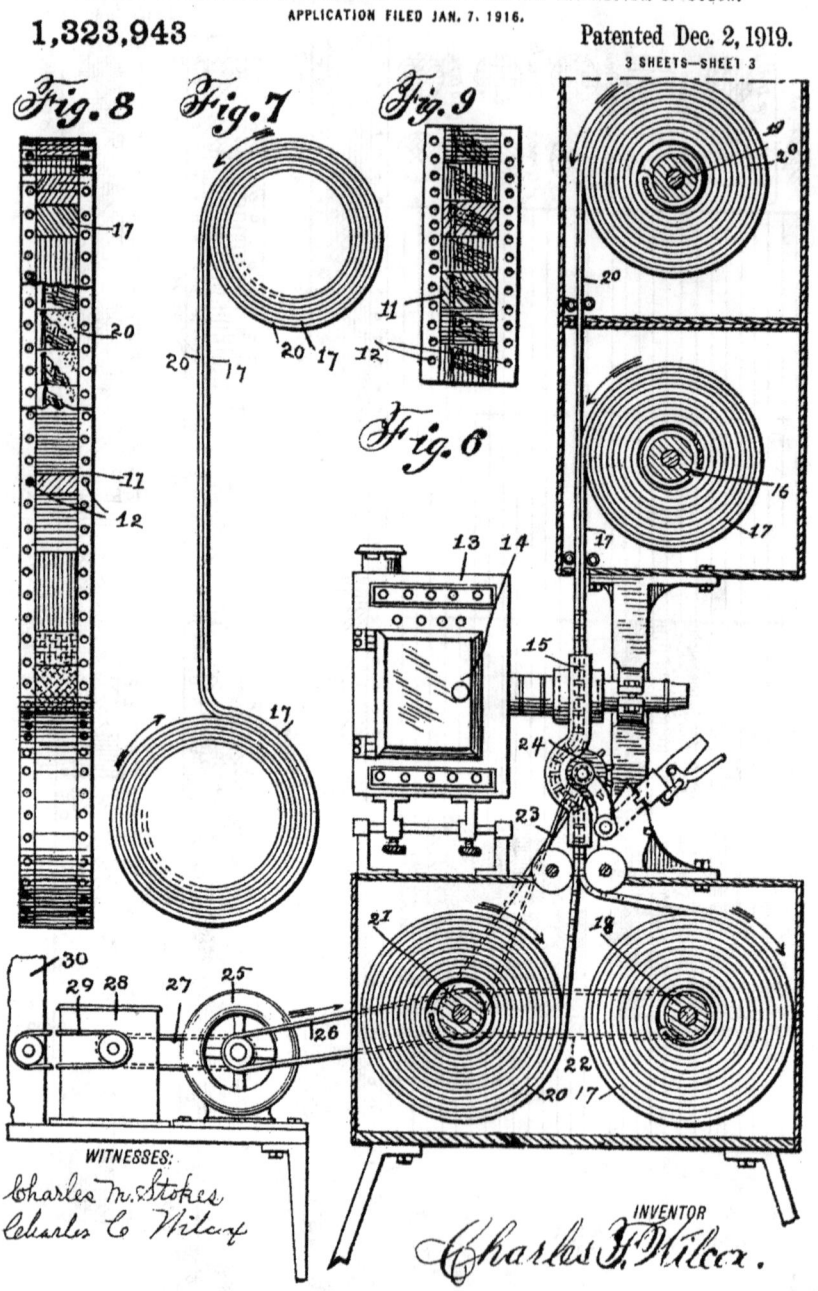

UNITED STATES PATENT OFFICE.

CHARLES F. WILCOX, OF BROOKLYN, NEW YORK, ASSIGNOR OF FORTY-NINE ONE-HUNDREDTHS TO ALBINUS WILCOX, OF KINGS COUNTY, NEW YORK.

METHOD OF PRODUCING MUSICAL COMPOSITIONS THROUGH THE MEDIUM OF COLOR.

1,323,943. Specification of Letters Patent. Patented Dec. 2, 1919.

Application filed January 7, 1916. Serial No. 70,763.

To all whom it may concern:

Be it known that I, CHARLES F. WILCOX, a citizen of the United States, residing in the borough of Brooklyn, in the city of New York, in the county of Kings and State of New York, and whose post-office address is Box 271, Brooklyn, New York, have invented certain new and useful Improvements in Methods of Producing Musical Compositions Through the Medium of Color, of which the following is a specification.

This invention relates to the method of producing musical compositions, or accompaniments for musical compositions, or other rhythmical effects, auricular or spectacular, essentially for entertainment, as instrumental music, singing, marching, dancing or dramatic action, by and through the medium of color which is presented to the eye as a changing rhythmical light of different colors projected upon a screen a stage or other object or it may be so contrived and arranged that the effect will be projected directly to the eye from the source of light.

My invention is based upon the scientific theory of the relation between sound vibrations and vibrations of light, the varying rapidity of vibrations of each causing the phenomena of color perception in the case of light and of the perception of pitch or tone in the case of sound.

The correlation or analogy between color and sound as I prefer to designate the phenomena of effects upon sight and hearing respectively, is evidenced by the fact that the rays of light revealed by the spectrum are broadly divided into seven degrees or colors of light, as; indigo, blue, violet, or purple, red, orange, yellow and green, which through the organ of sight the eye through the retina and the optic nerve affect the consciousness, subconsciousness and the subjective sense of the observer; and similarly the gamut or musical scale is likewise broadly divided into seven degrees or subdivisions of tones, as C, D, E, F, G, A, B, the seven tones in the octave in the key of middle C. It should be noted that while there are eight tones in each octave, yet the eighth tone of the octave is a repetition of the first tone in a higher key, and the first tone in the next octave above the lower octave.

Thus the broad division of the spectrum and the gamut are identical in number and therefore the varying effects that can be produced upon the eye and ear respectively by different arrangements and combination may be facilitated by the similar division of both into seven parts. The nice adaptation of the colors of the spectrum to synchronous presentment with the tones of the gamut or musical scale, is further illustrated by the arrangement and presentment of the colors of the spectrum to the eye in the sequence or order in which they may be disposed, as indigo, blue, purple, red, orange, yellow, green, making seven, and then repeating the first of the seven making the eighth, the color being repeated in a higher key, similarly to the manner of repeating the first tone of an octave to complete the octave, so that the first tone repeated in a higher key stands as the eighth tone of the first octave and the first tone of the second octave. By this it is seen that the colors of the spectrum may be disposed in octaves of color, precisely in the same manner as the gamut or musical scale is divided, by repeating the first color of the color octave in a higher key, that is, a lighter tone or tint, as the last or eighth color of the first octave and the first color of the second octave.

I do not limit myself to any particular code for the arrangement of the colors as corresponding identically with certain tones of the musical scale, and have only suggested the order above given as a convenient mode of defining the principle and theory of my invention. Should it be assumed that the above arrangement or order might be adopted as either a correct or arbitrary code of correspondence, it will be perceived that by following the code in the interpretation of a musical composition that only effects of consonance or concord between the musical tones and the colors would be produced in the interpretation; whereas it is often desirable in esthetic effects to produce effects of dissonance or contrasted effects approaching a discord. In view of this principle, I have provided for arranging the code of corresponding colors and tones arbitrarily for variation. In all cases however it should be remembered that whether an effect of consonance or dissonance between colors and tones be desired, that both colors and tones are subordinated to the law of rhythm and meter, with as much fidelity as the musical tones of instruments playing in concert, which is made possible by the method I employ by subordinating various colors to voluntary control for the purposes set forth and in the manner described.

While I have described in the foregoing only a correspondence between the tones in middle C and the primary tones of the spectrum, making no allusion to the adaptation of colors for correspondences with the tones of the scale in other keys than the natural or middle C and higher and lower octaves, and have only illustrated the correspondence between the colors and the tones of middle C, yet this is for expedience only and for the purpose of rendering the specification more simple and intelligible than would be possible if the drawings and specification were involved with a detailed illustration and description of all the various keys and the varying tones in each scale of a different key and an attempt to illustrate the correspondance of all the various colors with each musical tone of whatever scale or key.

Therefore while I have not attempted and will not attempt in this specification to define and explain in detail the exact correspondence of each particular musical tone in the gamut, with any particular color I will state that the correspondence of the colors with semi-tones, as sharps and flats is determined by a code which is prearranged so that the corresponding tones and colors may be produced in the keys in which sharps and flats occur as well as in the natural key as illustrated in the drawings and described in the specification. This is accomplished by blending two colors corresponding with two musical tones between which a sharp or flat may occur, so as to produce a neutral tone or tint of color which will correspond with the sharp or flat between the two musical tones with which the two original colors thus blended are assumed to correspond; and to make the prismatic colors and the blended colors correspond with the tones in the higher and lower octaves or scales.

I am aware that other persons have promulgated theories of correspondence between color and sound and have proposed to produce colors as an interpretation of music or as an accompaniment to music, but I do not concede to their assumed basis of correlation or the code of correspondence proposed by them as being accurate and absolute and believe that in every case the persons have assumed an arbitrary code which they allege to be absolute and based upon physical law. I am prepared to admit that there may be a correspondence that is absolute based upon the rapidity of vibrations of light waves and of sound waves, and do not doubt that some pleasing effects could be produced by synchronously producing such corresponding colors and tones in a rhythmical harmony, but I cannot concede that the production of other colors and tones synchronously would produce any less pleasing effect, or that it might not produce a more pleasing effect. This I base upon the fact that a different motive in esthetic effects justifies different treatment. As an illustration of this I will assume that for one thoroughly educated in physics and knowing the exact degree of rapidity of vibration of light for each particular color, and the degree of rapidity of vibration of sound waves in each musical tone as nearly as scientific investigation may determine the same, might find great pleasure in hearing a musical composition produced synchronously with light effects arranged according to a code of correspondence based upon the comparative rapidity of vibration of light and sound waves respectively, as in this case the motive would be to note the effect upon the objective or even the subjective sense of the colors and sounds corresponding according to the code of correspondence based solely upon the rapidity of vibrations of light and sound waves.

But to assume another motive a much more pleasing effect might be obtained. For example, assuming as a basis for a code of correspondence between colors and tones, that the tone most universally sounded by the human voice, or that most universally sounded by the musical voice common to both sexes, or to men or women only, should be assumed as the predominating tone in a code and given the first place in the natural key or middle C, if such it proved to be; it is believed that this would be a fair criterion for ascertaining the basis for a code of musical tones with which to marshal or class by analogy or similitude the colors of the spectrum; this much having been established and disregarding any and all abstsruse and didactic theories of physical relationship based upon rapidity of vibrations, it would seem quite consistent to assume as a basis for determining the corresponding colors of the spectrum for the tones in the scale, an analogous rule to that adopted in determining the basis for determining the predominating color in the chromatic scale, namely the law of universality or frequency with which the color is seen in general, or in particular pleasing and beautiful scenes or surroundings as in landscapes natural scenery, or in certain fields of art. Based upon the principle of universality, or frequency, the prevailing or predominating color to correspond might be said to be the ultramarine blue of the ocean or the cerulean blue of the sky, or perchance the emerald green of the verdure; or seeking for a color in the rainbow, or in the field of art red might be selected as the predominating color and therefore the correlative, analogous or corresponding color to middle C. The correspondent for the first musical tone in the scale being ascertained I assume that ordinarily the relative position of the colors as seen in the rainbow, or spectrum should be followed in the ascending scale the first color being repeated as the eighth in an octave and the semitones, or sharps and flats being indicated by a blending of the colors corresponding with the tones above and below the sharp or flat as before described.

The octaves or scales above middle C in accordance with my method are represented by the same colors as the tones of middle C and the semitones or sharps and flats in that octave, with the exception that the color is diluted to a tint of the color which represents the corresponding tone in the lower octave; and correspondingly the octaves or scales below middle C are represented by the same colors as the tones in the middle C, with the exception that the colors are more dense or are mixed with black or other pigment, or more nearly approach black or darkness where all color perception is dissolved.

More specifically my invention relates to the method of producing musical compositions, or accompaniments for musical productions or other rhythmical auricular or spectacular effects essentially designed for entertainment, as instrumental music, singing, marching dancing or dramatic action, by and through the medium of changing color effects presented to the eye by means of filaments of different colors disposed in the path of rays of light projected from a source of light, in accordance with a code of correspondence between the colors and the tones of a musical scale or the gamut, each color or combination of color being successively presented to the view in rhythmical succession and for an interval corresponding with the time of the musical tone or chord with which it is assumed to correspond in the musical production.

My invention consists in the method employed for producing the rhythmical changing color effects desired, inexpensively and with accuracy by means of machinery now in common use thus obviating the necessity of constructing special machinery for the purpose of controlling color effects for interpreting musical compositions or as accompaniment for music or other rhythmical productions.

I attain this object by the method illustrated in the accompanying drawings and more fully described hereinafter.

Referring to the accompanying drawings, Figure 1 is a verse of the national song America, set to music and written in the natural key or middle C.

Fig. 2, is a diagrammatic view illustrating the comparative length of the time of the notes by an elongated space between two lines, the beginning and end of the tones being indicated by a vertical line across the space between the two lines said inclosed elongated spaces being disposed upon the staff in the same relative position as the notes in Fig. 1;

Fig. 3 represents an assumed color scale in which the tones are each represented by shading or hatching in accordance with the code or key shown in Fig. 5, instead of the usual system of notation in which the tones of the scale are written upon the lines and in the spaces between the lines;

Fig. 4 represents a film adapted for being conveyed through a projecting lamp such as is commonly employed for projecting motion pictures upon a screen, and is charged with colors in accordance with my assumed code of correspondence between colors and musical tones, for interpreting in color the tune America, as illustrated in Fig. 1 in the key of middle C;

Fig. 5 is a plurality of roundels taken collectively as one figure and shaded or hatched substantially in accordance with the rules laid down in the Rules of Practice of the United States Patent Office to indicate colors in drawings and serves as a key or code for interpreting the coloring of the spaces in the drawings;

Fig. 6 illustrates one method of employing my specially colored films for projection upon a screen in conjunction with a motion picture film; wherein each film is wound upon a separate delivery reel and conveyed through the machine simultaneously and then wound upon a separate receiving reel, also showing one method of connecting the projecting apparatus with other instruments as a phonograph and a mechanical piano player;

Fig. 7 is a view illustrating another method of using my specially colored film in conjunction with another film wherein both films are wound upon the same delivery reel in superposed relation and after being transmitted are rewound in the same manner upon a receiving reel;

Fig. 8 is a front view of the films and fragmentary rolls shown in Fig. 7; and

Fig. 9 represents a section of a film charged with impressions for moving picture effects and also charged with colors in accordance with my special method for the purpose of interpreting a musical composition in color as set forth.

The scale or code represented in the drawings and employed in the representation of the method herein described is not presented as being technically correct or complete, but is arbitrarily assumed and embraces or illustrates only tones on the natural scale or that of C. The drawings are made to embrace only these tones for the sake of simplicity and clearness, for the reason that middle C is the natural key and no sharps or flats occur in the octave, so it is only necessary with this scale to represent the true colors of the spectrum as given in my assumed code, as they are assumed to correspond with the tones in middle C, so it is unnecessary to represent in these drawings any sharps or flats, as would be necessary if another scale were used.

It is assumed for the purpose of illustration of the method that blue corresponds with middle C, indigo with D, purple with E, red with F, orange with G, yellow with A, green with B, and lighter blue with second C.

To produce these notes in the higher octaves a lighter shade of the same colors are employed, and to produce the tone in the octaves below middle C the tones are deepened or darkened by shading toward black or darkness where all color effects are dissolved and lost.

To express the sharp and flat tones the two colors representing the natural tones first above and below the semi-tone are blended in suitable proportions so as to make a neutral color or tint which represents the sharp or flat to be denoted.

In Fig. 2, I have omitted the notes of the ordinary system of musical notation and in the place thereof have drawn parallel lines with cross lines which represent the tones of the scale and also represent the time or interval of each respective tone; in this figure however the exact proportional length of the notes is not assumed to be expressed in the comparative length of the spaces but it is assumed that they are proportionally of the proper length to express the comparative intervals of time of the notes they represent. I adopt this mode of illustrating the tones and time to illustrate in a simple manner how an elongated strip or space may be employed to represent time in notation, and assuming that the position or tone of each note for its proper interval may be indicated by the color with which the portion of a strip of film or space is charged, it is apparent that by varying the lengths into which a film is divided the time of music may be determined, and by the color of the different portions or sections thereof the various tones of music may be denoted in accordance with a predetermined code of correspondence.

In Fig. 2, I have not colored the spaces to indicate the tones they represent as they occupy a position upon the staff to denote their tone, and for the further reason that the spaces are too small to admit of hatching successfully. As blank spaces it will be assumed that they represent varying lengths of a continuous film such as is used for motion pictures, the variations in length being in exact proportion on the film with the variation in the length of the time of the tones in the musical tones they represent.

Referring to Fig. 3, it will be obvious that by coloring these subdivisions of the film in accordance with the scale or code there represented in accordance with the key shown in Fig. 5 of the drawings that the film will be susceptible of denoting the tones of the musical composition through the medium of their color, and the time by the length of the portion of film charged with the color. In Fig. 3 I have represented the treble clef as extending over two bars on the staff which is to indicate that the colors may be extended entirely across the staff and the notes of music indicated thereon as a method of notation, and in the bass clef I have shown the colors as extending only to one bar which indicates that the color code may be placed at the beginning of each staff only and the musical notation written upon the plain paper across the page the length of the staff as is now customary.

The difference in the depth of the color that expresses the higher or lower octaves is suggested by the strength of the shade lines and the comparative depth of shading or hatching which denotes the colors.

By reference to Fig. 4, a practical illustration of the method I employ will be seen. In the figure, the numeral 11 represents a continuous film of transparent material and having parallel perforated edges 12, whereby it may be transmitted through the ordinary projecting machines used in motion picture work. The film may be assumed to be drawn to a scale of one half the actual width and one eighth of its lineal length per foot as subdivided in the drawing.

Further assuming that the film will be usually transmitted through the projector at an average speed of 1 foot per second and assuming also that the usual time for a whole musical note is one second it will be seen that the film moving at one foot per second would travel one foot in the time of one whole note of music, one half a foot in the time of a one half note and one fourth of a foot in the time of a one fourth note, &c.

In the drawing one and one half inches lineal length represents one foot of the film and accordingly in indicating the coloring by the shading or hatching one and one half inches represents one foot or the length of film which will be transmitted through the projector in one second of time, and shorter or longer spaces in like proportion, as one second, one second and one half, one half a second and one fourth of one second, &c.

The tune America transposed to the key of middle C is indicated upon the film shown in Fig. 4. For simplicity only the air is given.

The first tone is middle C and accordingly the color of the first subdivision of the film must correspond with middle C which according to the code given in Fig. 3, is blue, and as there are two half notes in the tone of C the time of both notes is equal to one whole note and therefore the length of film which will be transmitted through the projector in one second of time or the time of two half notes is colored blue, the color here shown as representing middle C. The next tone is D, a half note, and that portion of the film which will be transmitted in one half a second should be colored indigo blue, which is the color here represented as corresponding with D.

To denote the pauses or rests in the music a suitable length of the film is colored black or some other color distinguishable from the colors representing the musical tone, so that the pause will be denoted by the time it requires for the portion so colored to be transmitted through the projector.

In the last line of the song there are glides or slurs or notes tied together as at the word "every" and "let" The first slur or glide is from F to E and from E to D. The film is charged at the beginning of the portion denoting the time of the beginning of the tone, with the color representing F, which is red, the latter portion is charged with the color representing E, which is purple, and a part of the film between the beginning and latter portion of this section of the film is colored a shade of color neutral between red and purple so that the change from the red to purple will be graduated and will resemble the glide of the tone from F to E. Like treatment is given to the film to simulate the glide from E to D, excepting that the colors are indigo and blue and likewise in the last bar, where the tone of the word "let" begins on A and glides to E, the colors representing these tones according to our assumed code being orange and yellow and a neutral color between them.

In practising the method herein described I not only charge transparent films with colors to express musical compositions, but films charged with impressions for projection upon screens, whereby illustrated songs and other compositions, dramatic or rhythmical productions or effects may be presented synchronously with the color interpretations of a musical composition as an accompaniment to music or as a color interpretation independently of other musical expression.

When it is desired to present my color interpretation of music simultaneously with pictures I employ several modes one of which is shown in Fig. 6 of the drawings, in which the numeral 13 indicates a projecting machine shown partly in section, having a lamp within a casing 14, guides for a film 15, a delivery reel 16 above the guides and supported by the frame on which the reel is wound a picture film 17, said film being adapted to be transmitted through the guides 15 of the projector, a receiving reel 18 on which the film is wound after being transmitted through the projector and a second delivery reel 19 is superposed upon the frame above the delivery reel 16, and on which is wound one of my color films 20 which is transmitted through the same guides as the picture film simultaneously therewith and then wound upon a separate receiving reel 21 mounted on the frame contiguous to the receiving reel 18.

By this method I can transmit one film at a higher rate of speed than the other by regulating the speed of the transmitting gearing of the projector and the reels, which is an advantage in certain cases. It is also possible by this method to transmit the two films simultaneously for a time and stop one of them or unthread one from the guides and project the colors or impressions charged upon one only for a period of time.

By connecting the driving mechanism of the projector with the mechanism of a phonograph, a mechanical piano player, or with both or with other similar instruments I have found that musical tones from the instrument, and the color of the films projected upon a screen or stage or other object may be presented synchronously without error or defect as the speed of the projector, the phonograph and instrument may be exactly regulated so as to operate in unison. A simple and practicable means of connecting the mechanisms of the devices is illustrated in Fig. 6. The receiving reels 18 and 21 are connected by a belt 22 indicated in dotted lines, and the reel 19 is connected by a belt 23 with a sprocket 24 which conveys the film through the guides 15 of the projector. A motor 25 is provided which is connected by a belt 26 with the receiving reels 21 and 19 and serves to drive the mechanism of the projector 13 to convey the film through the machine so that the film will move across the path of rays of light emitted from the light. The belt 27 connects the motor with the phonograph 28 and in a similar manner the belt 29 connects the mechanical piano player 30 with the motor, whereby all the mechanism of the various devices so connected may be operated in unison so that synchronous phonographic records, piano music, motion pictures and color accompaniment or interpretation of music may be produced.

It is contemplated that when it is desired to present synchronously the records taken by a phonograph, and motion pictures with instrumental music and my color interpretation of music as described that a camera will be substituted in the place of the projector shown in the drawings and the film taken while the music of the instrumental player is being produced, or while a phonographic record is being made to synchronize with the scenes of the motion picture or while both such phonographic record and piano or instrumental music are being produced. The film for the color effects may then be made to correspond with the musical composition by any process found most desirable and projected with the picture and phonographic record and other musical effects as desired.

By this means the speed of the phonograph and the speed of the camera may be regulated and when the pictures are exposed or projected the mechanism running at the same relative speed will insure perfect synchronism of phonographic records and picture projections. The use of the mechanical piano player will also enable the operators to time the picture and phonographic record while preparing them so that there will be a perfect rhythm and synchronous effect throughout.

I do not deem it necessary to multiply views in the drawings in order to show a camera in operation in the place of the projecting machine as the mechanism is so designed that the one can be substituted for the other in the system of machinery, and the speed of the mechanism is regulated by means commonly employed in such mechanism.

In presenting the color interpretation of a musical composition simultaneously with the impressions upon a motion picture film, I prefer to place the color film between the source of light and the picture film so that no filament will pass between the picture film and the screen or other object upon which the projection is thrown, which might tend to obscure the clearness of the pictorial effects of the film and prevent a perfect reproduction of the delicate impressions registered on the picture film by the camera. This is avoided by placing the color film between the source of light and the picture film for although the colors of the color film will modify the strength and color of the light passing through the picture film, the light as so modified after reaching the picture film has an unobstructed path from the picture to the screen, and clear sharp definition of picture impressions upon the screen will result.

In Fig. 9 I have shown a portion of a picture film charged with colors denoting a musical composition, as well as picture impressions. It will be seen that where the picture film is thus charged with color and where a color film only is employed for projection that no unusual provision need be made for projection, but the film is transmitted in the ordinary manner through the projector.

As a code of correspondence between colors and musical tones I propose to employ and present them as follows: middle C=indigo, D=blue, E=purple, F=red, G=orange, A=yellow, B=green, C 2nd=light blue, C sharp=neutral between indigo and blue, D sharp=neutral between blue and purple, F sharp=neutral between red and orange, G sharp=neutral between orange and yellow, A sharp=neutral between yellow and green, and B sharp=neutral between green and indigo.

To produce the corresponding tones in higher octaves I produce lighter tints or shades of the same colors as those employed in the key of middle C; and to produce the corresponding colors in the lower octaves I employ darker shades of color the same as those used in middle C, merging toward black or utter darkness.

As a secondary code of correspondence between colors and musical tones, I substitute blue for indigo in the above and foregoing code, and indigo for blue.

As a third code of correspondence for color and musical tones I present them as follows: middle C=green, D=indigo, E=blue, F=purple, G=red, A=orange, B=yellow and C 2nd=green lighter in shade. The sharp and flat or semi-tones are produced by blending these colors as assumed to represent their corresponding tones, to produce a color to correspond with the sharp or flat or semi-tone between the colors represented by the corresponding prismatic colors.

The same treatment is employed as above described to produce colors to correspond with the tones of the higher and lower octaves or scales than middle C.

While I have described certain mechanical means for producing the effects sought to be produced through my invention and while I have at length described certain details in explaining my methd of producing color interpretations of music or color accompaniments for musical or other rhythmical productions, I do not wish to limit myself to any of the specific means or methods employed for producing these novel and beautiful effects but claim as my invention all the slight modifications and variations which reasonably fall within the scope of my invention as more specifically pointed out in the annexed claims.

I claim—

1. The herein described method of producing a color harmony as an accompaniment for music or other rhythmical optical or other form of entertainment, comprising the fixing upon a continuous movable medium adapted to be employed in conjunction with a lamp, of a color scale, whereby the light

from the lamp may be modified so as to produce a rhythmical and harmonious changing color effect in the rays of light from the lamp, substantially as and for the purposes set forth.

2. The method of producing a color harmony as an accompaniment for music or other form of entertainment, auditory or spectacular, comprising the fixing upon a transparency adapted to be employed in conjunction with a lamp of a color scale, whereby the light may be modified so as to produce a rhythmical and harmonious changing color effect in the rays of light emitted from the lamp or projected upon a screen, a stage or other object, as an interpretation of music through the medium of color substantially as and for the purposes set forth.

3. The method of producing a color accompaniment for music or other form of entertainment, auditory or spectacular, by fixing upon a continuous film adapted to be conveyed through guides provided upon a lamp, of a color scale, whereby the light from the lamp may be modified so as to produce a rhythmical and harmonious changing color effect, substantially as and for the purposes set forth.

4. The method of producing color music synchronously with other forms of entertainment, auditory or spectacular; comprising the fixing upon a medium adapted to be employed in conjunction with a light, of a color scale whereby the rays of light may be modified by the colors of the scale in metrical and rhythmical succession by the continuous and regular movement of the medium, so as to produce a rhythmical and harmonious changing effect through the changing colors of the rays of light and the intervals of duration of the respective color effects, substantially as and for the purposes set forth.

5. The method of producing color music synchronously with other forms of auditory or spectacular entertainment; comprising the fixing upon a transparency adapted to be employed in conjunction with a light, of a color scale, whereby the rays from the light may be modified by the colors of the scale in metrical and rhythmical succession, by the continuous and regular movement of the transparency, so as to produce a rhythmical and harmonious color effect on the rays of light.

6. The method of producing color music synchronously with other forms of auditory or spectacular entertainment; comprising the fixing upon a continuous film adapted to be conveyed through guides provided upon a lamp of a color scale, whereby the rays of light emitted from the lamp may be modified by the colors of the scale, in metrical and rhythmical succession, by the continuous and regular movement of the film through the guides, so as to produce a metrical, rhythmical and harmonious changing color effect upon the rays of light emitted from the lamp or projected upon a screen, a stage or other object, substantially as and for the purposes set forth.

7. The herein described method of translating a musical composition through the medium of color; comprising the fixing upon a medium adapted to be disposed in the path of the rays of light from a lamp or other source of light of a color scale corresponding with the musical tones in a scale of music, said medium being adapted to be conveyed continuously across the path of the rays of light so as to produce a rhythmical and harmonious changing color effect upon the rays emitted from the light or projected upon a screen, a stage or other object, substantially as and for the purposes set forth.

8. In a method of translating music through the medium of color, the mode of producing the desired changes in color and rhythmical succession, by fixing upon a continuous film adapted to be conveyed across the path of rays from a light at a given speed, a color scale, in which each musical tone is represented by a certain color as determined by a prearranged code of corresponding colors and musical tones, and in which the time of each musical tone is represented by the extent of the film of the color representing the tone upon the film so that the prolonged time of any tone will be represented by a greater length of time of exposure of light through the portion of film being charged with such color and the shorter tones by a shorter exposure of light through a less extent of the film being charged with such color as corresponds with the musical tone, substantially as and for the purposes set forth.

9. In a method of translating music through the medium of color; the mode of producing the required changes in color and the rhythmical variations in time, by fixing upon a film adapted to be conveyed through guides provided upon a lamp and across the path of the rays of light from the lamp at a given speed, of a color scale, in which each color represents a tone in a musical composition and the extent of the film charged with the color relatively corresponds with the interval of time which the tone should be held, whereby the rays of light will be modified as to color, and the rhythmical succession of time will be regulated by the transmission of the movable film across the path of the rays of light at an even rate of speed, substantially as and for the purposes set forth.

10. In a method of translating a musical composition through the medium of color, as an accompaniment to instrumental music,

singing, dancing, marching or dramatic action, or pictures projected upon a screen, a stage or other object, the mode of producing the requisite changes in color and rhythmical succession by fixing upon a continuous film, adapted to be conveyed continuously across the path of rays of light from a projecting lamp or other source of light, of a color scale as determined by a code of correspondence between colors and musical tones, in which each color represents a certain tone in a musical composition and in which the time or intervals of the music is represented by varying exposure of light through varying length of film charged with a given color, so that the time of a one fourth note will be represented by exposure of light through an extent of film one fourth that which would represent a whole note; whereby a translation of music through the medium of color may be produced by modifying the rays of light and regulating the duration of each color effect produced to correspond with the changes of pitch and time in a musical composition.

11. In the herein described method of producing a rhythmical and harmonious color accompaniment for music; the mode of dividing a continuous film which is adapted to be conveyed across the path of rays of light from a lamp or other source of light; whereby each subdivision of the film is made to correspond in length with the interval of time of the corresponding tones in a musical composition in accordance with a code, so that a given length of film represents a full note, and a fractional part of such length represents an equivalent fractional part of a whole note, and another certain extent of the film represents a pause or rest of a certain duration, each subdivision of the film being charged with a certain color corresponding with the tone of music with which it corresponds in time, in pitch in accordance with the code.

12. In the herein described method of producing music through the medium of color; means for varying the pitch and time; comprising a continuous transparent film, adapted to be transmitted through a projecting machine for motion pictures, said film being charged with colors in accordance with a code of correspondence between colors and musical tones, the extent of the film charged with each color corresponding relatively in length, to the extent of time of each note of the musical composition, whereby a rhythmical and harmonious color effect is produced for projection upon a screen, a stage or other object, substantially as and for the purposes set forth.

13. In the herein described method of producing a musical composition through the medium of color; means for successively emitting rays from a constant source of light through successive portions of a continuous transparent film charged with different colors, in accordance with a code of corresponding colors and musical tones, in rhythmical succession, substantially as and for the purposes set forth.

14. The herein described method of interpreting a musical composition through the medium of color, in accordance with a code of corresponding colors and musical tones, in which; middle C equals indigo blue, D equals blue, E equals violet, F equals red, G equals orange, A equals yellow, B equals green, and C 2nd equals indigo reduced in intensity; and the semi-tones are represented by a color produced by blending the colors representing the two tones next above and below the semi-tone; the same colors being employed in varying degrees of density brilliancy, depth and clearness to represent the scale above and below the scale of middle C, whereby the higher scales are denoted by lighter tints of color and the lower scale by darker shades of color.

15. The herein described method of interpreting a musical composition through the medium of color by successively emitting rays of light from a constant source of light through transparencies of different colors in accordance with a code of correspondence between colors and musical tones, in which middle C equals green, D equals indigo, B equals blue, F equals violet, G equals red, A equals orange, B equals yellow and C 2nd equals lighter green; C-sharp equals neutral between green and indigo, D-sharp equals neutral between indigo and blue, F-sharp equals neutral between violet and red, G-sharp equals neutral between red and orange, A-sharp equals neutral between orange and yellow; and the tones in the scales or octave above middle C are represented by lighter tints of the same colors as those representing the tones in the scale or octave of middle C; and the tones in the scales or octaves below middle C are represented by deeper or darker shades of the same colors as those representing the tones in middle C, the higher tones being graduated into white or white light and the lower tones being graduated in the black or darkness or absence of all light.

16. In a method of translating music through the medium of color by a rhythmical successive presentment to view, by projection upon a screen or other object, of variously colored lights in accordance with a scale of corresponding colors and musical tones, in which middle C equals blue, D equals indigo, E equals violet, F equals red, G equals orange, A equals yellow, B equals green and C2nd equals lighter blue; the semitones are simulated by blending the colors which represent the next tone above and below the semitone; and the tones of the

scales or octaves above middle C are represented by lighter tints of the colors representing the tones in middle C, graduated toward white or white light, and the tones in the scales or octaves below middle C are represented by deeper or darker shade of the colors representing the tone in middle C graduated toward black or darkness or absence of all light.

17. In the herein described method of interpreting a musical composition through the medium of color comprising the system of exposing or projecting a light through a variously colored continuous film in rhythmical succession in accordance with a prearranged arbitrary code of correspondence between colors and musical tones; means for denoting a glide or slur comprising the mode of coloring a section of the film of a given extent or length corresponding with the tones of the glide or slur so that a part of such section will be charged with the color denoting the first note of the slur or glide and another section slightly removed therefrom will be charged with the color representing the succeeding note, and the section of film between the two sections will be charged with a color gradually blended from the first color to the second color, *ad seriatim* through all the notes embraced in the glide or slur, whereby there will be no abrupt cessation of one color but a gradual merging or transition from the first to the second color by the blending of the colors together in the interval of space between the two.

18. In the herein described method of interpreting a musical composition through the medium of color in accordance with a code of corresponding colors and musical tones the mode of denoting a pause in a staff of music by changing a section of a continuous color film prepared in conformity with the code, with a color darker than the colors denoting the tones in the music immediately preceding or succeeding the pause the length of the section so colored to denote the pause being regulated in proportion to the length of the pause or rest in the music, substantially as and for the purposes set forth.

19. The herein described method of interpreting a musical composition through the medium of color by successively exposing a light through a continuous transparent film of different colors, of a continuous transparent film, said film being colored in accordance with a prearranged code, defining a natural law of harmony between colors and musical tones, the intervals of time being denoted by the relative extent of film of a given color and the time of exposure of the light through each color corresponding with its correlative tone, while such part of the film is passing at a given speed across the path of the rays of light from the projector to be projected upon a screen, a stage or other object.

20. The method of producing a harmonious color accompaniment to songs, instrumental music, motion pictures and phonographic records, in rhythmical time, by means of a continuous transparent color film charged with colors in accordance with a prearranged code of corresponding colors and musical tones, synchronously by operating the mechanism of the projector, the phonograph and mechanically played instrumental music, at the same relative speed in unison by a common motor or motor generator, substantially as and for the purposes set forth.

In testimony that I claim the foregoing as my invention, I have signed my name in presence of two witnesses, this thirtieth day of December, one thousand nine hundred and fifteen.

CHARLES F. WILCOX.

Witnesses:
CHARLES M. STOKES,
CHARLES C. WILCOX.

HENRY FITCH TAYLOR

Means for Determining Color Combinations (1917)

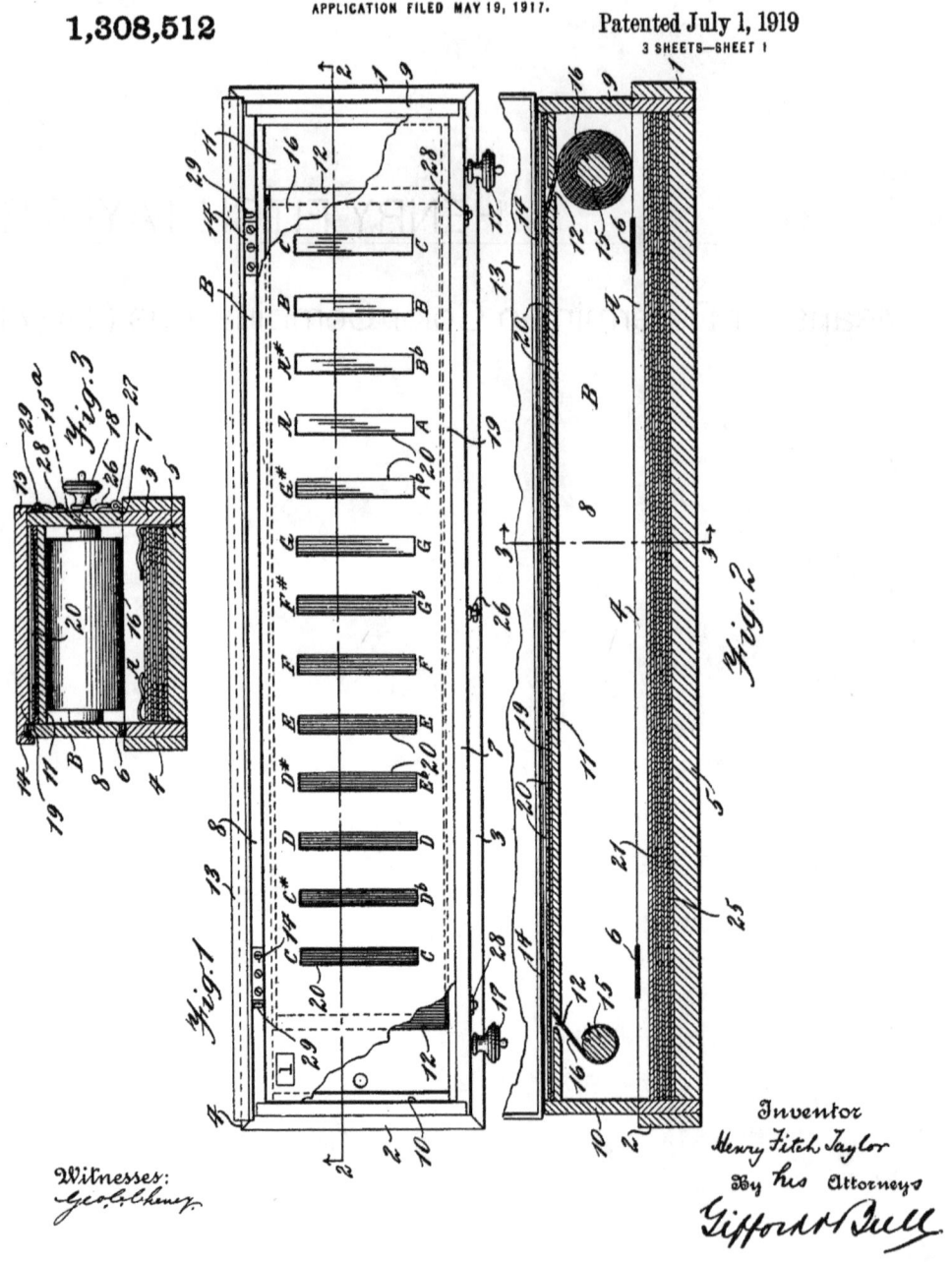

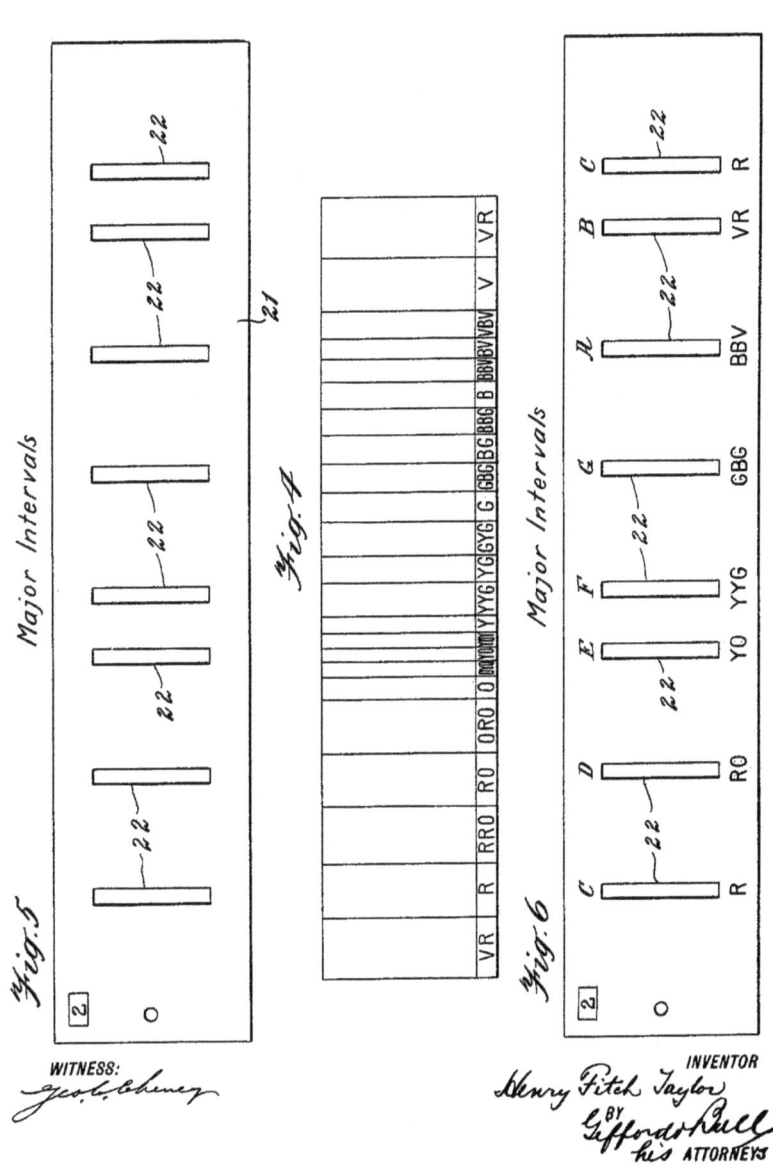

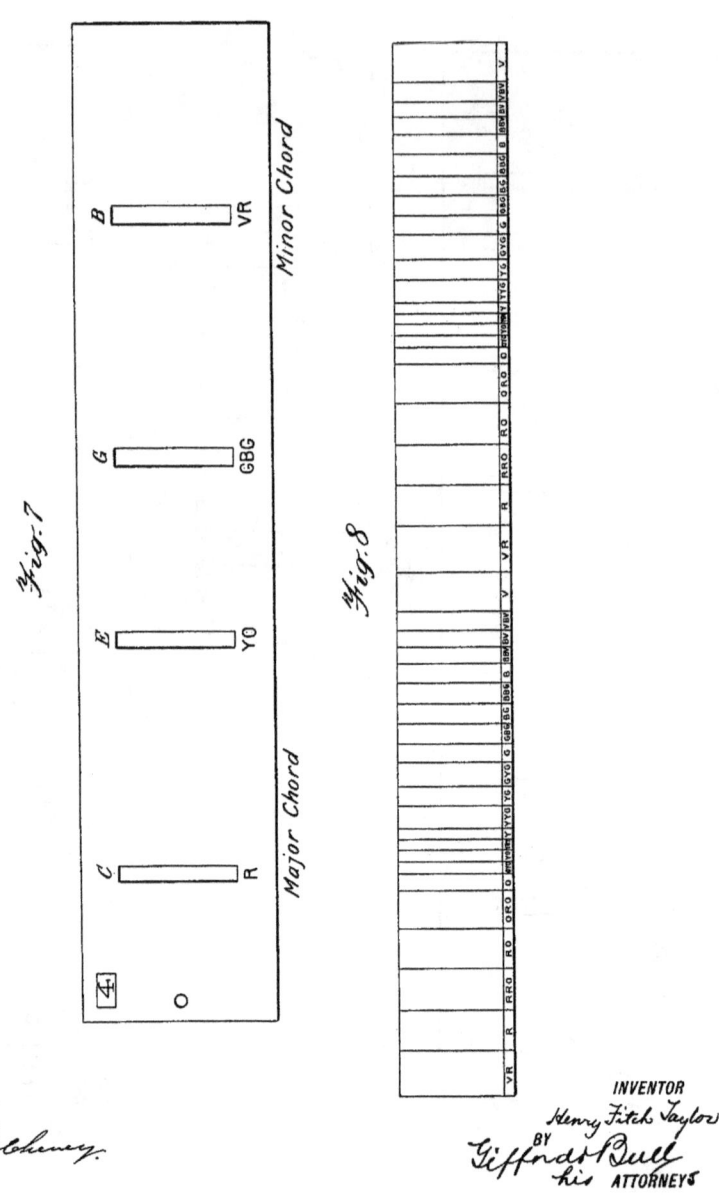

UNITED STATES PATENT OFFICE.

HENRY FITCH TAYLOR, OF NEW YORK, N. Y.

MEANS FOR DETERMINING COLOR COMBINATIONS.

1,308,512.   Specification of Letters Patent.   **Patented July 1, 1919.**

Application filed May 19, 1917. Serial No. 169,611.

To all whom it may concern:

Be it known that I, HENRY FITCH TAYLOR, a citizen of New York, residing at New York city, borough of Manhattan, in the county of New York and State of New York, have invented certain new and useful Improvements in Means for Determining Color Combinations, of which the following is a specification.

My invention relates to new and useful improvements in means for ascertaining and determining combinations of colors, or shades, or tints of colors, which will be in proper harmony.

It has long been believed that musical tones and colors are correlated, although as far as I am aware no means has ever been devised, or principle established, whereby any supposed correlation could be definitely ascertained and employed to determine proper color combinations. I have discovered that the chromatic scale, as employed in music, bears a definite relation to color as the same exists within the visible limits of the solar spectrum, and that proper harmonies produced by combinations of musical tones existing in the chromatic musical scale find their equivalent or response in harmonious color combinations selected from the solar spectrum, so that combinations of musical tones which are in proper harmony can be employed for the purpose of selecting and correlating colors from the solar spectrum which will be in proper harmony.

In carrying out my invention, I employ the solar spectrum, or a representation of it, of any given length, in which the colors bear the proper relation to each other, for instance, the spectrum of Fraunhofer, and provide means whereby the spectrum may be divided in accordance with the tones of the octave of the chromatic musical scale, and produce or determine harmonious color combinations by selecting those color areas or divisions which find harmonious counterpart in tones selected from the chromatic musical scale. In other words, indicating means is provided determined in accordance with harmonious combinations of tones in an octave of the chromatic musical scale, and is made applicable to the solar spectrum in such way that harmonious color combinations may be ascertained by reference to the said harmonious tone combinations in the indicating means.

The invention is of wide importance because it provides a guide by which, not only those versed in the proper selection of color combinations, but also those entirely ignorant of such combinations, may by its practice ascertain definitely and invariably combinations which will be correct for use for artistic purposes, such as pictorial paintings, but also for decorative purposes, in fact, in any situation where a correct combination of colors is desirable or essential. It can also be employed to visualize music and make the reading of it easier and more interesting.

The invention consists in the improvement to be more fully described hereinafter, and the novelty of which will be particularly pointed out and distinctly claimed.

I have fully and clearly illustrated in the accompanying drawings a preferred embodiment of an apparatus for practising my invention, and wherein—

Figure 1 is a plan view of the apparatus;

Fig. 2 is a longitudinal sectional view on the line 2—2 of Fig. 1;

Fig. 3 is a section on the line 3—3 of Fig. 2;

Fig. 4 is a view of a solar-spectrum, showing the divisions according to the Fraunhofer divisions or lines;

Fig. 5 is a plan view of a plate or mask applied to the spectrum, and showing the colors or tints of colors selected according to the major intervals of the chomatic scale;

Fig. 6 is a view of the same mask shown in Fig. 5, but showing the same as applied to sections of two adjoining spectra;

Fig. 7 is a plan view of a plate or mask applied to a spectrum, and having openings therethrough disclosing the colors or tints corresponding to the intervals of the major chord or the minor chord of the chromatic scale, and

Fig. 8 is a view of a plurality of spectra placed end-to-end in sequence and of varying intensity or degrees of color if desired.

Before proceeding with a detailed description of the apparatus employed for practising my invention, I desire to make it understood that I do not limit myself to the particular apparatus shown and described, as the invention in its application is capable of wide variation without departing from the spirit and scope thereof.

Referring to the drawings by numerals of reference, A designates a base-box preferably oblong in shape, and consisting of end walls 1, 2, and longitudinal front and rear side walls 3, 4, and a bottom wall 5. Hingedly connected, as at 6, to this base-box is a rectangular oblong box or frame B, consisting of longitudinal side walls 7, 8, and end walls 9, 10, which form vertical extensions of the end walls and side walls of the base-box, as clearly appears in Figs. 1 and 2. The box or frame B is provided with a table or platform 11 closing the top of said box frame and provided adjacent its ends with transverse slots 12, 12, for a purpose to be presently described. The box frame B described may be provided with a cover 13 of any suitable construction, preferably hinged as at 14 to the wall 8. Within the box frame B, beneath the platform or table 11, and adjacent the ends thereof, are arranged rotatable reels or drums 15, 15, having their axes of rotation extending transversely of the box B, upon which drums are wound the opposite ends of a band or web 16 carrying the spectrum or spectra from which the color combinations are to be determined and selected. From said reels or drums, the web 16 passes upward through the said slots 12, 12, and the intermediate portion of said web lies flat upon the platform of table 11 heretofore mentioned. This web or band may carry a spectrum or any number of spectra desired in accordance with the range of capabilities it is intended the apparatus to have. If more than one spectrum is employed, they are arranged end-to-end lengthwise of the band or web, and may be, and preferably are, of gradually decreasing or graded tones, that is, the first spectrum, say that at the left-hand end of the web, may be low and deep toned, and the other spectra gradually lightening or rising in color pitch toward the right, so that a range of colors and tints or shades will be available, either of high or low key or intermediate key as may be desirable.

The forward ends of the shafts or pintles 15ª, of the drums 15, 15, may be provided with hand-knobs 17, by means of which said drums may be rotated to pay out and wind up the web 16, so as to bring any desired area thereof in position upon the platform or table 11. By the means just described the desired spectrum or portions of adjacent spectra may be located on the table to permit the selection of the desired combinations of color.

The web or band 16, in the embodiment illustrated, preferably bears seven (although it may bear more or less than this number) representations of the solar spectrum which, beginning at the left end, are low and deep toned and gradually lighten or rise in pitch as they progress toward the right-hand end of the band. I preferably employ a transverse division line to mark the beginning and ending of each representation of the spectrum and within the area between the adjacent lines lies what I term "an octave of color."

In Figs. 4 and 8 wherein are shown one spectrum and also a strip embodying three spectra, I have indicated by letters or initials the names of the various colors shown, which will be clear from the following:

V R indicates violet-red; R indicates red; R R O indicates red-red-orange; R O indicates red-orange; O R O indicates orange-red-orange; O indicates orange; O Y O indicates orange-yellow-orange; Y O indicates yellow-orange; Y O Y indicates yellow-orange-yellow; Y indicates yellow; Y Y G indicates yellow-yellow-green; Y G indicates yellow-green; G Y G indicates green-yellow-green; G indicates green; G B G indicates green-blue-green; B G indicates blue-green; B B G indicates blue-blue-green; B indicates blue; B B V indicates blue-blue-violet; B V indicates blue-violet; V B V indicates violet-blue-violet; V indicates violet.

I will now proceed to describe one means for determining or indicating harmonious color combinations upon a spectrum or combination of spectra, for instance, such as indicated on the said band 16, and in order that the same and its operation will be fully understood, I would first state that it is well-known that every visible graduation of pure color is to be found within the bounds of the solar spectrum, and that every known gradation of tone is contained within the octave of the chromatic musical scale. With these well-known facts in mind, I provide means for dividing the spectrum into twelve divisions equally spaced, and proportioned to the twelve half-steps or tones of the chromatic musical scale. In order to make this clear, I have illustrated in Fig. 1 a mask 19 having a plurality of openings 20 which are equally spaced apart from each other, and are of such area as to expose the colors on that portion of the spectrum directly beneath the said openings. These openings 20 are twelve in number and correspond to the twelve half-steps of the chromatic musical scale, as clearly indicated in Fig. 1, and a thirteenth opening to repeat the first to make it complete and convenient to obtain an octave of color. When an octave of color is to be determined, the mask and the spectrum may be moved lengthwise relative to each other, so that the black line at one end of the spectrum comes under the left-hand edge of the first opening 20 at the left of the mask 19, so that the twelve openings through the mask expose a scale of color which corresponds to the chromatic scale in music, and the thirteenth repeats the first. If a higher pitch octave of color is desired, the band may be moved to the left, while a lower pitch octave may be obtained by moving the band to the right. This description serves to indicate the manner in which the chromatic musical scale is to be applied to the spectrum to ascertain or determine the divisions or areas of color in the spectrum corresponding to the chromatic scale. It will be understood that the colors exposed through the openings 20 of the mask 19 do not as an aggregate make or indicate any selection or combination of colors as regards the harmonious effect desired.

With the scale or octave of color determined in the manner just described, I am able to apply the principle for making of musical harmonies to the making of color harmonies, by the selection of those openings or indications. The corresponding colors exposed through said openings, will be found to be in correct harmony as combinations of color. For instance, from the standpoint of harmonious musical tone it is known that the notes or musical intervals of the major scale are the foundation for composition of harmonious tone, and this is also true when the colors of the spectrum show through the openings 20 corresponding to the intervals of the musical scale. That is, if the portions of the spectrum exposed through the openings 20, corresponding to a harmonious tone combination of notes selected from the notes or tones C, D, E, F, G, A, B are combined or used together, they will be in color harmony. In order to facilitate such a selection I employ a mask or indicating means such as shown at 21 in Fig. 5, in which appear only those openings or indications 22 which correspond to the intervals of the major scale. This mask 21 may be laid over the spectrum in the same manner as described with reference to the use of the mask 19, and a group of colors will be exposed which are in harmony, and from which harmonious color combination can be made. In this mask, there are contained eight openings, the last one at the right corresponding to C of the next octave higher. This mask 21 may be employed not only to determine those colors in a single spectrum which are in harmony, but also any harmonious color combination including any key color in the spectrum. For instance, if one wishes to find the harmoniously related colors to orange or green, or any other color of the spectrum, it is only necessary to adjust the web until the required key color appears in the first opening at the left, and it will be found that this color, with the others exposed, will form a harmonious group. This result is indicated in Fig. 6, in which red is made to appear at the first opening, and at the other openings, will appear red-orange, yellow-orange, yellow-yellow-green, green-blue-green, blue-blue-violet, violet-red, and red, all of which will be in harmony. Red in the next octave of color is repeated at the eighth or last opening. In the case where orange or green, for example is the key color, by bringing that desired color to the first opening at the left, the exposure forms the harmonic group of that color, the mask covering and exposing portions of two representations of the spectrum.

I do not desire to limit myself to the number of indicators or masks shown in the drawings, and described herein. From the indicator or mask of Fig. 1 indicating the twelve (12) half steps in the solar-spectrum corresponding to the twelve half steps in the musical octave known as the chromatic scale, may be developed, if desired, various other indicating means or masks, for instance, a mask showing the major intervals, a mask showing the melodic minor, a mask showing the chromatic minor, a mask showing minor and major chords (illustrated in Fig. 6), a mask showing diminished sevenths, and a mask showing the eccentric chords used by some of the modern composers of music. All of these are included within the mask (shown in Fig. 1) indicating the chromatic scale. By means of this mask (shown in Fig. 1) any musical composition arranged for the pianoforte may be translated into color.

In Fig. 7 I have shown a mask containing but four openings which represent a means of obtaining the major and minor chords of the key shown in mask 19. By the use of this indicating means the major and minor chords of harmonious color may be selected, for instance, the colors appearing through the first three openings from the left will be a major chord of colors in harmony, and the first three colors from the right will be a minor chord of colors in harmony. The band or web may be shifted from right to left to any position relative to the openings, but no matter what position it reaches there will be exposed a major and minor chord of color harmony.

It will thus be seen that a harmonious combination of musical tone may be, and is employed in accordance with my invention to ascertain or determine a group of colors the individuals of which are harmoniously correlated.

It will be understood that I do not limit my invention to the use of a mask or masks as the indicating means, as other means operating on the same principle involved may be employed without departing from the spirit and scope of my invention. I also do not desire to be limited to the mounting of the spectrum or spectra upon a band, but merely show this means as being a convenient one, and one which lends itself readily to the mounting of several spectra in proper relation to each other.

The arrangement or construction of the apparatus shown and described is merely by way of exemplification in order to provide a convenient and self-contained device. It will be noted that the base-box structure 5 serves as a container for those indicating devices, for instance, the masks which may not be in use, as indicated in Fig. 5.

In Fig. 1 it will be noted that the side and end walls of the box or frame B are extended above the level of the platform 11, so as to provide a peripheral flange which serves to properly locate the mask on the platform, so that the openings through the mask will be in proper relation to the corresponding areas of the underlying spectrum band. The intermediate frame B may be provided with hooks 26 adapted to coöperate with eyes 27 on the base-box A, whereby the parts A and B may be secured together. The box B may also be provided with hooks 28 to cooperate with eyes 29 on the cover, whereby the latter is held closed.

I have illustrated in the drawings a representation of the spectrum by indicating the primary colors, shades and tints by means of definite areas of the same, but it will be understood that this method of illustration is adopted because of the inability to depict the spectrum in its true form by means of black ink, and that while such representation is within the scope of my invention, the invention also contemplates in the actual instrument the correct representation of the colors and gradual blending or transition thereof as they appear in the true spectrum.

The openings in the masks are preferably limited in width so that individually they may be adjusted not to show more than one area of color of the spectrum. It will be understood, that the color harmonies are not limited to those exposed by the masks described, which for example, are only for half-tones in the chromatic, because harmonies will also be produced in case the masks be constructed to indicate quarter, eighth or any other value of note.

What I claim and desire to secure by Letters Patent of the United States is:—

1. An instrument of the character described, comprising a representation of the solar spectrum, and means comprising a representation of a musical tone harmony associated therewith for selecting a harmonious color combination.

2. A device of the character described, comprising a representation of the solar spectrum, and indicating means operable to selectively indicate harmonious combinations of color corresponding to harmonious tone combinations of the notes of an octave of the chromatic scale.

3. A device of the character described, comprising a representation of the solar spectrum, and a mask adapted to lie over the spectrum and having openings spaced according to the notes of the chromatic scale which are in harmony.

4. A device of the character described, comprising a representation of the solar spectrum, and a mask adapted to lie over the spectrum and having openings corresponding to harmonious tone combinations of an octave of the chromatic scale.

5. A device of the character described, comprising a representation of the solar spectrum, and a mask adapted to lie over the spectrum and having openings spaced to correspond to a combination of harmonious notes of an octave of equally spaced notes of a chromatic scale coextensive with the spectrum.

6. A device of the character described, comprising a plurality of representations of equal length of the solar spectrum, and a mask having openings spaced from each other to correspond to a combination of harmonious notes of an octave of equally spaced notes of a chromatic scale coextensive with one of said spectra.

7. A device of the character described, comprising a plurality of representations of equal length of the solar spectrum, a mask having openings spaced from each other to correspond to a combination of harmonious notes of an octave of equally spaced notes of a chromatic scale coextensive with one of said spectra, and means for causing a relative movement of said mask and spectra longitudinally of the latter.

8. A device of the character described, comprising a representation of the solar spectrum, a mask adapted to lie over the spectrum and having openings spaced to correspond to a combination of harmonious notes of an octave of equally spaced notes of a chromatic scale coextensive with the spectrum, and means for causing a relative movement of said mask and spectrum longitudinally of the latter.

9. A device of the character described, comprising a representation of the solar spectrum, and indicating means operable to selectively indicate harmonious combinations of colors to correspond to a combination of harmonious notes of an octave of equally spaced notes of a chromatic scale coextensive with the spectrum.

10. A device of the character described, comprising a plurality of representations of the solar spectrum of equal lengths, and indicating means operable to selectively indicate harmonious combinations of colors to correspond to a combination of harmonious notes of an octave of equally spaced notes of a chromatic scale coextensive with the spectrum.

11. A device of the character described, comprising a representation of the solar spectrum according to the Fraunhofer divi-

sions and means for indicating a color combination thereon in accordance with a musical tone harmony.

12. A device of the character described, comprising a representation of the solar spectrum, and indicating means dividing said spectrum into areas of color, said means consisting of indicia spaced according to the notes of a chromatic scale coextensive with the spectrum.

13. A device of the character described, comprising a representation of the solar spectrum, and indicating means coöperable therewith to select colors to correspond to a combination of the notes of an octave of equally spaced notes of a chromatic scale coextensive with the spectrum.

14. A device of the character described, comprising a casing, drums in the casing, a web wound on the drums, said web bearing a representation of the solar spectrum, and indicating means coöperating with the spectrum for determining a harmonious color combination thereon in accordance with a musical tone harmony.

15. A device of the character described, comprising a casing, drums in the casing, a web wound on the drums, said web bearing a representation of the solar spectrum, and a mask adapted to lie over the spectrum and having openings spaced according to the notes of a chromatic scale coextensive with the spectrum.

16. A device of the character described, comprising a casing, drums in the casing, a platform over the drums, a web wound on the drums and lying on the platform, said web bearing a representation of the solar spectrum, and indicating means coöperating with the spectrum to indicate thereon a combination of harmonious colors corresponding to a combination of harmonious notes of an octave of equally spaced notes of a chromatic scale coextensive with the spectrum.

17. A device of the character described, comprising a casing, drums in the casing, a platform over the drums, a web wound on the drums and lying on the platform, said web bearing a representation of the solar spectrum, and a mask adapted to lie over the spectrum and having openings spaced according to the notes of a chromatic scale coextensive with the spectrum.

In testimony whereof I have hereunto signed my name in the presence of two subscribing witnesses.

HENRY FITCH TAYLOR.

Witnesses:
C. G. HEYLMUN,
E. M. LOCKWOOD.

Copies of this patent may be obtained for five cents each, by addressing the "Commissioner of Patents, Washington, D. C."

ALEXANDER BURNETT HECTOR

Color-Music Apparatus (1917)

Color-Music Apparatus (1917)

Color-Music Apparatus (1922)

Color-Music Apparatus (1927)

Color-Music Apparatus (1927)

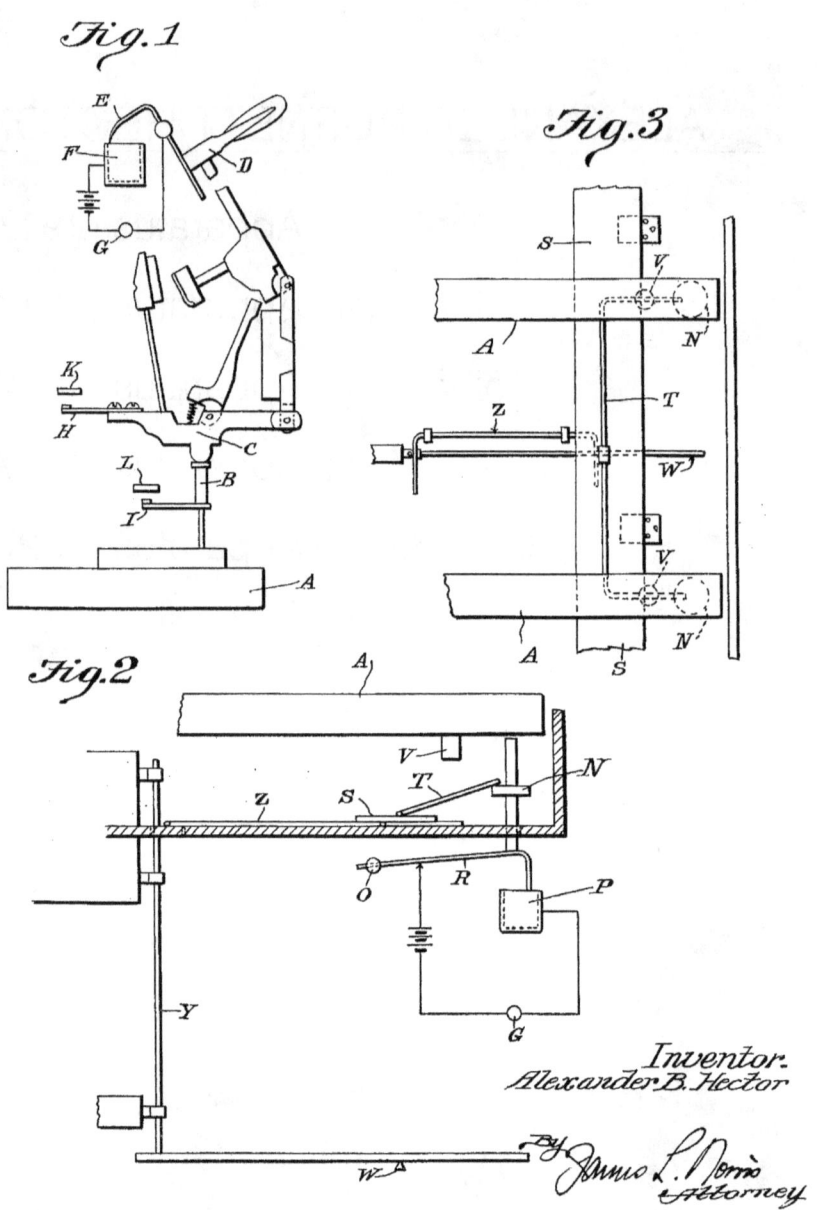

VISUAL MUSIC INSTRUMENT PATENTS (I)

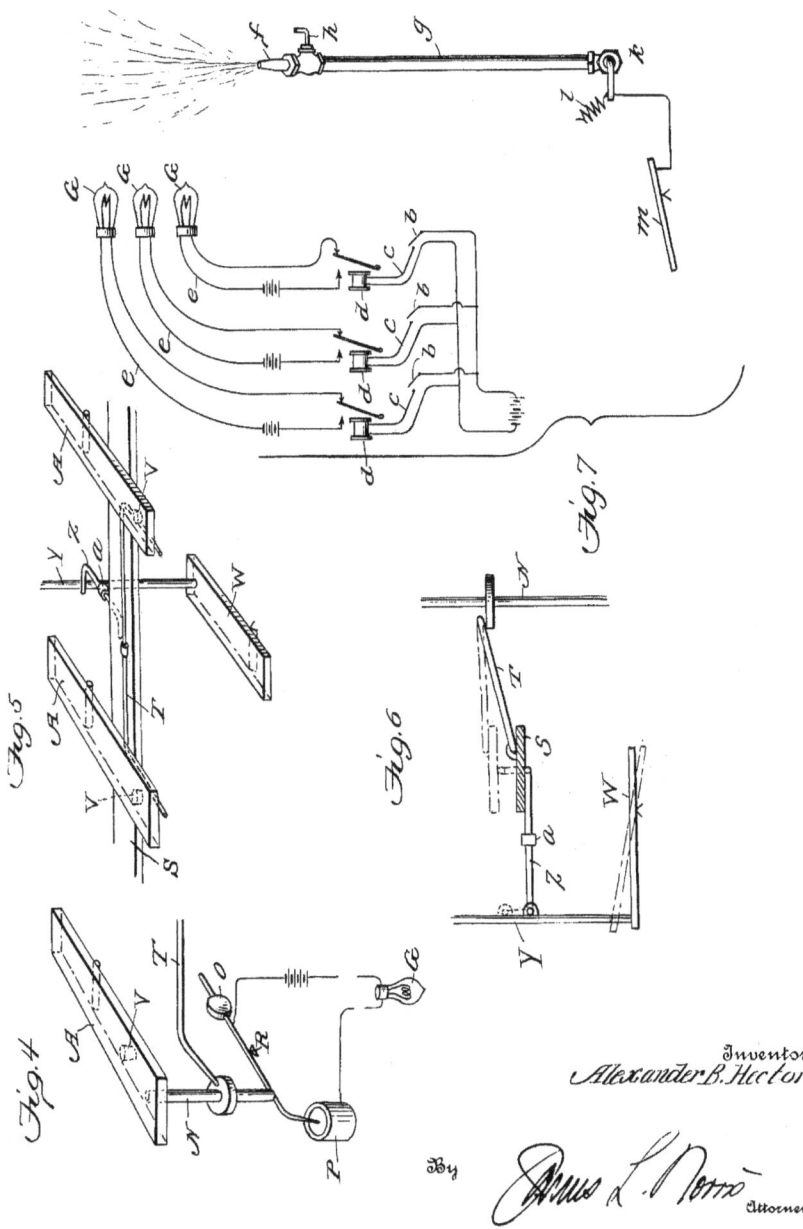

UNITED STATES PATENT OFFICE.

ALEXANDER BURNETT HECTOR, OF GREENWICH, NEAR SYDNEY, NEW SOUTH WALES, AUSTRALIA

APPARATUS FOR PRODUCING COLOR-MUSIC.

1,388,706. Specification of Letters Patent. **Patented Aug. 23, 1921.**

Application filed July 9, 1917. Serial No. 179,460.

To all whom it may concern:

Be it known that I, ALEXANDER BURNETT HECTOR, a subject of the King of Great Britain, residing at Greenwich, near Sydney, in the State of New South Wales, Commonwealth of Australia, have invented certain new and useful Improvements in and Relating to Apparatus for Producing Color-Music, of which the following is a specification.

This invention has reference to improvements in and relating to the production of color music and other spectacular effects and apparatus therefor as described in my prior British Patent No. 29615 of 1912, also my recent prior applications for Letters Patent of the United States of America, filed June 8, 1917, Serial Nos. 173,671 and 173,672, in which the movements of the keys of a piano, piano player, and organ are made to operate a series of switches so as to light a series of lamps in connection with the production of color music.

When the key of a piano, or combined piano and player, is depressed, the hammer moves forward and strikes a given set of wires producing an individual note of music; this movement of the hammer is utilized to complete the electric circuit of a given switch and light a given lamp or series of lamps. By repeating this for every hammer of the piano and suitably coloring the various lamps color music is made possible as already described in my said prior applications for Letters Patent.

The present invention has for its general objects to provide improved circuit-closing means for apparatus of this character, to provide means for producing sustained and octave effects, and to provide for the sympathetic control of water, steam, smoke, or other fluid on which to project and reflect the colors.

The foregoing and other objects of the invention, together with means whereby the same may be carried into effect, will best be understood from the following description of one form or embodiment thereof illustrated in the accompanying drawings, in which:

Figure 1 represents in elevation the various parts of a piano movement at the rear of the keys and to which the contact devices of this invention have been attached.

Fig. 2 is a sectional elevation showing the invention fitted to the forward end of one key.

Fig. 3 is a plan showing the coupling bar between two keys, one octave apart.

Fig. 4 is a detail perspective view, partly diagrammatic, of the circuit closing means shown in Fig. 2.

Fig. 5 is a detail perspective view and Fig. 6 a fragmentary sectional view of the octave coupling means shown in Figs. 2 and 3.

Fig. 7 is a fragmentary detail view, partly diagrammatic, of the fluid projecting means and the lamp controlling relays.

In Fig. 1, A is a piano key which is pivoted in the usual manner and on being depressed causes the extension B to lift. This extension in turn raises the wippen C which throws forward the hammer D which by striking a tuned string produces a note of music. As the hammer D moves forward to strike the string the end of the contact lever E which is suitably weighted or controlled by a spring drops into the mercury cup F and thus completes an electric circuit through the lamp G. At the same time and by the same movement of the key A two other independent circuits may be closed by the contact arms H and I, which are carried by the wippen C and extension B, respectively, and make contact on the metal strips K and L. When pressure is removed from the key A the hammer D drops and strikes the lever E causing it to break the electric circuit through the lamp. At the same time the wippen C and extension B drop back to their normal position thus breaking the circuits through I and H.

From the foregoing it will be seen that advantage has been taken of the hammer movement to control a plurality of circuits by the operation of a single key, and that the arrangement is especially suitable for use in connection with combined piano players wherein the space within the case is very largely occupied by the player mechanism. It will also be observed that the construction and arrangement of the lever E is such that it follows the hammer D through the full extent of the movement of the latter, thus insuring electrical contact during the whole period of the depression of the controlling key.

When a note, or chord, of a piano is struck, and the sustaining pedal is depressed at the same time, wires of the octaves of these notes are set vibrating by the well known principle of resonance. To obtain a somewhat similar effect in color, the following mechanism is provided:

In Figs. 2 to 6, each, key A on being depressed acts on the plunger N, which in turn tilts the weighted lever O into the mercury cup P thus completing an electric circuit through the lamp. When pressure on the key A is removed the weighted lever O which is pivoted at R falls back to its original position thus breaking the electric circuit through the lamp. In addition along the underside of the whole length of the keyboard is a hinged coupler board S on which are fixed a series of coupling levers or rack shafts T only one of which is shown in the diagrams. The bent end of each lever rests on the flange of the corresponding plunger N and when the coupler board is in the position shown in Fig. 2, these bent arms are out of reach of the buttons V carried by the several keys A when said keys are depressed. When the octave or sustaining pedal W is operated it causes the rod Y to lift. This rod is fitted with a projecting piece on which rests one arm of the rock shaft or bent lever Z pivoted at a and the other arm of which is under the coupler board S. The action of the pedal in lifting the rod Y causes the coupler board to be raised, as shown in dotted lines in Fig. 6, and brings the bent arms of the lever T into a more or less horizontal position so that when the key A is next depressed the button V pressing on one arm of the lever T causes the opposite end to depress the plunger one octave higher and complete an electric circuit through a second lamp.

The complete sequence of movements is, first, the depression of the sustaining pedal W which acts through the rod Y and lever Z to raise the coupler board S, second, the depression of the given key A and the simultaneous depression of the corresponding plunger N which acts to close the corresponding switch P—R, and, third, actuation by the button V on the depressed key of the corresponding lever T the other end of which acts on the plunger N under the key an octave higher on the scale. Consequently, when the sustaining pedal is depressed, each key is made to control two lamps or two series of lamps, and, by the multiplication of the arms of the individual levers T, three or more octaves may be operated at the same time by the depression of a single key.

The circuit closing devices E—F, H—K, I—L, and P—R, above described, may, if desired, control the circuits to the lamp G directly, as shown in Figs. 1 and 2. Preferably, however, and as shown in Fig. 7, these circuit closing devices (three of which are generically indicated by the letter b in the latter figure) are arranged to control circuits c to magnetic relays d which, in turn, control circuits e to the several lamps G. The relays d are preferably of a well known type involving a time element, whereby a sustained effect in the display of the colors is produced.

In order to obtain a varying body or form on which to project and reflect the light, fountains of water, steam, or smoke may be employed. Thus, as shown in Fig. 7, the light from the lamps G is projected upon a spray or jet from a nozzle f supplied with fluid from any suitable source through a pipe g. Flow from the nozzle f may be controlled by a hand operated valve h, but is preferably regulated by a valve k controlled by a spring l and operated, through suitable connections, by one or more pedals m which may be the loud or soft pedals of the instrument, or both, whereby the volume of the spray or cloud will be in sympathy with the pianissimo, piano, mezzoforte, forte, and fortissimo of the music.

The apparatus hereinbefore described is preferably utilized in conjunction with the definite tempered color scales described in my said prior applications for Letters Patent.

Having thus described my invention what I claim as new and desire to protect by Letters Patent, is:—

1. In an apparatus of the character described, the combination with a keyed musical instrument, of means for displaying a variety of colors corresponding to the several notes struck, circuit closing devices operated by the several keys for controlling said displaying means, each of said circuit closing devices comprising a mercury cup and a lever having a portion adapted to dip into said cup, and a coupler mechanism coöperating with said controlling devices for causing a plurality of said colors to be simultaneously displayed upon operation of a single key.

2. In an apparatus of the character described, the combination with a musical instrument and means controlled thereby for producing varied color effects in accordance with the notes sounded by said instrument, of means under the control of the player and including one or more electric contacts and one or more electro-magnetic relays having a time element for varying the operation of said color producing means to produce a sustained effect therein.

3. In an apparatus of the character de-

scribed, the combination with a musical instrument and illuminating means controlled thereby for projecting a variety of colors in accordance with the notes sounded by said instrument, of means controlled by said instrument for discharging a body of fluid upon which said colors are projected.

In testimony whereof I have hereunto set my hand in presence of two subscribing witnesses.

ALEXANDER BURNETT HECTOR.

Witnesses:
CHARLES E. ENHAM,
HENRY W. CLARKE.

VISUAL MUSIC INSTRUMENT PATENTS (I)

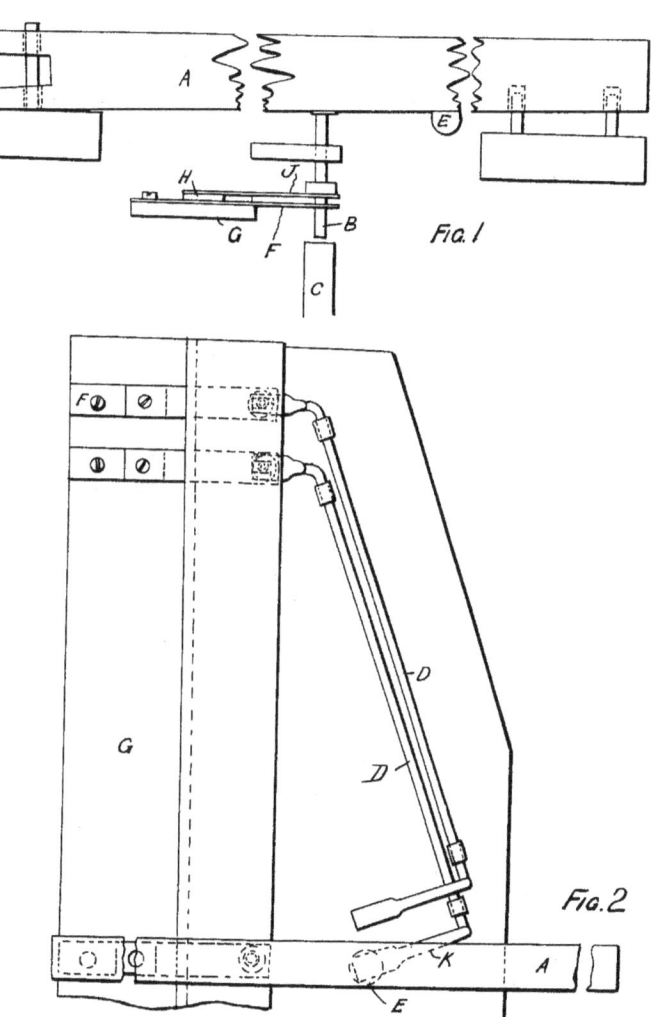

A. B. HECTOR.
PRODUCTION OF COLOR MUSIC AND OTHER LUMINOUS EFFECTS AND APPARATUS THEREFOR.
APPLICATION FILED JUNE 8, 1917.

1,432,552

Patented Oct. 17, 1922
5 SHEETS—SHEET 1

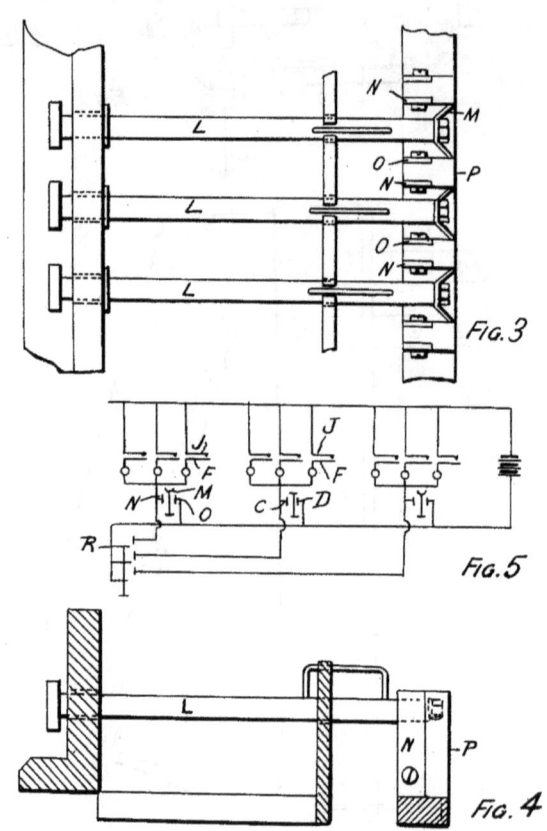

VISUAL MUSIC INSTRUMENT PATENTS (I)

A. B. HECTOR.
PRODUCTION OF COLOR MUSIC AND OTHER LUMINOUS EFFECTS AND APPARATUS THEREFOR.
APPLICATION FILED JUNE 8, 1917.

1,432,552

Patented Oct. 17, 1922.
5 SHEETS—SHEET 3

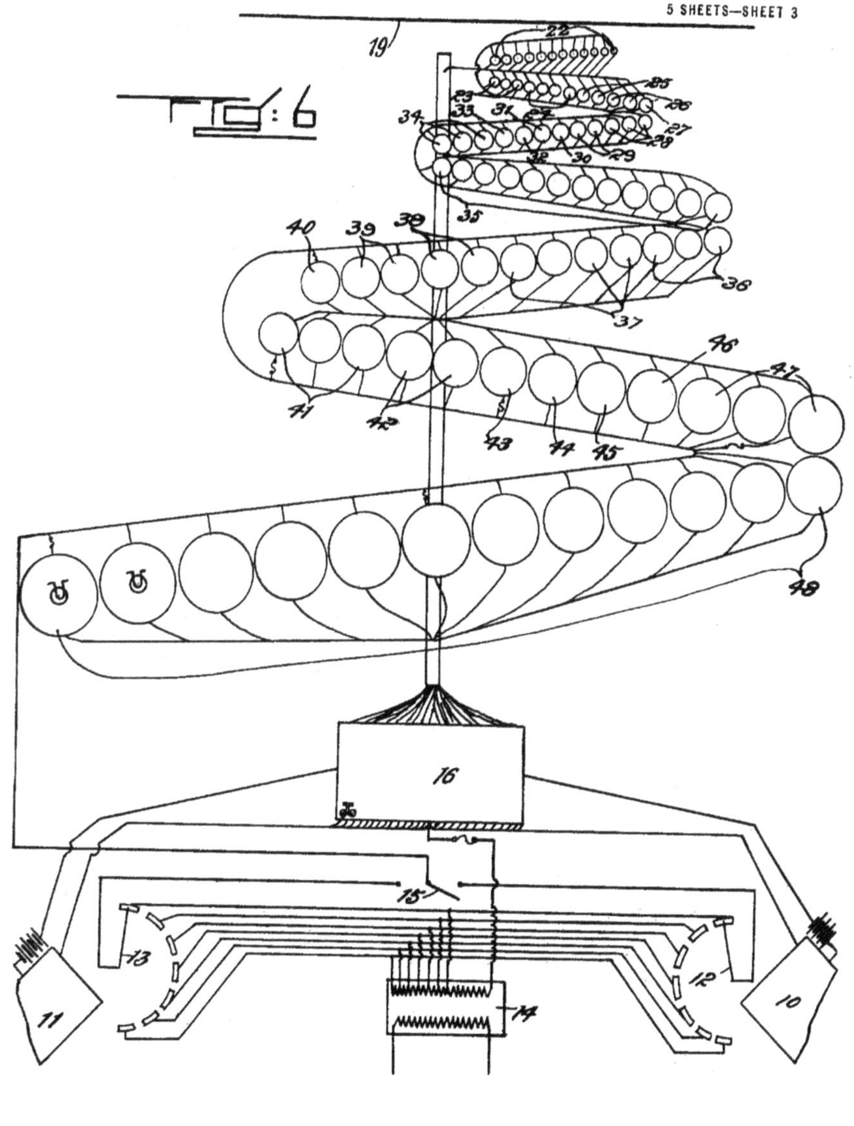

FIG. 6

Witnesses:

Inventor
Alexander B. Hector
by
Attorney

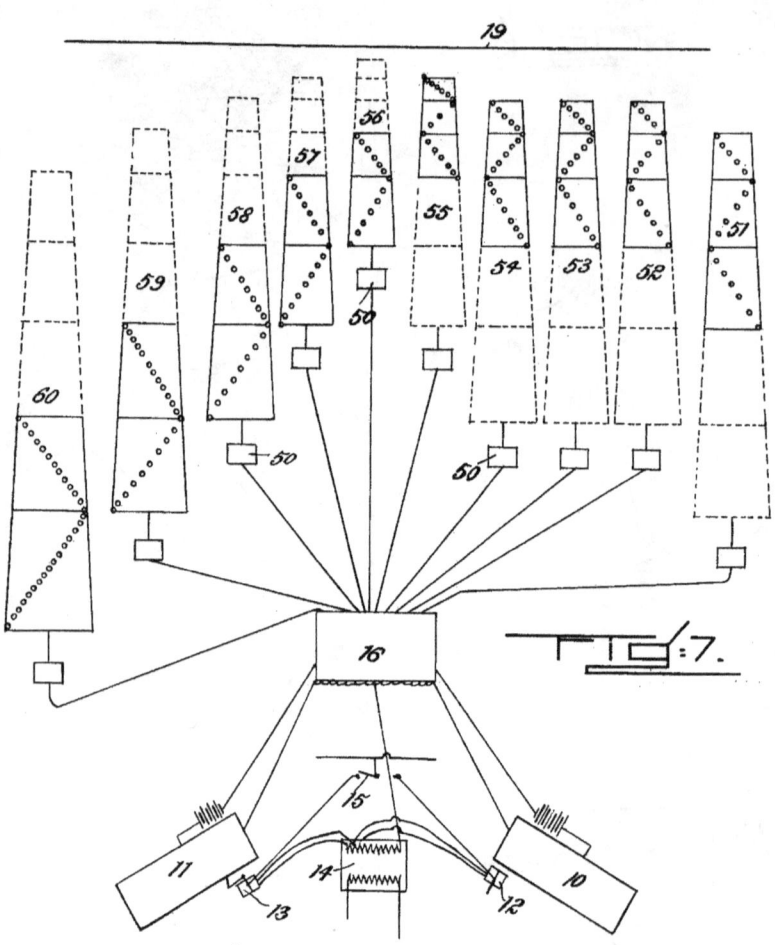

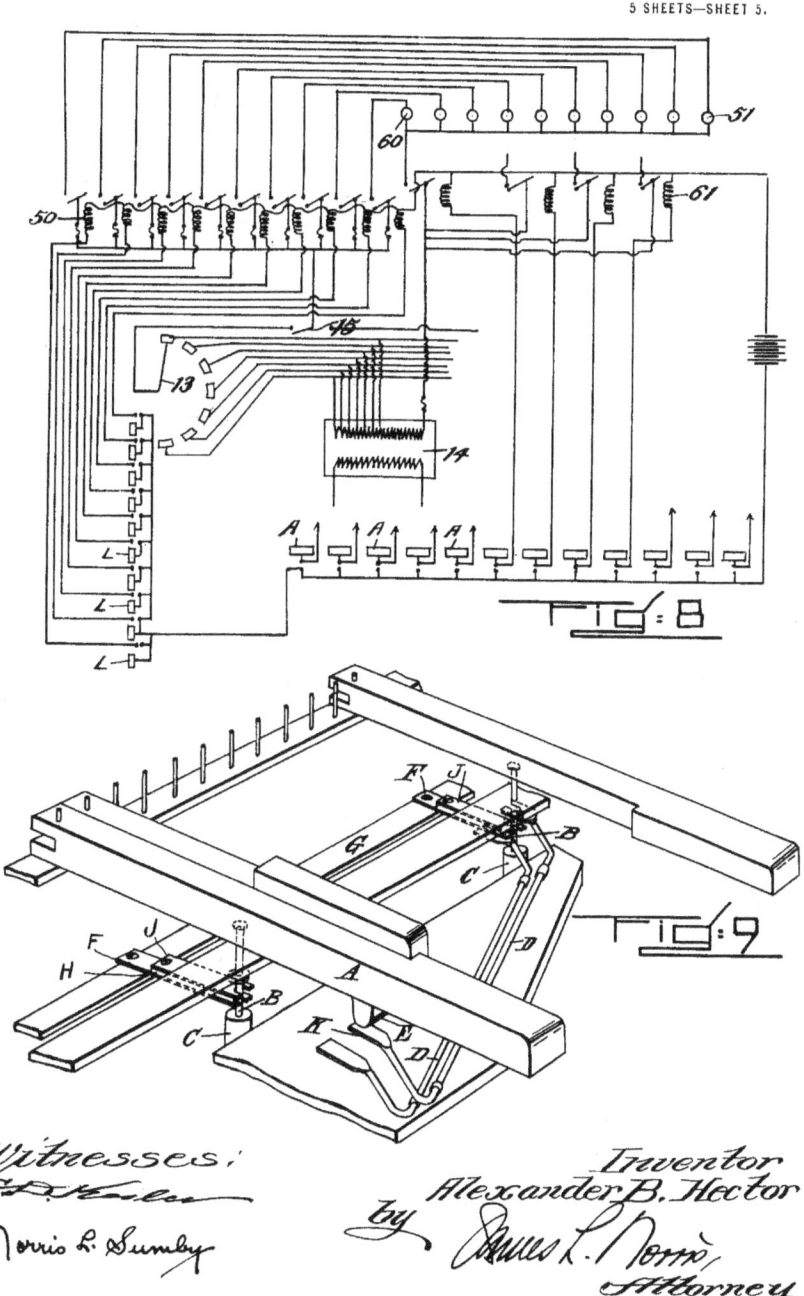

Patented Oct. 17, 1922.

1,432,552

UNITED STATES PATENT OFFICE.

ALEXANDER BURNETT HECTOR, OF GREENWICH, NEAR SYDNEY, NEW SOUTH WALES, AUSTRALIA.

PRODUCTION OF COLOR MUSIC AND OTHER LUMINOUS EFFECTS AND APPARATUS THEREFOR.

Application filed June 8, 1917. Serial No. 173,672.

To all whom it may concern:

Be it known that I, ALEXANDER BURNETT HECTOR, a subject of the King of Great Britain, residing at Greenwich, near Sydney, in the State of New South Wales, Commonwealth of Australia, have invented certain new and useful Improvements in the Production of Color Music and Other Luminous Effects and Apparatus Therefor, of which the following is a specification.

This invention relates to improvements in my prior British Patent No. 29,615 of 1912 and to improvements covered by a further application for patent filed June 8, 1917, Serial No. 173,671 and consists firstly in the means for forming what I term "scales of colors" controlled by the individual keys of an organ, piano, or other keyed instrument in definite ratios of space occupied by the various colors in the normal solar spectrum; secondly, in the means whereby the stops of an organ operate switches to illuminate electric lamps of a candle power and reflectors with an area in definite ratios; and, thirdly, in the particular apparatus whereby the various colored electric lamps so positioned and arranged are controlled by the keys to make and break contacts or diminish or increase the intensity of the lamps.

It is well known (see for example, "Modern Chromatics," by Ogden N. Rood, page 24) that if the space occupied by the normal solar spectrum be divided into, say, 1,000 parts, the various colors occupy different proportions of this space, the ratios for each color being as shown in the following table A.

Table A.

Red	330
Orange red	104
Orange	25
Orange yellow	26
Yellow	13
Greenish yellow and yellowish green	97
Green	87
Blue green	16
Cyan blue	51
Blue	74
Violet blue	117
Violet	60

In applying these ratios to form my scale of colors controllable by the keys of an organ, I commence with the lowest bass note and proceed upwardly through the first four octaves or 48 notes as follows:—

Table B.

(Bass notes).	Keys.	Lamps or series of lamps.
Reds	15 =	15
Orange reds	5 =	5
Oranges	2 =	2
Orange yellow	1 =	1
Yellow	1 =	1
Greenish yellow and yellowish green	5 =	5
Green	4 =	4
Blue green	1 =	1
Cyan blue	2 =	2
Blue	4 =	4
Violet blue	6 =	6
Violet	2 =	2
(Treble notes).		

The remaining thirteen treble notes are tinted in varying degrees of violet pink and light pink, merging into white light.

The sub-base stop controls lamps of a hue descending from violets and purples to blues and greens of the deepest hue, the lowest note being greenish yellow, in the following ratios:—

	Keys.	Lamps or series of lamps.
Violet	3 =	3
Violet blue	6 =	6
Blue	4 =	4
Cyan blue	2 =	2
Blue green	1 =	1
Green	4 =	4
Yellowish green and greenish yellow	4 =	4

This arrangement of color in the ratios set forth would also apply in the case of a piano or other keyed instrument, it is of fundamental importance, and it would apply to all apparatus outlined in my prior British Patent No. 29,615 of 1912.

This scale of ratio of the spectrum colors may be arranged over the various keys and octaves in several ways to suit different classes of music. These arrangements are conveniently shown in the following, wherein x denotes any suitable constant:—

Table C.

Octaves (treble).	Color.	Hue.
1st octave 12 keys	White	Depth 1x
2nd octave 12 keys	} Violet to red	} Depth 2x
3rd octave 12 keys		
4th octave 12 keys		
5th octave 12 keys	} Violet to red	} Depth 4x
6th octave 12 keys		
7th octave 12 keys		
(Bass).		

Table D.

Octaves (treble).	Color.	Hue.
1st 12 keys	White	Depth 1x
2nd 12 keys	} Violet to red	} Depth 2x
3rd 12 keys		
4th 12 keys	} Violet to red	} Depth 4x
5th 12 keys		
6th 12 keys	} Violet to red	} Depth 8x
7th 12 keys		
(Bass.)		

Table E.

Octaves (treble).	Color.	Hue.
1st 12 keys	White	Depth 1x
2nd 12 keys	Violet to red	Depth 2x
3rd 12 keys	Violet to red	Depth 4x
4th 12 keys	Violet to red	Depth 8x
5th 12 keys	Violet to red	Depth 16x
6th 12 keys	Violet to red	Depth 32x
7th 12 keys	Violet to red	Depth 64x
(Bass.)		

It is well known that when a given stop is pulled out in an organ, sound of a given volume and quality is produced, the volume increasing as a 2 feet, 4 feet, 8 feet, 16 feet and sub-base or 32 feet stops and so on is operated upon. Arrangements are made so that these stops operate a given switch bringing into light lamps of a candle power, reflectors with an area, and color of a hue or shade in the following ratio, x denoting any suitable predetermined unit or constant which is the same throughout any given column, but not necessarily the same in different columns.

Table F.

Stops.	Ratios of candle-power.	Area of reflectors.	Depth of shade or color.	Thickness of lamp filament.
2 feet	2x	2x	2x	2x
4 feet	4x	4x	4x	4x
8 feet	8x	8x	8x	8x
16 feet	16x	16x	16x	16x
32 feet	32x	32x	32x	32x
64 feet	64x	64x	64x	64x

In the accompanying drawings,

Figures 1 and 2 are respectively, a side view and plan of part of an American organ illustrating my apparatus for effecting contact of each key to control its particular lamp.

Figures 3 and 4 represent in plan and elevation an arrangement of stops on an American organ for bringing in lamps of the required candle power.

Figure 5 is a diagrammatic drawing illustrating means for bringing in all the lamps simultaneously by a master switch actuated by the left knee swell.

Figure 6 is a diagrammatic view illustrating an arrangement of lamps in accordance with Table C.

Figure 7 is a diagrammatic view illustrating a series of banks of lamps.

Figure 8 is a diagrammatic view of the wiring for the series of banks of lamps shown in Figure 7.

Figure 9 is a perspective view of the parts shown in Figures 1 and 2.

The same reference characters indicate the same or like parts in the several views.

Referring to Figs. 1, 2 and 9 A is a key of an American organ which when depressed causes the plunger B to operate on a sticker C to release the air pressure and produce a given sound. Also when the octave coupler is pulled out it raises a series of levers D bringing them in contact with lugs E situated underneath each key A so that for every key depressed the octave above is also sounded.

In my apparatus I utilize these movements to close a series of electrical contacts placed underneath the plungers which contacts control one or more lamps for each plunger and consequently for each key.

To effect this I provide a piece of ebonite or other suitable insulating material G the length of the keyboard and to this is screwed a series of metal strips F equalling the number of keys. Above each of these is screwed another insulating piece H also bearing a metal strip J registering with the corresponding strips F, the several pairs of strips J and F being capable of being brought into contact by the movements of the various plungers B when the corresponding key A is depressed. I thereby form a series of switches arranged in parallel with a common return and a lamp or series of lamps is illuminated by the current on the depression of each key A. When an octave coupler as D is pulled out as will be understood the arm K is brought close to the lug E so that when the key A is depressed the octave key corresponding to A is depressed by the coupler rod. At the same time the two sets of contacts F, J (Fig. 5), are closed and two lamps or series of lamps—corresponding to key A and its octave—are illuminated.

In Figures 3 and 4 are illustrated devices controlled by the stops of an organ for bringing in lamps of the desired candle power. L represents the stops to the end of each of which is fixed a contact piece M capable of completing an electric circuit between the contacts N and O when one of the stops is pulled out, the contacts N and O being carried on the insulated support P. These contacts N and O are connected in the lamp and battery circuit as shown in Fig. 5, and upon pulling out any stop and completing the circuit through N M and O the current from a battery or other source is made to flow to one side of each switch under a certain number of keys corresponding in number to those controlled by the stop which is withdrawn. On depressing any key the electric circuit is completed through the switch under the key as shown clearly in Figure 5.

By means of the master switch R actuated by the left knee swell all the lamps may be illuminated simultaneously, as will be understood from Fig. 5.

An embodiment of the invention in a complete system is diagrammatically illustrated in Figures 6, 7, and 8.

Referring to Figure 6, 22 represents twelve white lamps, the first of which is spaced $1x$ (x being any suitable unit distance) from the screen 19, the remaining eleven lamps being gradually spaced up to about $2x$. Then follows:—

23, representing 3 violet colored lamps, 24, representing 4 violet blue colored lamps, 25, representing 2 blue colored lamps, 26, representing 2 cyan blue colored lamps, 27, representing 1 blue green colored lamp, spaced from $2x$ to about $4x$.

28, representing 3 green colored lamps, 29, representing 2 yellowish green colored lamps, 30, representing 1 greenish yellow colored lamp, 31, representing 1 yellow colored lamp, 32, representing 1 orange yellow colored lamp, 33, representing 1 orange colored lamp, 34, representing 3 orange red colored lamps, spaced from $4x$ to about $8x$.

35, representing 12 red colored lamps varying in intensity of hue, spaced from $8x$ to about $16x$.

36, representing 3 violet colored lamps, 37, representing 4 blue violet colored lamps, 38, representing 2 blue colored lamps, 39, representing 2 cyan blue colored lamps, 40, representing 1 blue green colored lamp, spaced from $16x$ to about $32x$.

41, representing 3 green colored lamps, 42, representing 2 yellowish green colored lamps, 43, representing 1 greenish yellow colored lamp, 44, representing 1 yellow colored lamp, 45, representing 1 orange yellow colored lamp, 46, representing 1 orange colored lamp, 47, representing 3 orange red colored lamps, spaced from $32x$ to about $64x$.

48, representing 12 red colored lamps, spaced from $64x$ to about $128x$ distance from the screen.

Referring to Figure 7, 10 is a player piano and 11 an organ having controllers 12 and 13 respectively operated by the sound volume varying means of the instrument, 14 is a transformer, 15 a double throw switch, and 19 the screen.

50 (see also Fig. 8) represents master relays controlled respectively by the switches M, N, O, (Figs. 3 and 4) of the several stops L. Each of the relays 50 controls one of a series of banks of lights 51 to 60 similar respectively to the single bank or unit illustrated in Figure 6 and varying in size and distance from the screen 19 in ratio to the sound or size of pipe or reed used on withdrawing a given draw stop or stops of the organ. Each of the instrument keys A controls, through its switch F, J, a lamp relay 61. Each lamp relay 61 controls all lamps of the same color value but of different sizes and intensities, while each master relay 50 controls all lamps of the same intensity but of different colors.

In Figure 7 the lamps shown in full lines may be operated by a draw stop in the same way as the reeds or pipes of an organ. An individual stop of some organs controls the whole of the sixty one notes of the organ, while in other organs the stops are divided into bass (twenty-four keys) and treble (thirty-seven keys). The precise arrangement of the apparatus may be considerably varied in accordance with the particular construction of organ or other instrument, a lamp being added for each individual reed or pipe employed. The main object has been to provide apparatus which synchronizes sound and color in accordance with the geometrical progression set forth in the foregoing tables. It will, of course be understood that the figures given in these tables are merely illustrative and that others may be adopted according to the requirements so long as the fundamental proportions are maintained.

Having thus described my invention what I claim as new and desire to protect by Letters Patent, is—

1. An apparatus of the character described comprising a musical instrument having a series of keys embracing a range in excess of a single octave, and a series of devices for displaying lights of different colors, means for controlling said devices from the respective keys of said series, the relative arrangement of said keys and color displaying devices being such that as the several keys of the complete series of keys are successively operated in the order of the note scale the colors will be displayed in the order in which they appear in the solar spectrum, such lights progressing geometrically in intensity relatively to increases in the sounds produced by the different notes of the note scale.

2. An apparatus of the character described comprising a musical instrument having a series of keys embracing a range in excess of a single octave and means for varying the volume of sound produced by said instrument, a series of devices for displaying lights of different colors, means for controlling said devices by the respective keys of said instrument, the relative arrangement of said keys and devices being such that as the several keys of the complete series of keys are successively operated in the order of the note scale the colors will be displayed in the order in which they appear in the solar spectrum and the intensity of the lights will progress geometrically relatively to increases in the sounds produced by the different notes of the note scale, and means operatively connected with the sound volume varying means of said instrument for relatively varying the intensity of the light displayed.

3. An apparatus of the character described comprising a musical instrument having a series of keys representing a plurality of octaves, a series of devices for displaying lights of different colors, and means for controlling said devices from the respective keys of said series the devices controlled by the keys of different octaves displaying colors of different hues and the lights controlled by the keys of each octave progressing geometrically in intensity relatively to increases in the sounds produced by the key of the respective octave.

In testimony whereof I have hereunto set my hand.

ALEXANDER BURNETT HECTOR.

Witnesses:
CHARLES E. GRAHAM,
HENRY W. CLARKE.

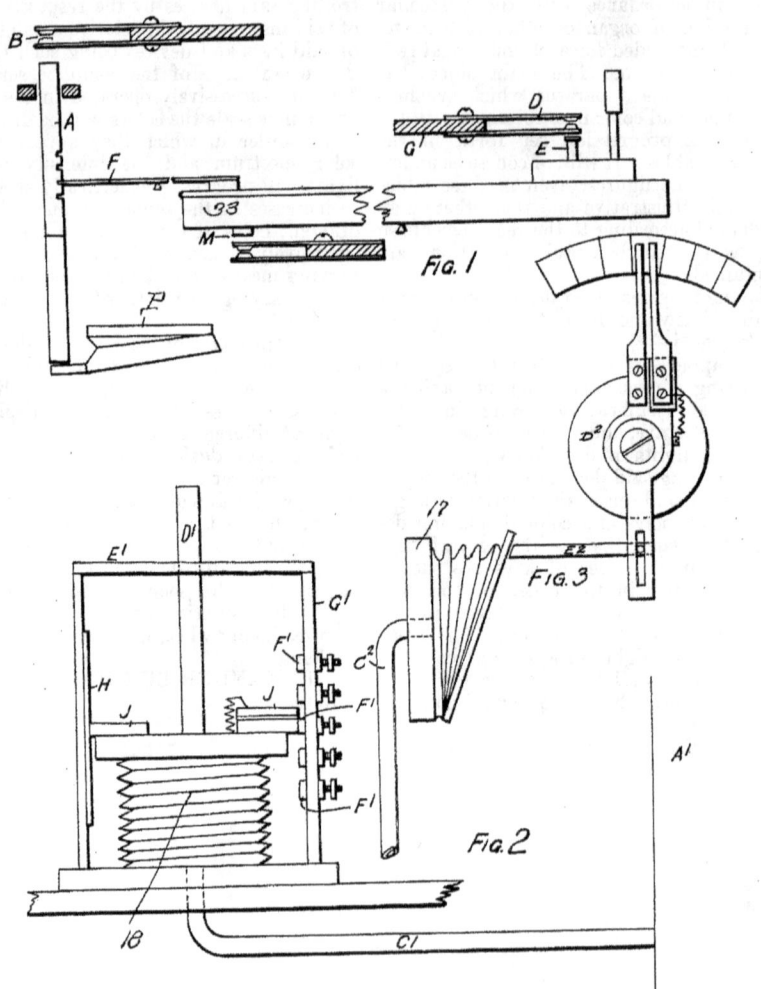

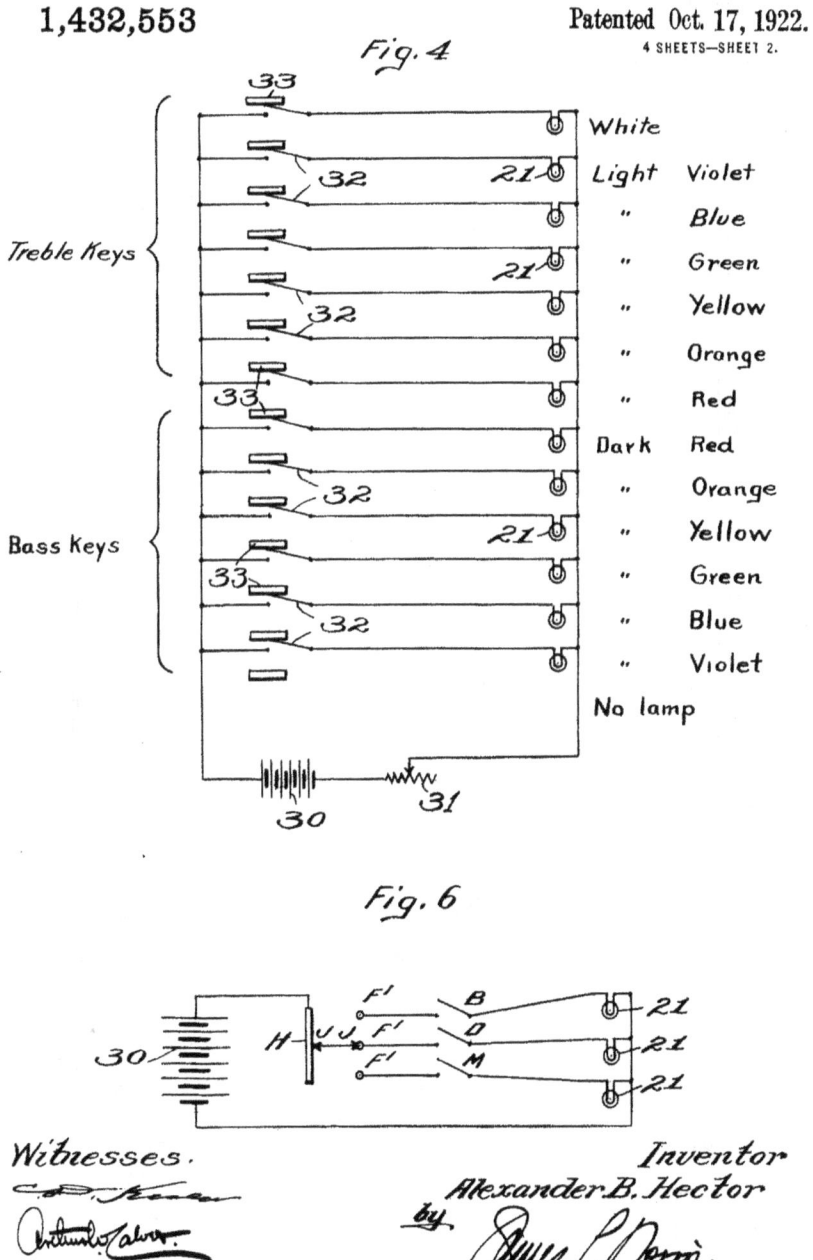

A. B. HECTOR.
PRODUCTION OF COLOR MUSIC AND OTHER LUMINOUS EFFECTS AND APPARATUS THEREFOR.
APPLICATION FILED JUNE 8, 1911. RENEWED JULY 11, 1922.

1,432,553 — Patented Oct. 17, 1922.

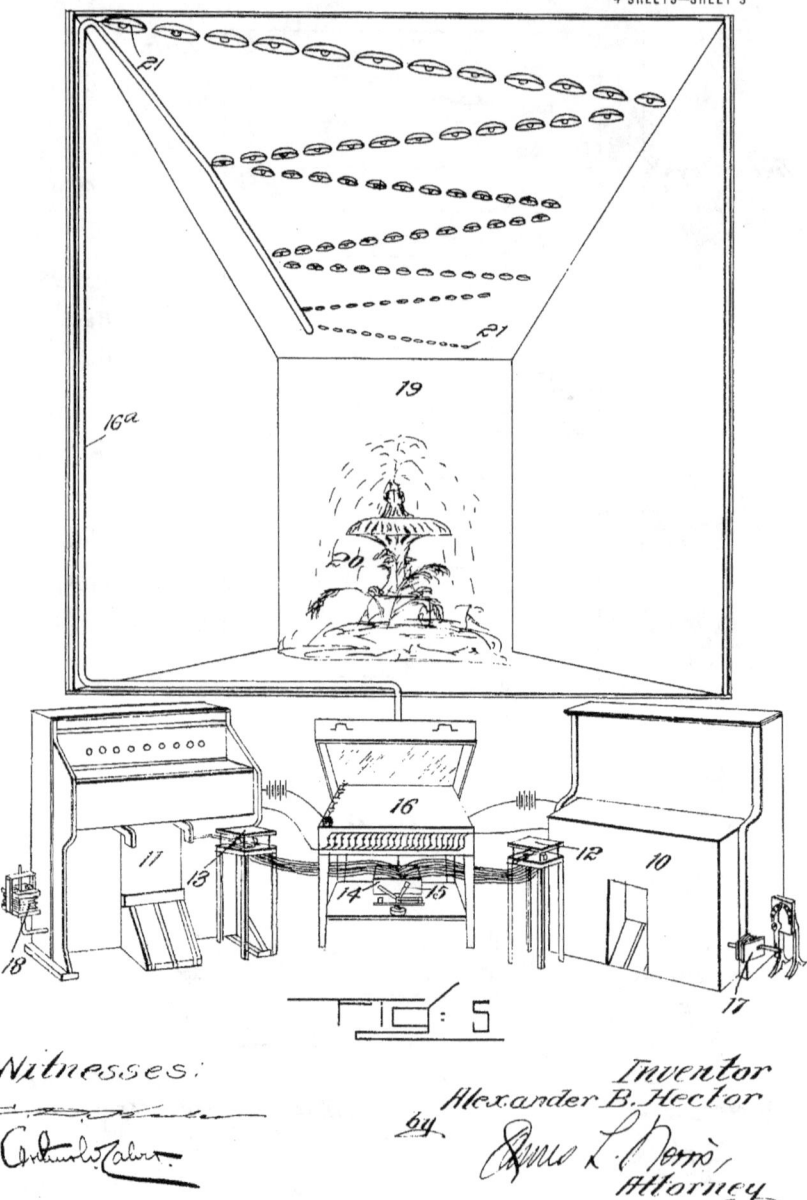

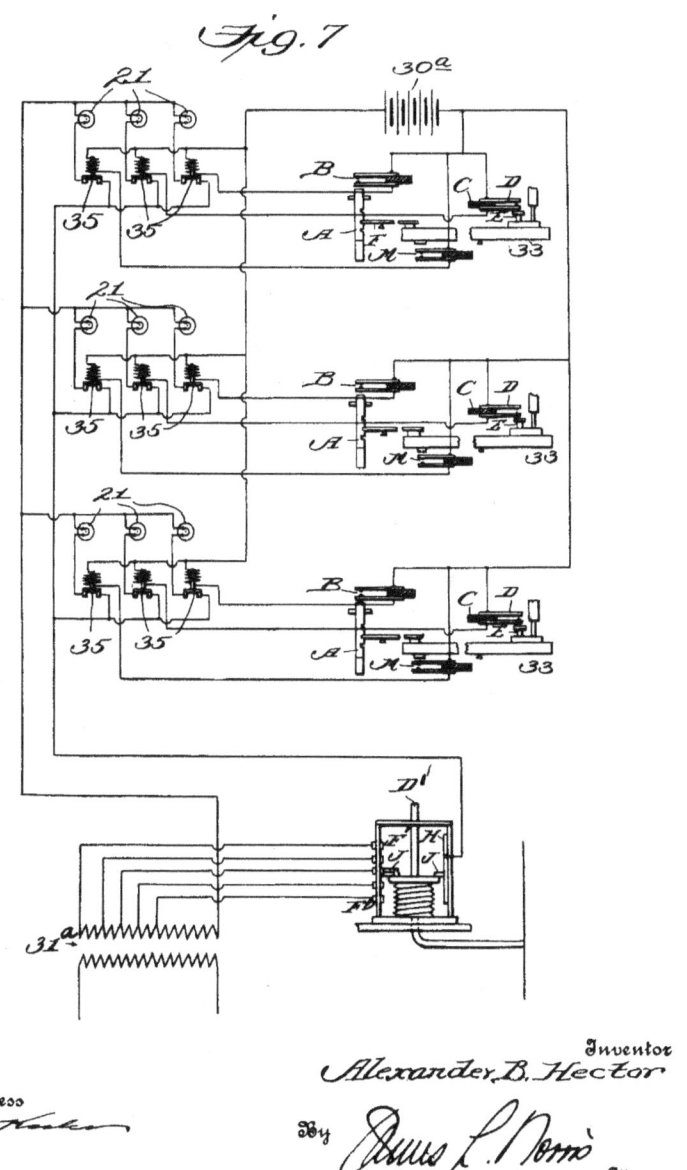

UNITED STATES PATENT OFFICE.

ALEXANDER BURNETT HECTOR, OF GREENWICH, NEAR SYDNEY, NEW SOUTH WALES, AUSTRALIA.

PRODUCTION OF COLOR MUSIC AND OTHER LUMINOUS EFFECTS AND APPARATUS THEREFOR.

Application filed June 8, 1917, Serial No. 173,671. Renewed July 11, 1922. Serial No. 574,283.

To all whom it may concern:

Be it known that I, ALEXANDER BURNETT HECTOR, a subject of the King of Great Britain, residing at Greenwich, near Sydney, in the State of New South Wales, Commonwealth of Australia, have invented certain new and useful Improvements in the Production of Color Music and Other Luminous Effects and Apparatus Therefor, of which the following is a specification.

This invention relates to improvements in the production of color music and other luminous spectacular effects and apparatus therefor, the colors having mathematical relation to the musical notes produced and forming a color harmony in mathematical relation to the musical harmony produced as described in my prior British Patent No. 29615 of 1912.

The present invention consists firstly in the arrangement of a color scale of treble and bass notes, secondly, in the apparatus whereby the mechanism of piano players, organs, or other keyed wind instruments may be conveniently utilized to obtain the desired effects in conjunction with such arrangement, and thirdly, in the means for the reflection and diffusion of light and production of shadows.

It is well known that when a double rainbow is seen, the colors of each bow follow a definite sequence thus: Upper rainbow—from outer to inner edges=violet to red; lower rainbow—from outer to inner edges= red to violet, and that the various colors occupy a definite ration in space of the whole.

Advantage of this is taken by me to construct what I term a "color scale" of treble and bass notes in accordance with either of the tables as follows:—

Table A.

Treble notes.

7th octave.
3 light violet.
6 " blue violet.
4 " blues.
2 " cyan blue.
1 " blue green.
4 " greens.
5 " greenish yellow and yellowish green.
1 " yellow.
1 " orange yellow.
2 " orange.
5 " red orange.
Middle octave. Middle "C" 15 " red.
15 dark red.
5 " orange red.
2 " orange.
1 " yellow.
5 " greenish yellow and yellowish green.
4 " greens.
1 " blue green.
2 " cyan blue.
4 " blue.
1st octave. 6 " blue violet.
3 " violet.

Bass notes.

Table B.

Treble notes.

7th octave.
12 white or light fluorescent tints.
Light violet
  to   } Spaced in same ratio as
light red.   Table A.
Middle octave. Middle "C"
Dark red
  to   } Spaced in same ratio as
dark violet.   Table A.
1st octave.
Blackness.
(No lamps attached.)

Bass notes.

In the accompanying drawings,

Figure 1 is a side elevation partly in section of a switch of a piano player and its switch contacts according to my invention and adapted to be utilized in connection with my color scale.

Figure 2 is a side elevation of an auxiliary bellows, its connection with the main bellows and the contacts for obtaining variations in the intensity of the light in sympathy with the variations in sound intensity.

Figure 3 is a plan view illustrating an alternative apparatus for operating a rotary type of regulating switch to obtain the same result.

Figure 4 is a diagrammatic view illustrating, in a simplified form, the general principles of the complete system.

Figure 5 is a general perspective view of an apparatus for a normal instrument of seven octaves provided with one bank or unit of lights, showing how it may be operated on by a piano or organ, either alternately or simultaneously.

Figure 6 is a diagrammatic view illustrating one unit of the portion of the system for varying the intensity of the light.

Fig. 7 is a diagrammatic view of so much of the complete system as is required for co-operation with three keys of the musical instrument.

In Figure 4 is illustrated diagrammatically a system comprising a source of electric energy 30 and a circuit leading therefrom, said circuit including voltage varying means 31 and a series of differently colored lamps 21 connected in parallel and controlled respectively by circuit closers 32 operated by the keys 33 of the piano, organ, or other instrument. The voltage varying means 31 is, as hereinafter more fully explained, operated by the means for varying the volume of sound produced by the instrument. The lamps 21, in their relationship to the keys 33, are arranged in accordance with the color scale above set forth in Table A or Table B. It will be understood that in Figure 4 only a selected few of the keys 33, distributed throughout the scale, and their connected lamps 21, are shown, the remaining keys and lamps being omitted in order to simplify the illustration.

In Figure 1, A is part of a piano player action actuated usually by a player pneumatic and F a finger operated thereby. B is a series of electric spring contacts above, and M a switch placed under each key 33. G is an ebonite or other insulating piece, D spring contacts and E a switch at the rear of the piano.

In the "cabinet" piano player, when the mechanical finger F of the player delivers the blow to the key 33 of the piano, the part A operating the end of finger F moves upwards to a slight extent. By arranging a series of electric contacts B in parallel, each upward movement of the part A closes an individual contact and this in turn operates an individual electric lamp or series of lamps; when a piece of music is played on the mechanical player electrical contact is made for every note struck and the corresponding lamp is illuminated simultaneously, these lamps, being suitably coloured to produce the effect known as "color music." Each individual switch is suitably wired with insulated wire and brought to a common distributing board placed at the end of the "cabinet" player or other suitable position. It is also proposed to use the similar pneumatic movements of the "combined" piano player which operates the hammer of the piano so that when an individual note is struck an individual electric light is produced. Suitable modifications of the frame work of the "combined" player are made to provide for this added arrangement of switches.

In my British specification No. 29615 of 1912 I indicate how the downward movement of the piano or organ key can be utilized to close a switch M under each key, and I now wish to provide for the upward movement of the back of the key. The attached drawings will show this graphically. It will be seen that a piece of ebonite or wood G, the whole length of the piano, is supported on suitable supports. On each side are fixed a pair of spring contacts D, the number of pairs corresponding with the number of keys; on the back of each key a striker E is fixed in such a manner that when an individual key is depressed the striker causes the brass strips to make electrical contact and illuminate a lamp. It is thus possible to have three sets of lamps brought into glow simultaneously, that is, one from the "cabinet" piano player, one underneath the key of the piano and one at the back of the piano operated by the upward movement, so that by arranging the lamps of different candle power three different degrees of illumination are obtained.

Another special improvement is the arrangement illustrated in Figure 2 and which has for its object to vary the intensity of the light so that it will be in strict sympathy with the variations of the intensity of the sound produced.

To produce this result a small secondary bellows 18 is connected with the bellows A^1 of the "cabinet" player by a tube C^1. On the top of the secondary bellows B^1 is fixed a guide rod D^1 passing through the guide block E^1. On one side of the bellows a series of contacts F^1 are fixed to an insulating support G^1 and on the other side a contact strip H is similarly supported.

As the secondary bellows become inflated or deflated electrical connection is made between the strip H and one of the contacts

F¹ through the sliding contacts J—J which are electrically connected. The respective contacts F' may be arranged in circuit with the circuit closers B, M and D (Fig. 1) of the several keys so that when the contacts J, J are in one position, operation of the keys will cause circuits to be closed through the several circuit closers B; when the contacts J, J are in another position the circuits will be closed through the circuit closers M and so on, whereby, if the circuit closers B, M and D control circuits to lamps of different candle powers, movements of the contacts J, J will serve to control the intensity of the light. Thus, as shown in Figure 6, each of the circuit closers B, D and M is connected in series with one of the contacts F' and with a lamp 21, the several lamps 21 being of the same color but of different candle powers. In this figure the connections for one key only are shown, but it will be understood that the circuit closers B of all of the keys will control the supply of current to the respective lamps through one contact F', all of the circuit closers D will control the supply of current to the respective lamps through another contact F' and that all of the circuit closers M will control the supply of current to the respective lamps through a third contact F'.

The same result may be accomplished with a single circuit closer and a single lamp for each key by the use of suitable voltage varying means, as indicated diagrammatically in Figure 4, in which case the contacts F' may be connected with the terminals of a rheostat 31 or voltage varying device.

The latter arrangement is illustrated more fully in Figure 7, wherein voltage varying means 31ª controls the voltage of current supplied to all of the lamps 21 simultaneously, and the circuits to all of the lamps corresponding to any one key 33 are closed at once by relays or electromagnetic switches 35 which latter are controlled respectively by the circuit closers B, D and M operated by such key.

The voltage varying means may be of any well known character, variable resistance being indicated in Figure 4. Alternatively the voltage may be varied through the agency of cells which are switched in or out by the action of the bellows; or in the case of alternating currents tappings from a regulating compensator may be connected to the studs F¹ as shown at 31ª in Fig. 7. For manipulating larger currents relays or electromagnetic switches, similar to the switches 35 shown in Fig. 7, may be used. Such electrical devices being well known in the art are not shown in detail herein. The number of steps for voltage regulation is not limited, the precise number depending upon the requirements or the particular type of apparatus used. Thus, in the arrangement shown in Fig. 6, three contacts F', corresponding respectively to the circuit closers B, D and M are employed. In Figs. 2 and 7 five contacts F', providing for five variations of voltage, are shown. It will be clear that in the systems shown in Figs. 4 and 7 any desired number of variations might be provided for.

In the simplified forms of apparatus illustrated in Figs. 4 and 6, the main light circuits are directly controlled by the circuit closers 32 or B, D, and M operated by the instrument keys 33. Preferably however, and as shown in Fig. 7, the key operated switches control auxiliary circuits from a suitable source of current 30ª to the relays or electromagnetic switches 35 which in turn control the main light circuits.

An alternative arrangement of voltage varying device is shown in Figure 3, the auxiliary bellows 17 being connected to the main bellows by the pipe C². The regulating switch D² is operated by the bellows 17 through a lever or system of levers E². By these means the secondary bellows of a piano player is made to operate a rotary type switch in order to obtain the same result.

The lamps 21 may be provided with differently colored globes or, preferably, may be enclosed by polished parabolic reflectors in front of which are placed colored screens of varying hues; the screens being made of glass, gelatine or other suitable material. To produce efficient diffusion of the colors, the lamps are made to project on to a dull white surface. To break up the light and to produce pleasing shadows, palms, flowers, rocks, and figures are interposed between the lamps and the white surface. Alternately the lamps may be made to project their coloured lights on suitable semi-opaque glass structures, such as a gothic church window or the like. The light may be transmitted through semi-opaque glass or the glass may be silvered and the light reflected.

A suitable arrangement is shown in Figure 5, wherein 10 is a player piano and 11 an organ having their respective regulating switches 12 and 13, the former being hand operated and the latter knee operated. 14 is a transformer, 15 a double throw switch and 16 a relay cabinet (and in which any relay may be operated by current from the battery to bring in a current of high voltage to a particular lamp) through which pass all electrical connections between the keys of either musical instrument 10 or 11 and the lamps 21 through a suitable connecting cable 16ª. 17 is a bellows controlled switch like that shown in Fig. 3 attached to the player piano, whereby the intensity of the current may be automatically controlled. 18 is a bellows controlled switch like that shown in Fig. 2 and attached to the organ for the same purpose. 19 is a screen in front of which is positioned any suitable object or objects as 20 to be illuminated. The lamps 21 are shown as consisting of seven rows corresponding to seven octaves increasing in geometric proportion as regards sizes of the lamps, reflectors and distances from the screen. These rows of lamps are divided up into their various colors as exemplified in Table A.

Having thus described my invention what I claim as new and desire to protect by Letters Patent, is:—

1. An apparatus of the character described comprising a key-operated musical instrument and a series of color displaying devices controlled respectively by the several keys of said instrument, the order of the colors displayed by said devices being, with respect to the note scale of said keys, such as to correspond to the arrangement of colors in the double rainbow, the violets being at the ends of the scale and the reds in the middle, and the colors displayed by the devices controlled by the bass notes being of darker hues than those corresponding to the treble notes.

2. An apparatus of the character described comprising a musical instrument provided with means for varying the intensity of sound produced thereby, a series of devices controlled by said instrument for displaying lights of different colors in accordance with the notes sounded by said instrument, and means pneumatically controlled by said intensity varying means of said instrument for varying the intensity of the light displayed by said devices.

3. An apparatus of the character described comprising a key operated musical instrument, a plurality of electric lamps of different powers pertaining to and controlled by each of the keys of said instrument, and means for selectively closing the circuit to separate lamps of different powers to vary the intensity of the light produced.

4. A key-operated musical instrument comprising, in combination, a note-sounding key pivoted intermediate its ends, circuit closing devices operated respectively by the opposite ends of said key, a player having a mechanical finger for striking said key, and a third circuit closing device operatively connected with said finger.

5. An apparatus of the character described comprising a pneumatically controlled musical instrument, a series of electrically operated devices controlled by said instrument for displaying lights of different colors in accordance with the notes sounded by said instrument, and means for varying the intensity of the light displayed by said devices, said means including a series of contacts connected with said devices, a bellows connected with said instrument and controlled by pneumatic pressure, and a contact carried by said bellows and cooperating with said first named contacts.

In testimony whereof I have hereunto set my hand.

ALEXANDER BURNETT HECTOR.

Witnesses:
CHARLES E. GRAHAM,
HENRY W. CLARKE.

Sept. 17, 1929 A. B. HECTOR 1,728,860
PRODUCING COLOR MUSIC AND OTHER SPECTACULAR LUMINOUS EFFECTS
Filed July 7, 1927 4 Sheets-Sheet 1

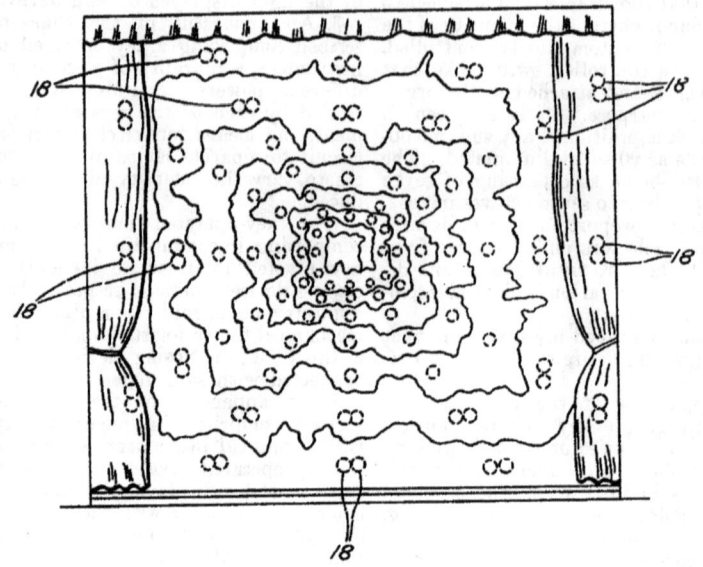

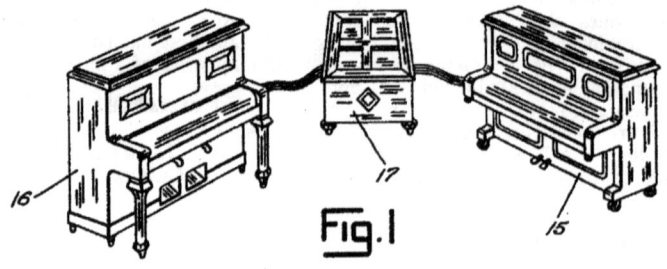

Fig.1

Inventor:
Alexander Burnett Hector.
by James L. Norris,
Attorney.

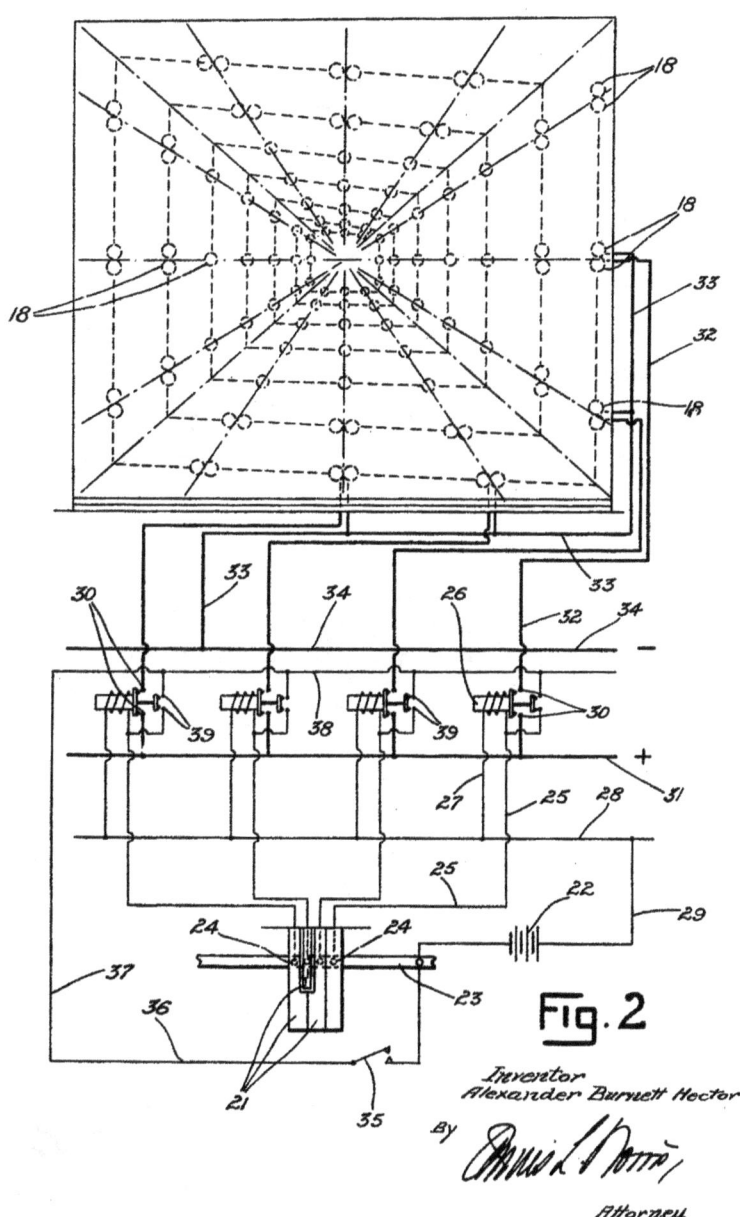

Sept. 17, 1929 A. B. HECTOR 1,728,860
PRODUCING COLOR MUSIC AND OTHER SPECTACULAR LUMINOUS EFFECTS
Filed July 7, 1927 4 Sheets-Sheet 3

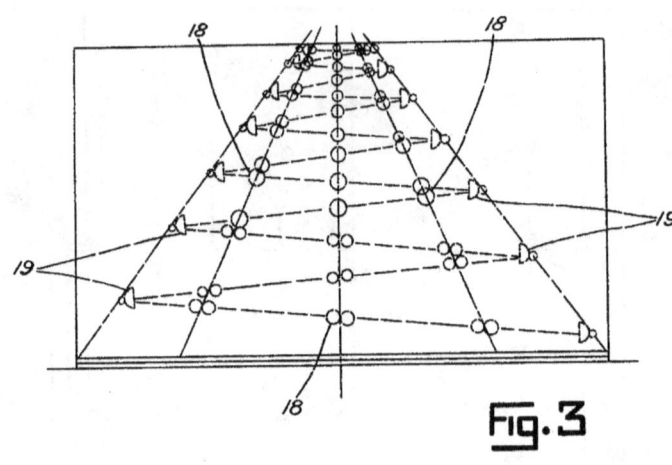

Fig. 3

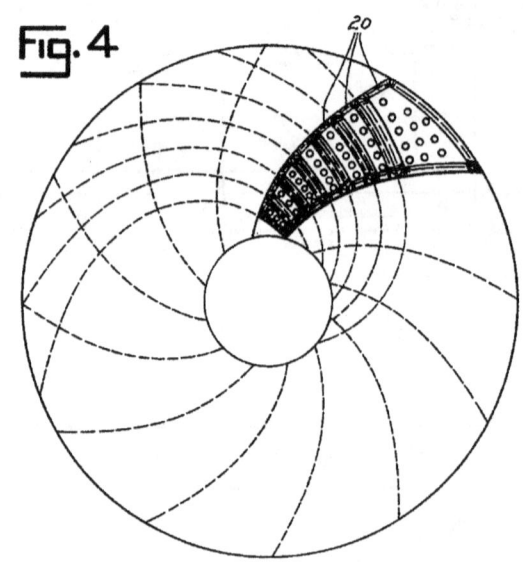

Fig. 4

Inventor:
Alexander Burnett Hector.
By [signature]
Attorney.

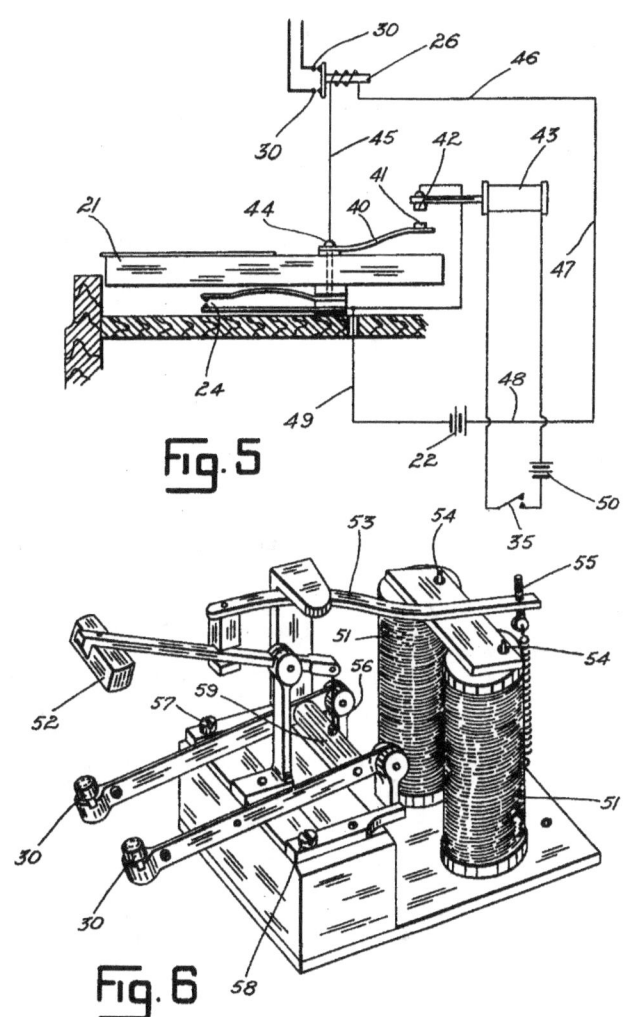

UNITED STATES PATENT OFFICE

ALEXANDER BURNETT HECTOR, OF GREENWICH, NEAR SYDNEY, NEW SOUTH WALES, AUSTRALIA

PRODUCING COLOR MUSIC AND OTHER SPECTACULAR LUMINOUS EFFECTS

Application filed July 7, 1927, Serial No. 204,086, and in Australia July 15, 1926.

This invention has reference to improvements in, and relating to the production of color music or the harmony of color and musical sounds, and other spectacular effects, and apparatus therefor in which the movements of the keys of a piano, piano player, organ, or other keyboard are made to operate a series of switches and/or relays so as to display or project colored lights in such manner as to harmonize with musical sounds.

The main object of the invention is to express more effectively by means of lights the emotions of a musician, through the keyboard of a musical instrument or the like. There may be used in some instances, a silent keyboard, that is, without the agency of sound, to produce luminous displays.

The invention consists briefly of the arrangements and/or projection of colored lights according to a color scale of treble and bass notes and in apparatus whereby the mechanism of piano players, organs, or other keyboard instruments may be conveniently utilized to obtain the desired effects, and in means for the reflection and diffusion of light and the production of shadows.

It is well known that if the space occupied by the normal spectrum be divided, the various colors occupy different proportions of this space. The ratios of each color may be determined and form the basis for a color scale.

Advantage is taken of this to construct what is termed a color scale of treble and bass notes.

In applying the color scale to the keys of a keyboard musical instrument I start at the lowest bass note and proceed upwardly.

The scale or ratio of the spectrum colors may be arranged over the various keys and octaves in several ways.

In applying the lighting effects the use of a spiral, known as the logarithmic spiral, the nebular hypothesis, the aurora borealis, or vortices is resorted to, that is to say, I have ascertained that all sound harmonics are curves or spirals and that the nearer the approximate curve or spiral is to the presentation of light, the closer the simultaneous harmonic effect of sound and light, and in this manner the form and color of music are rendered visible. In short the analogy of the "spinning electron" is followed.

The invention, in its simplest practical form, comprises a plurality of electric lamps arranged according to the chromatic scale of colors, in segments of a circle or spiral which segments or sectors may extend from the periphery to a center, and the color in each sector is graduated or shaded from the periphery to the center. Preferably, however, one or a plurality of electric lights of graduated size is provided to correspond with one or a series of pendulums of different lengths on which said lights are mounted or carried. By these means the lights take the swinging motion of their respective pendulums imparted from the keyboard until they slow down to a state of rest or are stopped by a pedal or other means controlled from the keyboard. The pendulums may be provided with universal joints whereby a vortex, to and fro, or other rhythmic movement, may be obtained.

The pendulums and the lamps thereon may be arranged in units of seven, the size varying geometrically. Twelve of such units, when fixed in a common circle, will be arranged to form a logarithmic spiral. The lights in a series may be shrouded from the other lights in that series.

The lights or lamps may be mounted on telescopic or lazy tong mechanism to vary the intensity or area of the lighting effect.

The apparatus may be portable and the keys or hammers of a keyboard instrument may be provided with metal contact strips to close an electric circuit on their depression.

However in order that the invention may be more readily understood, reference will now be made to the accompanying drawings, wherein:—

Figure 1 is a diagrammatic view of one form of the invention showing the arrangement of lights in the form of a logarithmic spiral and the musical instruments and relay box associated therewith.

Figure 2 is a diagrammatic view showing part of the circuit arrangement for controlling the lights from a keyboard, the disposition of the lights being in the form of a logarithmic spiral shown in elevation.

Figure 3 is a diagrammatic plan view of the logarithmic spiral shown in Figure 2.

Figure 4 is a part diagrammatic inverted plan view of the arrangement of lights in groups or clusters in a dome also in the form of logarithmic spirals.

Figure 5 is a sectional view of one of the keys of a keyboard instrument, illustrating an alternative circuit arrangement for producing a sustaining effect on the lights.

Figure 6 is a perspective view of a suitable form of quick acting relay for closing the lamp circuits.

Referring to Figures 1 to 6, the piano 15 and organ 16 are electrically connected in multiple to relays in the relay box 17. The relays may be of any suitable type but are preferably of the quick acting type shown in Figure 6. Each relay is controlled by a switch operated by one of the keys of the musical instrument and is adapted to complete the circuit for the respective lamps or groups of lamps under its control.

The lamps 18, which may have reflectors 19, are arranged in the form of a logarithmic spiral, shown in dotted lines in Figures 2 and 3, and diagrammatically as clusters of lamps in Figure 4. Each turn of the spiral represents one octave and is composed of twelve lamps or groups of lamps. For a seven octave keyboard instrument a seven turn logarithmic spiral in which each turn has twelve lamps or groups of lamps would be provided.

In Figure 4 seven clusters of lights 20 are shown, each of which is controlled by the same note in the seven respective octaves of the keyboard instrument. In a similar manner the other eleven notes of each octave would each control a cluster of lights arranged in a similar way to those shown in the drawing.

Beneath each note contacts are arranged, (see Figures 2 and 5). These are adapted on the depression of a note to complete a circuit for energizing a relay whereby a lamp, or group or cluster of lamps is lighted.

Referring to Figures 1 to 4, when one of the keys 21 of the piano 15 or organ 16 is struck by a musician or mechanical player, the following circuit is completed: from battery 22, contact bar 23, contact 24, wire 25, relay 26, wires 27, 28 and 29, back to battery 22. When the above circuit is completed, the relay 26 closes contacts 30 and completes the following lamp circuit: from positive main 31, wire 32, lamp or lamps 18, wire 33, to the negative main 34.

In order to sustain a particular lamp or lamps after a particular key has been played, additional contacts 39 are provided on the relay 26 in order to effect a locking circuit for the relay, which operates as follows. Upon the closing of a pedal or like operated switch 35, a circuit is completed as follows: from battery 22, switch 35, wires 36, 37 and 38, contacts 39, relay 26, wires 27, 28, 29, to battery 22. From the above circuit it will be seen that if a particular key is played and the respective relay contacts closed, the lamp will remain lighted provided the sustaining switch 35 is closed, causing the relay to be energized by the sustaining circuit. If the particular key returns to its normal position and opens switch 24, the particular lamp will remain lighted so long as the sustaining switch 35 is closed.

In the modified sustaining mechanism shown in Figure 5, each of the keys 21 of the keybard instrument has a back contact member 40 which is springy and has a soft iron tip or keeper 41. A soft iron bar 42 is supported by and capable of being magnetized by an electromagnet 43 mounted above the keyboard of the instrument and extending longitudinally thereof and which when magnetized is capable of retaining the tip or keeper 41 in contact therewith once a key has been depressed, and during such time as the sustaining switch 35 is closed by a pedal or like operating means to complete an independent circuit for energizing the electromagnet 43. When a keyboard instrument is installed with the modified arrangement shown in Figure 5, the lamp circuit closing relay is energized as follows. When a particular key 21 is depressed current flows from battery 22 by way of wire 49, contact 24, screw 44, wire 45, lamp circuit closing relay 26, wires 46, 47, 48, back to battery 22. The energization of the relay 26 causes the contacts 30 to close the lamp circuit of the particular lamp or group of lamps corresponding to the note struck.

If it is desired to sustain the lamp in lighted condition, the sustaining switch 35 is closed to energize the electromagnet 43 by means of current supplied from battery 50.

This has the effect of magnetizing the bar 42 so that when a particular key is struck the back contact member 40 is raised until the tip or keeper 41 engages the magnetized bar 42 against which it is held as long as the switch 35 is closed. Current will now pass from battery 22, wires 49, 51, bar 42, contact member 40, wire 45, relay 26, wires 46, 47, 48, back to battery 22, with the result that relay 26 maintains the lighting current of the particular lamp closed as long as the sustaining switch is closed, even when the note 21 returns to its normal position.

Figure 6 illustrates one of the lamp circuit closing relays 26 which are of the quick acting type. Each relay has electromagnetic coils 51 and contacts 30 which are bridged by the keeper 52. The operating arm 53 is secured to the armature of the relay and is loosely pivoted on pins 54, adjustment being effected by the screw 55. In operation, this relay works as follows. When the coils are energized the armature is attracted, causing the arm 53 to depress the keeper 52, and at the same time the coupling 56 raises the contacts 30 which, on engagement with the keeper, completes the circuit from terminal 57 to terminal 58. The contacts 30 are normally insulated from each other by a distance piece 59.

The lamps 18 with their reflectors 19 may be mounted on a universal joint 83 and be arranged to swing with a pendulum action when released by an electromagnet 84.

I claim:

1. In improvements in the production of color music and other spectacular luminous effects, the combination of a controlling keyboard of a musical instrument, a source of electrical energy, a plurality of circuits controlled by the keys of the keyboard, and a number of colored lights adapted to be controlled by the keys of the keyboard, said lights being arranged in the form of a logarithmic spiral.

2. In improvements in the production of color music and other spectacular luminous effects, the combination of a controlling keyboard of a musical instrument, a source of electrical energy, a plurality of circuits controlled by the keys of the keyboard, and a number of colored lights, representing a color scale corresponding to treble and bass notes, said lights being arranged in the form of a logarithmic spiral and each coil of the spiral representing one octave and comprising at least twelve lamps.

3. In improvements in the production of color music and other spectacular luminous effects, the combination of a controlling keyboard musical instrument, a source of electrical energy, a plurality of circuits controlled by the keys of the keyboard, and a number of colored lights representing a color scale of treble and bass notes, said lights being arranged in the form of a logarithmic spiral and adapted to be electrically controlled from the keyboard, and means common to each circuit for sustaining the energization of the lights at will.

4. In improvements in the production of color music and other spectacular luminous effects, the combination of a controlling keyboard musical instrument, a source of electrical energy, a plurality of circuits controlled by the keys of the keyboard, so that on depressing one of the keys of a keyboard an electrical circuit is completed, a relay in each circuit and contacting a lighting circuit for a colored lamp that forms part of a color scale corresponding to treble and bass notes arranged in the form of a logarithmic spiral, and a switch operable at will to close an independent circuit to the relays in order to sustain the lighting circuit in the closed position after the key is released and returns to its normal position.

5. In improvements in the production of color music and other spectacular luminous effects in combination, a keyboard musical instrument, a source of electrical energy, a plurality of circuits, a series of electric lamps arranged in the form of a logarithmic spiral, at least one lamp to a key, electrical contacts closed by the keys of the musical instrument to close a circuit including a lamp and the source of electrical energy, lamp circuit closing relays, one to each key, controlled by said contacts, and a manually operated switch adapted to complete a circuit for sustaining said relays in energized condition after the keys of the musical instrument have returned to the normal position.

6. In improvements in the production of color music and other spectacular luminous effects in combination, a keyboard musical instrument, a source of electrical energy, a plurality of circuits including said source, a series of electric lamps arranged in the form of a logarithmic spiral, normally open electrical contacts one to each key adapted to be closed by the keys, lamp circuit closing relays controlled by said contacts, one to each contact and its key, a manually operated switch adapted to complete a circuit for sustaining said relays in energized condition after a key has been depressed, closed its contacts to cause the energization of the relay and been released, and sustaining means comprising a manually operated switch and relay contact adapted to close a circuit for energizing the relay.

7. In improvements in the production of color music and other spectacular luminous effects in combination, a keyboard musical instrument, a source of electrical energy, a plurality of circuits including said source, a series of electric lamps arranged in the form of a logarithmic spiral, electrical contacts, one to each key, adapted to be closed by the keys, lamp circuit closing relays controlled by said contacts, one to each contact and its key, a manually operated switch adapted to complete a circuit for sustaining said relays in energized condition after a key has been depressed, closed its contacts to the keys to cause the energization of a relay and been released, and sustaining means comprising a contact blade on each key, said contact blade having a soft iron keeper adapted to retain the contact on a closed condition when attracted by an electro-magnetic bar under the control of an electro-magnet energized by closing said manually operated switch, said contact blade completing an independent circuit for energizing the lamp circuit relay.

In testimony whereof I have hereunto set my hand.

ALEXANDER BURNETT HECTOR.

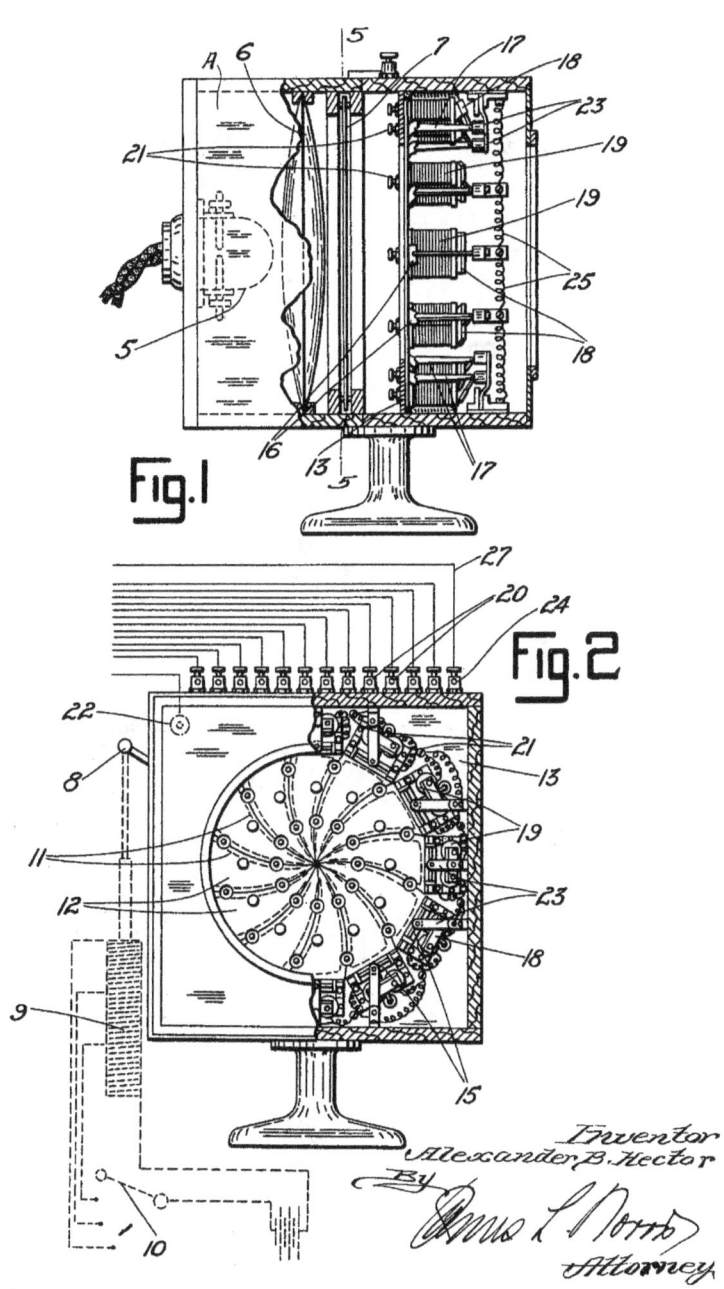

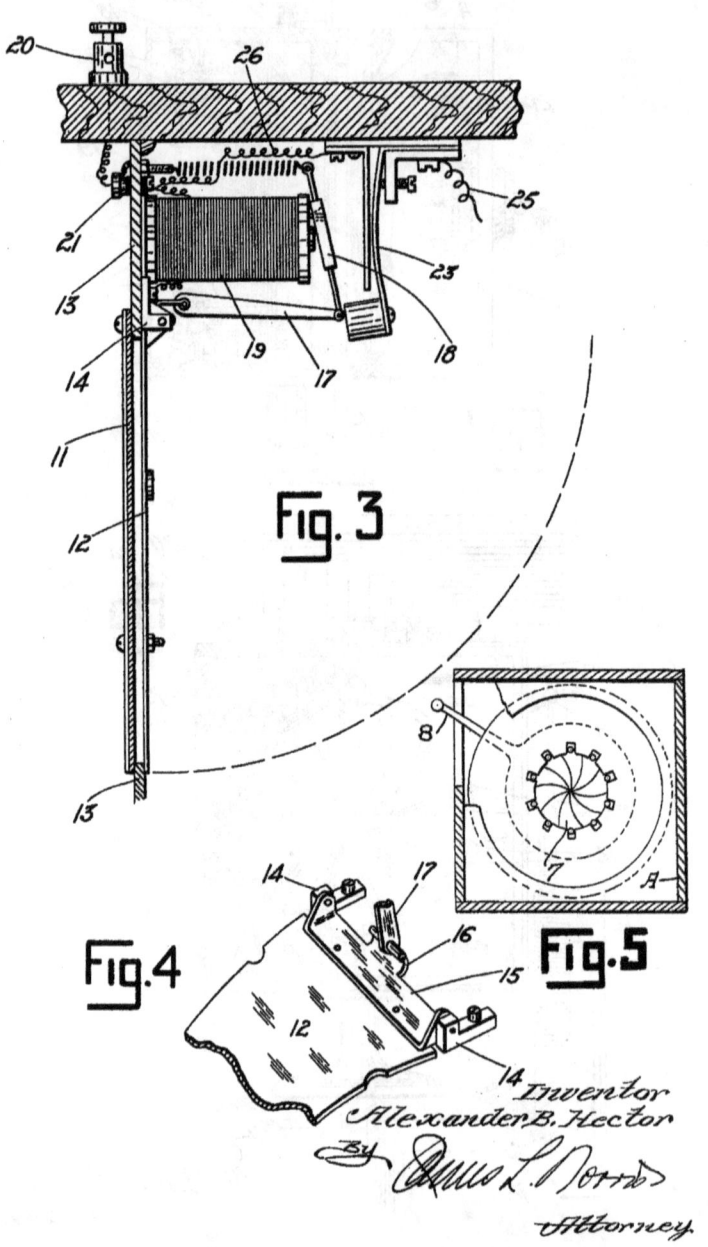

Patented Dec. 2, 1930

1,783,789

UNITED STATES PATENT OFFICE

ALEXANDER BURNETT HECTOR, OF GREENWICH, NEAR SYDNEY, NEW SOUTH WALES, AUSTRALIA

APPARATUS FOR PRODUCING COLOR MUSIC OR OTHER SPECTACULAR LUMINOUS EFFECTS

Original application filed July 7, 1927, Serial No. 204,086, and in Australia July 15, 1926. Divided and this application filed August 31, 1928. Serial No. 303,306.

This invention has reference to improvements in, and relating to the production of color music or the harmony of color and musical sounds, and other spectacular effects and apparatus therefor in which the movements of the keys of a piano, piano player, organ, or other keyboard are made to operate a series of switches and electromagnets so as to display or project colored lights in such manner as to harmonize with musical sounds.

The main object of the invention is to express more effectively by means of lights the emotions of a musician, through the keyboard of a musical instrument or the like. I may in some instances use a silent keyboard, that is without the agency of sound, to produce luminous displays.

The invention consists briefly of the arrangement and/or projection of colored lights according to a color scale of treble and bass notes and in apparatus whereby the mechanism of piano players, organs, or other keyboard instruments may be conveniently utilized to obtain the desired effects, and in means for the reflection and diffusion of light and the production of shadows.

It is well known that if the space occupied by the normal spectrum be divided the various colors occupy different proportions of this space. The ratios of each color may be determined and form the basis for a color scale.

Advantage of this is taken by me to construct what I term a color scale of treble and bass notes.

In applying the color scale to the keys of a keyboard musical instrument I start at the lowest bass note and proceed upwardly.

The scale or ratio of the spectrum colors may be arranged over the various keys and octaves in several ways.

According to the present invention a series of projector apparatus is used to display colored lights under the control of a musician or mechanical player by the use of electromagnetically controlled shutters which may be of varying sizes according to the respective areas of the different colors shown in the spectrum.

The apparatus may be portable and the keys or hammers of a keyboard instrument may be provided with metal contact strips to close an electric circuit on their depression.

But in order that the invention may be more readily understood, reference will now be made to the accompanying drawings wherein:—

Figure 1 is a side elevational view, partly in section, of one of a number of projectors having electromagnets controlled from a keyboard.

Figure 2 is a front elevational view thereof, also partly in section.

Figures 3 and 4 are detail views, on an enlarged scale, of parts of the shutter mechanism of Figures 1 and 2.

Figure 5 is a view of the iris diaphragm taken on the line 5—5, Figure 1.

The construction illustrated shows one of the series of projectors used to display colored lights under the control of a musician or mechanical player. Electromagnetically controlled shutters of various sizes according to the respective areas of the different colors shown in the spectrum are used to display the colors, one source of light being utilized to display twelve colors or the representation of one octave in color music. A keyboard instrument having seven octaves would require seven of the projectors illustrated in Figures 1 to 5.

Each projector comprises a casing A in which is mounted a source of light 5 and a condenser 6 in front of which is an "iris", or contracting diaphragm 7 having a lever 8 adapted to be controlled by a solenoid 9 and a three position switch 10 which may be arranged as a swell pedal on the keyboard instrument.

The color screens 11, twelve in number, one for each note of an octave, are arranged in sections in front of the diaphragm 7, as best shown in Figure 1, and are covered by electromagnetically controlled shutters 12. Each shutter is hinged to the partition 13 by lugs or brackets 14 and has secured to it a member

15 having an extension 16 which is connected to a coupling 17 adapted to be depressed on the attraction of the armature 18 of the electromagnet 19.

In this invention relays are not provided for operation by each note of the keyboard instrument, the instrument being connected directly to the electromagnet of its particular color screen. The connecting wires for one octave are shown in Figure 2 leading to the terminals 20. Each of these terminals is connected to its respective insulated terminal 21 leading to the coil of the particular one of the twelve electromagnets.

The return wire from each electromagnet is grounded to its respective lug brackets 14, the path leading by way of the metallic partition 13 to the return terminal 22.

The sustaining of the shutters in their open position is effected by a switch 23 controlled by the coupling 17 which is so arranged that on raising a shutter 12 the switch is closed allowing current to flow to the respective relay from a common terminal 24 by way of a common wire 25 connected to each of the switches 23. The opposite sides of the switches 23 are connected by wires 26 to their respective insulated terminals, the return circuit being completed by way of the earth terminal 22.

The common terminal 24 of the sustaining switches is connected by a wire 27 to a suitable sustaining switch capable of being operated from the keyboard instrument.

I claim:

1. In improvements in the production of color music and other spectacular luminous effects, a source of light, a series of color screens in front of the light, a condenser and contracting diaphragm between said screens and light, shutters for covering and uncovering the color screens, electromagnetic means for actuating said shutters, means for sustaining any of the shutters in the open position and electrically actuated means for operating the diaphragm.

2. Apparatus according to claim 1 wherein the electromagnetic means for actuating the shutters comprises an electromagnet for each of the shutters and an armature for each of said electromagnets, each of said armatures being operative when its associated electromagnet is energized, to move its associated shutter into open position, and wherein the means for sustaining the shutters in open position comprises a plurality of electric switches each associated with one of the shutters and operable by the opening movement of such shutter to close the electric circuit to the electromagnet associated therewith.

3. In an apparatus for the production of color music and other spectacular luminous effects, a source of light, a series of color screens in front of said source of light, a light condenser and a contractible diaphragm between said color screens and said source of light, and shutters selectively operable for exposing and covering said color screens.

In testimony whereof I have hereunto set my hand.

ALEXANDER BURNETT HECTOR.

MARY HALLOCK-GREENEWALT

System of Notation (1919)

Sarabet (1918, reissued 1924)

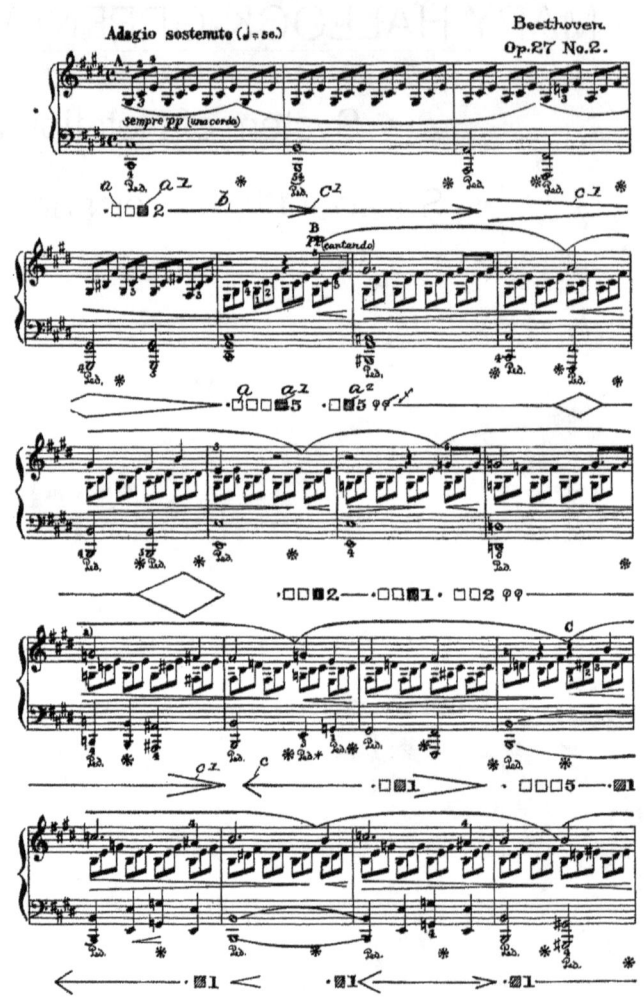

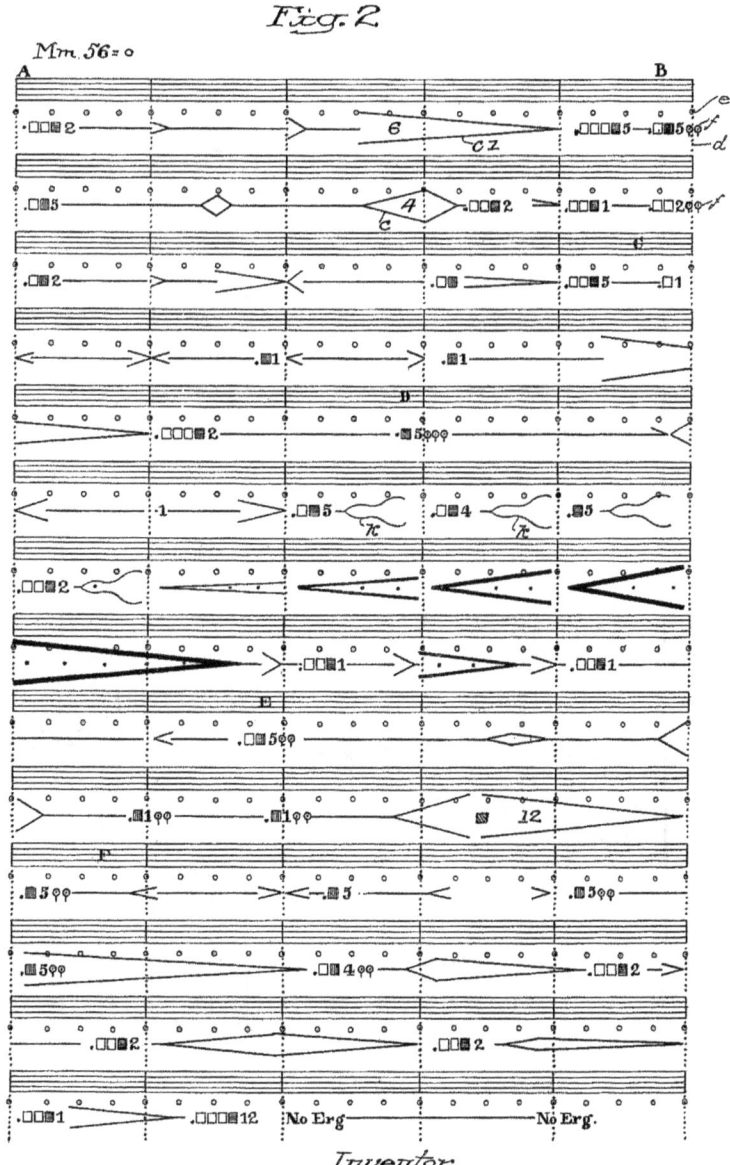

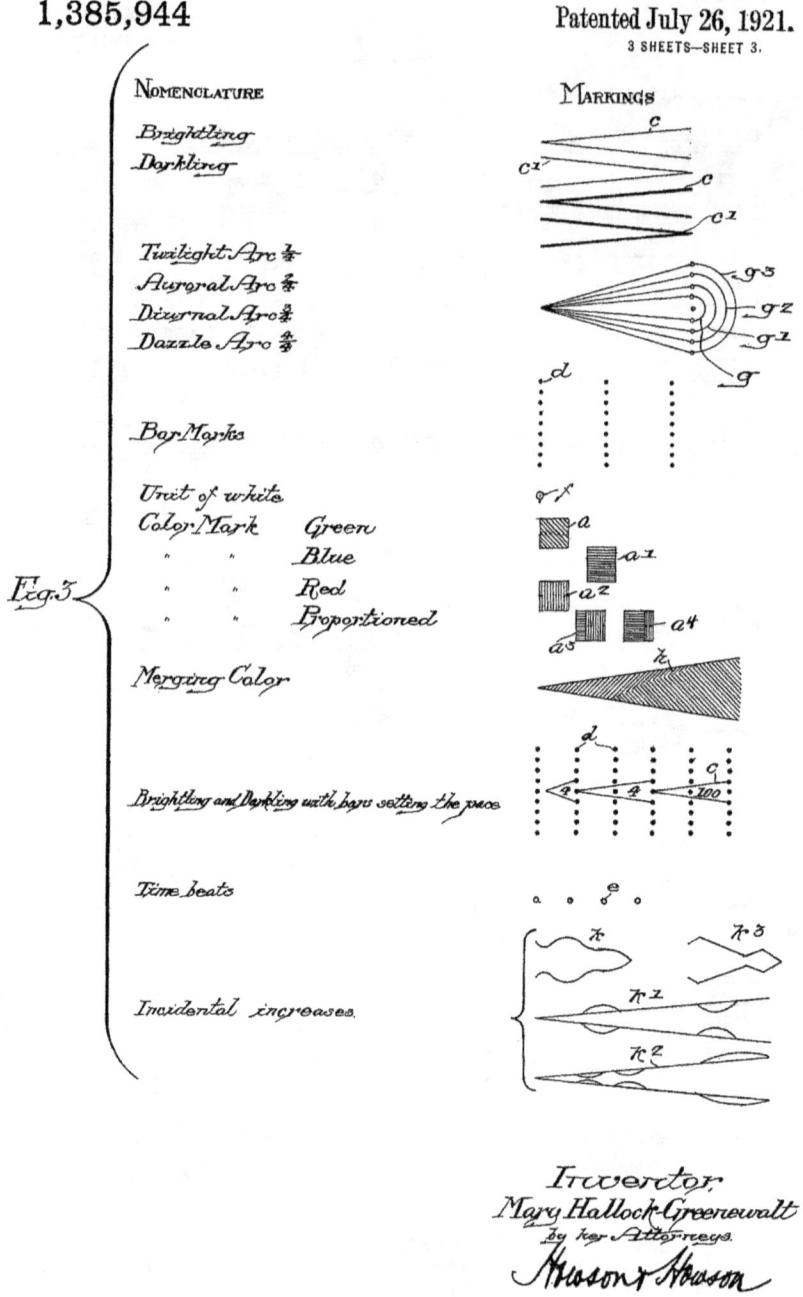

UNITED STATES PATENT OFFICE.

MARY HALLOCK-GREENEWALT, OF PHILADELPHIA, PENNSYLVANIA.

NOTATION FOR INDICATING LIGHTING EFFECTS.

1,385,944. Specification of Letters Patent. **Patented July 26, 1921.**

Application filed August 18, 1919. Serial No. 318,393.

To all whom it may concern:

Be it known that I, MARY HALLOCK-GREENEWALT, a citizen of the United States, residing in Philadelphia, Pennsylvania, have invented an Improved Notation for Indicating Lighting Effects, of which the following is a specification.

My invention relates to notation whereby lighting effects progressively or otherwise intended either as an accompaniment for musical sounds or an independent display may be produced by an operator controlling such lighting effects in a more or less arbitrary relation to the musical sounds, or to the effect desired, in the case of an independent display; this light notation may be written in or disposed adjacent the staves of a musical score if used with music, or placed on an independent sheet if used for the independent display, or placed upon perforated sheets employed with mechanically operated musical instruments.

I have set forth in a prior application for patent, filed August 30, 1918, Serial No. 252,133, the idea of employing light, with and without color, as an accompaniment to music; musical compositions being susceptible of coördination and synchronization with a lighting system, with and without color. The object of my present invention is to provide a score comprising names, numerals, marks, symbols, hieroglyphs or the like, constituting a chart or record sheet for denoting or interpreting a lighting sequence or succession to accompany music to be used independently or to be used in conjunction with any other means of esthetic expression. By this the intensity of the lighting effect, its timed succession, the scheme, sequence, character or intended effect of the same may be understood by the performer, or by an assistant. Such light in any intensity, and with or without color, is to be distributed in the manner and throughout the space for which it is intended, which may be an auditorium or any other place adapted for esthetic pleasure.

In carrying out my invention and using the same as an accompaniment to music, the light and color notation is preferably placed between the musical staves when applied to the score, and, of course, bears a definite and more or less arbitrary relation to the musical notation thereon. If used without music, the notation may be arranged upon a sheet or other suitable surface, either alone or in conjunction with any other forms of expression.

These and other features of my invention are more fully described hereinafter, reference being had to the accompanying drawings, in which:

Figure 1, shows a part of the score of Beethoven's "Moonlight Sonata," with lighting notation embodying my invention disposed between the staves of the musical notation.

Fig. 2, is a diagrammatic view illustrating lighting notation placed with reference to musical staves wherein the notes are omitted, and

Fig. 3, is a view illustrating certain arbitrary details of the lighting notation.

The light notation hereinafter described and forming the subject of my invention is intended not only to indicate the lighting and color effects desired, but also their intensity and the gradations of such intensity in increasing and diminishing effect, or any contrasted succession; all in relation to recurrent time.

For the purpose of indicating the quantity of light desired, I may employ rectangular figures or symbols a, each of which may represent a definite unit of intensity when used alone, and with which modifying characters or numerals may be employed to represent intensity.

For the purpose of indicating colored light, the figures or symbols a, as well as any modifying characters accompanying the same, may be arbitrarily marked to represent color in accordance with any recognized scheme; thus blue, will be indicated by filling the rectangular figures and the supplemental symbols with horizontal lines; red, by vertical lines; green, by diagonal lines, and so on; and these markings may be combined in any desired proportion, or intelligibly combined, shortened or condensed, as space or convenience may require. The uncolored light may be indicated by blank spaces, and by special symbols for adding white to the color in definite amounts.

When the lighting or color effect is designed to remain unchanged over a period indicated by one or more bars or parts of one or more bars of the music, the continuation of such color with its light intensity may be indicated by straight lines b following the color indication. Increase or decrease in the intensity of the color effect may be indicated by the use of forked or diverging lines shown at c; their length across the lines of vertical dots shown at d indicating the time in which the ultimate increase and decrease is to occur; the inclosed numeral representing a certain light quantity together with the length giving the abruptness as well as leisureliness of the increase of the light and its decay; those lines diverging or opening to the right being designed to indicate intensification or brightening, and those converging toward the right a decrease or darkening in the intensity which may be sharply defined or diminish gradually; depending upon the length of the marks and the symbols indicating intensity changes for light quantity which they hold.

As an assistance to the eye, the scale of light may be arbitrarily divided into sections marked with such descriptive titles as "twilight arc", "daylight arc," &c. For the purpose of designating these more or less arbitrary divisions, the whole vertical space between the staves may be sub-divided into a plurality of unit spaces, the temporal or bar divisions being marked at intervals by lines of dots d, which may be alined with the lines dividing the musical bars. Thus in Fig. 2, the space between the staves is sub-divided into unit spaces of equal width, giving a range of intensity from that indicated by a single median width which may represent a crepuscular lighting or low range value of any color employed, to an intensity represented by all the spaces or full range; an increase in intensity which may reach a dazzling or superbright degree.

Mm. $56 = $ "o", in Fig. 2, refers to the metronome time underlying the orderly change of light. The "o", indicated at e represents the unit of beat underlying the play of that light score. A denoting of time, finer than the eye requires to establish a color, is incompatible with the synthetic nature of the light.

This particular light score to the Moonlight Sonata opens up at a light intensity equaling two ten-thousandths of a lambert. That light remains unchanged through four units of beat or four "oooo". At the opening unit of beat or first "o" of the second bar, the light may dip one step. Esthetically there would be choice as to whether the light shall begin to dip before the sound makes a step down or exactly with the lowering in pitch of the sound. This would be one of the many ways in which fine esthetic choice would enter into the use of time in conjunction with light.

In Fig. 1, the symbol ". ☐ ☐ ▦ 2" (two ten-thousandths of a lambert or two-tenths of a milli-lambert) indicates the quantity of light; also coloration.

At the second bar, Fig. 2, the light continues the same over the remaining three "ooo" (beats) of that bar. At the third bar, the light dips again with the first "o" or beat, and dips still a greater step at the third "o" or beat; gradually making its way down in intensity until it reaches a quantity of light denoted by . ☐ ☐ ☐ ▦ 5, (or five hundred-thousandths of a lambert or five-hundredths of a milli-lambert). At the fourth "o" of the fifth bar, the light in conjunction with the entering of the melody (at B) changes ino a higher quantity of light indicated by . ☐ ▦ 5 (five-thousandths of a lambert shaded for red. Since that red is to be diluted into pink, denotation is made that two units of white light, indicated at f, are to be added to the red light being filtered through. This pink light continues through bar No. 6, and one-half of bar No. 7, where it increases in brightness; decreasing again at the beginning of the following bar, making at the third "o" or beat of bar No. 8, a still greater increase and decrease down to the final note of the melody. There the light dips and changes in tint till it reaches the opening quantity of light and its shade of color.

In Fig. 3, I have indicated diagrammatically various elements of the nomenclature comprising the marks to be applied to a sheet of music and the meaning thereof.

The forked lines c are intended to indicate a brightening or increase of the light; the forked lines c' are intended to indicate a darkening; the character indicated at g indicates a range of light equivalent to the "twilight arc;" the character indicated at g' represents a range of light equal to the "auroral arc;" the character indicated at g^2 indicates a range of light equal to the "diurnal arc," and the character represented at g^3 indicates a "dazzle arc." Other arcs may be added as "starlight arc," "moonlight arc," etc.

Bar marks are shown at d. The units of white light are indicated at f. These may be multiplied for the amount of light required. The colored squares a, a', a^2, are in accordance with the usual color markings of the heraldic scale. When the colors are proportioned, the blocks or other symbols will include the lines representing different colors, as at a^3 and a^4. Merging color may be shown as indicated at h; being disposed within diverging lines.

The time beats are indicated at e. Where it may be desired to effect momentary changes in the light or color in ultimately increasing or decreasing ranges of the same, I may employ characters such as shown at k, k', k^2 and k^3.

Since the spectral colors are not found in equal amounts in artificial light, the intensities of the lighting and colors will vary at the same point of scale value so that the amount of coloration of one color at a given intensity of the light scale will differ from the intensity exhibited by another color at the same point of intensity measure for the one light source. The person making the light creation may provide for leveling of these natural discrepancies when this is wished. Color cannot be considered in steps as notes since its increment of quantity is insensible. Intensity of light, gradually increasing, gradually decreasing, carries the color and not color the intensity since color is only a form of intensity.

As may be further understood, any color may follow another and in passing from one to another there may be periods of time when the colors will blend and produce a third color or shade which is dispelled when the first color is cut off. These combinations or blending effects may be illustrated on any of the symbols by the use of arbitrary color indications according to the scheme employed, and proportioned for the end desired: half and half; much of one color; little of another; a third of this; a fourth of that, etc., so much time of this; so much time of that, and so on. It takes time to merge color and this merging cannot be denoted by notes of music, neither can colors follow each other with the "rapidity of change" of notes in music.

In addition to the markings above described, there may be occasion for a lighting effect in which the gradations of intensity may fluctuate or proceed in angular steps in their increasing or decreasing effect, and to indicate these fluctuating conditions, I may employ a symbol of the character indicated at k, k', &c., where wavy lines are shown. The wavy lines may be changed to angular form where this may be wanted.

The forked lines displayed thus " 4 > "
are intended to represent decrease in the intensity of the light or color effect, with a gradual diminution of the same, as the lines converge to the unit intensity of the light or color the point reaches, in use with any portion of the music with which it is coördinated. The forked lines disposed "< 3 "
are intended to represent a gradual increase in the intensity of the light or color employed, with a change to the unit intensity at the extreme point of divergence or, when combined thus: "< 2 2 >" to a gradual change beyond and back to any unit intensity. The intensity of the color indicated by the forked lines may be further indicated by the relative thickness of the same.

The forked lines used in this light notation, because of the wide range of light to be considered, require in all instances for quantity and numeral value denotation, since the numerals here would refer to the number of steps in a light scale as the note on the music staff refers to the note scale of an instrument.

The forked lines with thin incidental curves denote the time and manner of the growth only, which also is indispensable. It is plain that a plotting of the light fluctuations used in any light score may be made by one or two line graphs, continuous or cursive, for use in some required direction. Such plotting would stand in relation to light scoring as any diagram of relationship stands to the matter it portrays.

These light markings will connote esthetic qualities, attributes, expressions and uses of feeling, speed, matters of taste, climax and anti-climax, emotional and dynamic.

The unit value of intensity of the symbols employed may be based upon any table or scale of brightness. In the present case I have used the term "lambert" as the unit of measure of the light intensity, it being understood that "lambert" is the centimeter gram second unit of brightness, or the brightness of a perfectly diffusing surface radiating or reflecting one lumen per square centimeter.

I claim:

1. A system of notation for indicating lighting effects in timed succession comprising a series of arbitrary symbols, certain of said symbols indicating light, and other symbols indicating the intensity of such light.

2. A system of notation for indicating lighting effects in timed succession, comprising a series of arbitrary symbols representing units of light, and other symbols associated therewith and designed to represent increment and decrement in the intensity of such light.

3. A system of notation for indicating lighting effects, comprising a series of arbitrary symbols representing degrees of intensity.

4. A notation for indicating lighting effects comprising a series of arbitrary symbols representing the intensity and color of the light.

5. A notation for indicating colored lighting effects in timed succession, comprising a series of arbitrary symbols representing degrees of intensity, and other symbols in association with the first named symbols for indicating color.

6. A system of notation to indicate the timed succession of lighting effects in conjunction with rythmic expression, comprising a series of arbitrary symbols, certain of

said symbols indicating the intensity of such color.

7. A system of notation to indicate the timed succession of lighting effects in conjunction with rythmic expression, comprising a series of arbitrary symbols, certain of said symbols indicating color, and other of said symbols indicating the increase and decrease in the intensity of said color.

8. A system of notation to be used in timed succession with a form of rythmic expression comprising symbols indicating color, other symbols indicating the intensity of such color and means for indicating the timed sequence of the color and color intensities.

MARY HALLOCK-GREENEWALT.

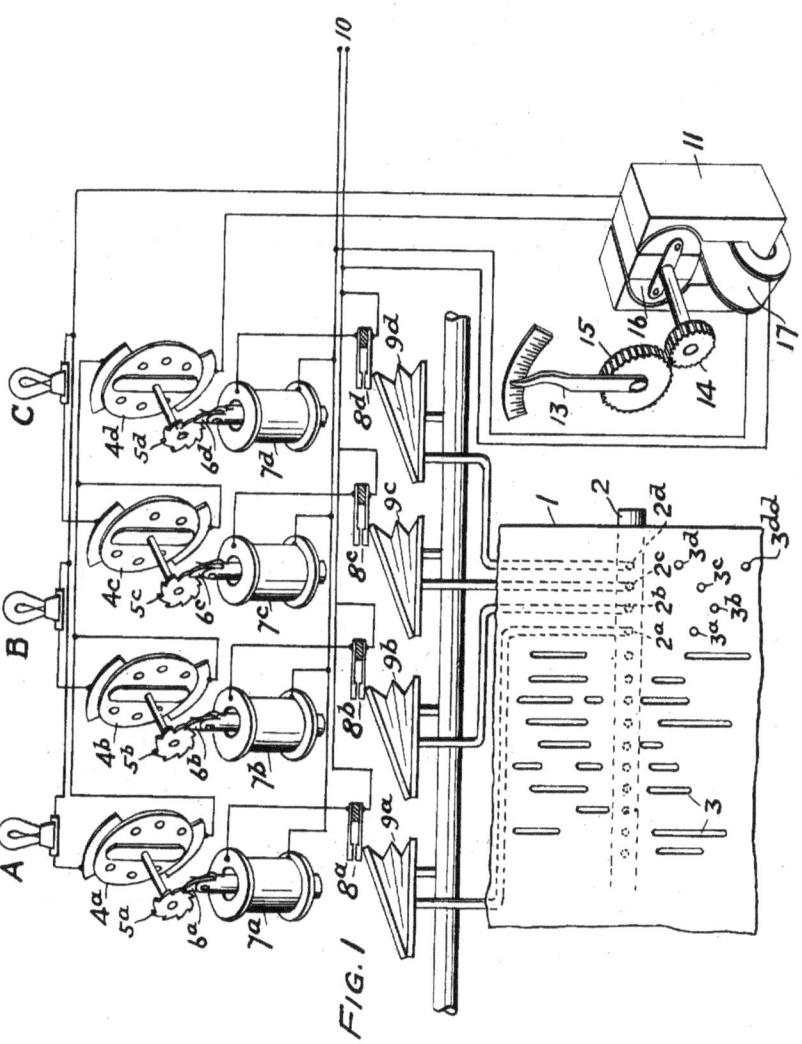

Dec. 20, 1927.
M. H. GREENEWALT
Re. 16,825
METHOD OF AND MEANS FOR ASSOCIATING LIGHT AND MUSIC
Original Filed Aug. 30, 1918 3 Sheets-Sheet 1

FIG. 1

WITNESS:
Rob.t P. Ketchel

INVENTOR
Mary Hallock Greenewalt
BY
Busser & Harding
ATTORNEYS

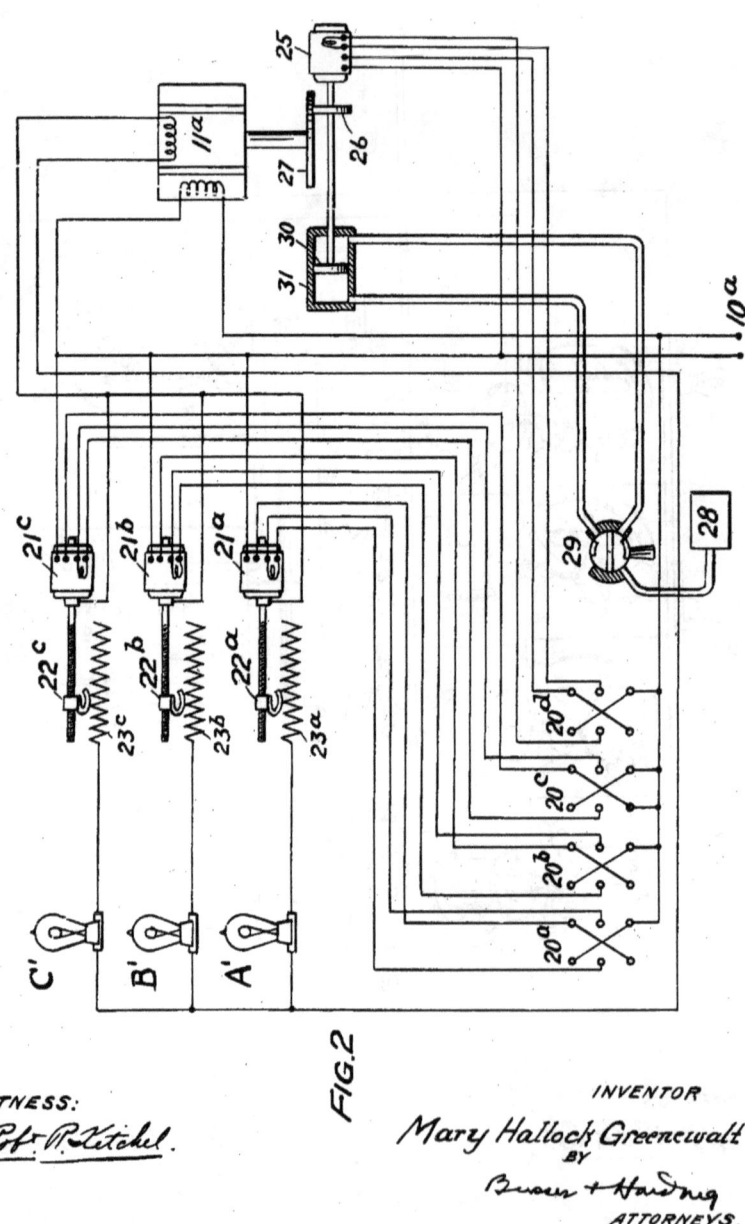

Dec. 20, 1927

M. H. GREENEWALT

Re. 16,825

METHOD OF AND MEANS FOR ASSOCIATING LIGHT AND MUSIC

Original Filed Aug. 30, 1918   3 Sheets-Sheet 3

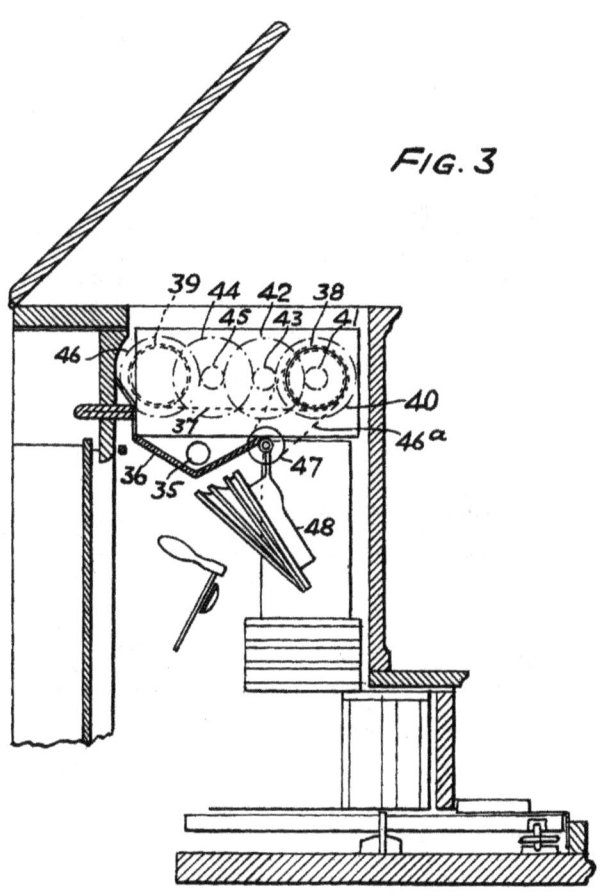

Fig. 3

WITNESS:

INVENTOR
Mary Hallock Greenewalt
BY
ATTORNEYS

Reissued Dec. 20, 1927.

Re. 16,825

UNITED STATES PATENT OFFICE.

MARY HALLOCK GREENEWALT, OF PHILADELPHIA, PENNSYLVANIA.

METHOD OF AND MEANS FOR ASSOCIATING LIGHT AND MUSIC.

Original No. 1,481,132, dated January 15, 1924, Serial No. 252,133, filed August 30, 1918. Application for reissue filed October 15, 1924. Serial No. 743,839.

My invention relates broadly to the associating of light in various shades or intensities, which may be accompanied by color indication or sensation, with musical notes or tones in various shadings. My invention includes means for producing what in some instances would be flood lighting, and in other instances spots or zones of light, with or without color accompaniment in each instance, and in all instances the means employed shall be capable of effecting desired gradations in the lighting effects produced, from those of the greatest light intensity to the various degrees of what may be termined shade or darkness.

The object of my invention is to associate with musical or articulate sounds in various tones or shades a certain arbitrary system of brightening or darkening effects, with or without color accompaniment, peculiarly adapted to express or to complement the emotions produced by musical notes and tones in order that the pleasure derived by the individual through the sense of hearing may be enhanced through the sense of sight.

It is obvious that the field in which my improved arrangements are available is very large, and it is also obvious that while under some conditions certain arbitrary matters must form part of any system having in view the correlation or complementing of light and shade and color with music, they should be capable of a large amount of flexibility or elasticity in the way of adjustment to meet the widely various conditions presented by the range of musical compositions.

There are many compositions or works of classical and other music whose themes suggest the tonal or color aspect of the atmosphere, whether brilliant light or shadow, twilight, or darkness, or anything between the highest intensity of light on the one side, and the deepest shade of night or blackness on the other side; and the essential object of my invention is the provision of means whereby the music, however interpreted or by whatever means, may be accompanied by changes in the degrees of light of the atmospheric and other surroundings properly associated with such music, and with or without the accompaniment of color.

The means employed for attaining this result must be highly sensitive or elastic in order that changes from high light to shade and the various light intensities, or vice versa, and from color to color, which may or may not be associated with the brilliant lighting or the deepest shades of darkness, may grow or ebb in insensible gradations as the loud and soft notes or tones of music can grow or ebb; or may blend with each other gradually; or may follow each other in sharp contrast, depending upon the arbitrary arrangement of the lighting or coloring to which any particular musical composition or theme is especially adapted to respond from the viewpoint of artistic and aesthetic beauty.

As may be readily understood, music of a light and airy character might well be complemented with lighting effects which include the paler shades of any of the primary colors of the spectrum rays; the majestic themes may have the higher intensities of light and the deeper or more intense coloration; and the heavy and sombre musical works the deeper shades and the darker tones. It is obvious further that many different forms and types of mechanism may be employed to accomplish these results.

These and other features of my invention are more fully disclosed hereinafter, reference being had to the accompanying drawings showing several forms of mechanism which may be employed within the scope of my invention, in which:

Figure 1, is a fragmentary diagrammatic view of a lighting system within the scope of my invention in which light producing means, which may be electric lamps, are controlled by a perforated sheet such as is employed in mechanical music players; the sheet so employed having a line of perforations, through the instrumentality of which, acting in connection with properly cooperative means or parts, instantaneous control of the lighting means is effected.

Fig. 2 is a diagrammatic view of other means which I may employ to produce the desired lighting effects, with or without color accompaniment, and

Fig. 3 is a diagrammatic view of a portion of a piano, organ or other key-played instrument having means whereby atmospheric coloring in various intensities or shades may be produced.

In Fig. 1, I have shown a method of varying the intensity of a plurality of light sources as represented by lamps A, B and C. The drawing shows automatic controlling means. For this purpose, I prefer to use a standard type of perforated music sheet to automatically throw on and off the light supplying medium or source, and to control the same, individually or collectively, by means of a suitable voltage regulator or any means capable of performing the desired function.

In the system diagrammatically illustrated in Fig. 1; 1 represents a perforated music sheet common to mechanical music players; the same passing over the usual tracker board 2, having the usual apertures 3 controlling the musical notes or tones. In addition such sheet is provided with additional rows of apertures 3^a, 3^b, 3^c and 3^d, designed to cooperate with apertures 2^a, 2^b, 2^c and 2^d of the tracker board 2 whereby the control of the lighting or darkening intensity may be effected.

Each light source may be controlled by a rotary switch 4^a, 4^b, 4^c or 4^d, and these switches carry notched disks 5^a, 5^b, 5^c and 5^d, which are actuated by ratchet pawls 6^a, 6^b, 6^c and 6^d, operatively connected to the cores of the magnetic solenoids 7^a, 7^b, 7^c and 7^d, when the latter are energized by the closing of the contacts 8^a, 8^b, 8^c and 8^d through the expansion of the bellows 9^a, 9^b, 9^c and 9^d.

The general operation is as follows:

A suitable source of current supply, indicated at 10 is provided for supplying current to the lamps A, B and C to the solenoids 7^a 7^b, 7^c and 7^d, and to the voltage regulator or other device 11. When the aperture or hole 3^d in the music sheet registers with the aperture 2^d of the tracker board, the bellows 9^d expands and closes the contacts 8^d, thus energizing the solenoid 7^d, and the plunger or core thereof moved upward, turning the ratchet disk 5^d by the pawl 6^d, and operating the rotary switch 4^d, which closes the main circuit.

When the aperture 3^a in the music sheet registers with the aperture 2^a of the tracker board, the bellows 9^a expands slightly, from the position shown in Fig. 1, in which its upper edge lightly bears against the lower surface of the contacts 8^a and on its expansive movement closes the contacts 8^a, thereby energizing the solenoid 7^a, and the plunger or core thereof moves upward, turning the ratchet disk 5^a by the pawl 6^a, and operating the rotary switch 4^a. This supplies current to the lamp A.

When the apertures 3^b or 3^c of the music sheet register with the complemental apertures 2^b or 2^c in the tracker board, the operation of the several elements to supply current to the lamps B and C is the same as that effected by the registration of the apertures 2^d and 3^d. When it is desired to throw off the main current, the rotary switch 4^d is to be turned, and this may be effected by providing an aperture 3^{dd} at the end of the music sheet, designed to register with the aperture 2^d of the tracker board and move the bellows 9^d to close the contacts 8^d and actuate the solenoid 7^d to close the switch 4^d. From the above, it will be seen that any number of apertures 3^a, 3^b, 3^c or 3^d may be made in the music sheet so as to automatically throw on and off any number of light sources or lamps at the exact instance desired, and the electrical mechanism is entirely disconnected when the final aperture 3^{dd} operates the main rotary switch 4^d.

While electric lamps are shown as the source of illumination, it will be understood that other forms of light producing elements may be employed under the control of the actuating mechanism which cooperates with the apertured music sheet 1.

The voltage regulator 11, which is a special means of varying the pressure or voltage supplied to the light sources or lamps A, B and C, is provided and arranged so that it can be controlled by a hand-lever 13 which, in this case, may also serve as an indicator of the light intensity. This may be connected by gears 14 and 15 to obtain the required sensitive movement of the coil 16, which is normally stationary but free to turn. The position of the coil 16 with respect to the magnetic field 17 gives the voltage applied to the light source, and the movement, therefore, provides a means of varying the light intensity.

While specific means are shown to obtain the desired adjustment in the relation between the coil 16 and the magnetic pole or field 17, any other means of turning the coil 16 may be provided. This movement might be effected by a pedal, or by fluid pressure under the control of a suitable valve, which could be operated automatically by the use of apertures in the music sheet 1, thus making the entire control of the light and its intensities automatic through the use of perforations or apertures in the music sheet, which perforations may be produced simultaneously with the perforations which control the musical notes.

While the arrangement indicated is shown as controlling individual lamps A, B and C: the switches being arranged to increase or decrease the intensity of light at will, the lights may be arranged in banks, clusters or other combinations and in various color tones or shades, and with color screens or other means so that any desired color effect may be produced to any desired intensity or degree, and the lighting effects so produced are complemental to the musical tones, although the arrangement may be more or less of an arbitrary one from an æsthetic or artistic standpoint.

Fig. 2 shows an arrangement which may be employed for the control of two or more high candle power lamps or other illuminating elements. Lamps A′, B′ and C′ may be single lamps of any wattage capacity, or they may represent any number of lamps operated in banks as individual units. Any number of units can be used and controlled in the manner shown.

Reversing switches 20^a, 20^b and 20^c here shown, may be arranged similar to the tilting tablet of an organ, or otherwise modified in design; the object being to provide two movements, one to close one circuit, and the other to open this circuit and close another circuit. A key arrangement could be employed for this purpose. These reversing switches may be arranged to control, respectively, the motors 21^a, 21^b and 21^c. When one of these switches is thrown in 20^a, for instance, the corresponding motor 21^a will run in one direction or the other, thus driving the sliding contact 22^a, and cutting in or out the desired amount of resistance in the resistance element or coil 23^a. When the switch is thrown in the opposite direction, the motor reverses and the operation of the sliding contact is likewise reversed. This provides means for increasing or decreasing the intensity of the lamps A′, B′ or C′; each lamp being controlled individually.

10^a may represent the source of current supply for the electrical circuit and equipment shown, and 11^a may represent a voltage regulator or other device capable of the same or similar function which may be controlled by a reversing switch 20^d, disposed adjacent the reversing switches 20^a, 20^b and 20^c. A tilting table key or any other mechanical means, arranged so that it will operate as a switch, may be employed. The position of the switch 20^d controls the operation of the voltage regulator 11^a in such a manner that the potential supplied to the lamps A′, B′ or C′ can be gradually increased or decreased automatically from any remote point at which the switch 20^d may be located.

The voltage regulator may be driven by a motor or other prime mover 25, and may be operatively connected therewith through a disk drive comprising the friction wheels 26 and 27. The switch 20^d controls the motor 25, which in turn actuates the voltage regulator mechanism.

A fluid pressure pump 28 may be provided and equipped with a suitable valve 29, which can be located at any desired point for controlling the position of the disk 26, which may be caused to move by supplying fluid under pressure to either side of the piston 30 in the chamber 31.

The valve, pressure cylinder, disk drive and its accompanying actuating means, a motor or other prime mover, form a means of varying "at will" the voltage supplied from the voltage regulator. With this arrangement, the change in speed either slower or faster can be obtained by the simple movement of the valve correlating the manner of growth of the dynamics of sound with the dynamics of light, which valve may be under the control of the musician or under the control of a perforated sheet or other means properly synchronized or correlated with the musical themes interpreted by the artist upon the instrument played.

The device or structure illustrated in Fig. 3, is designed to produce by simple means, such as may be readily attached to an organ or piano or similar musical instrument, a color flooding or shading of the atmosphere by disposing within or adjacent to the musical instrument suitable lighting means, a reflector, and a colored screen in the form of a translucent or relatively transparent ruled sheet through which the light may show; the structure being provided with driving means whereby the colored screen may be moved simultaneously with the progress of the music as played by the performer, or by an automatically actuated mechanical-player, under such conditions that the desired light diffusion or shadow with or without coloration, may be properly associated as to time with the musical notes or tones.

In this arrangement, a source of light such as an electric lamp indicated at 35 may be employed, which lamp may be backed by a reflector 36, and above the light a colored film 37 may be arranged; such film being carried by a roll 38 from which it may be unwound, with a roll 39 upon which it may be wound. The roll 39 may be positively driven from the roll 38, by a suitable train of gearing 40, 41, 42, 43, 44, 45 and 46; the roll 38 being positively driven by a chain or belt 46^a, from a wheel 47, which may be actuated by a suitable motor 48, by electromagnetic control or by any other suitable means.

For the coloring effect, as may be well understood, colored lamps may be employed, with or without previously determined or set sequence, or colored screens may be employed, or means may be arranged whereby the primary colors of the solar spectrum can be utilized with the aid of a suitable lens (or lenses), a filter (or filters), placed in proper relation with the lighting means and with the desired or necessary instrumentalities for cutting off portions of the spectral colors, or of blending two or more of the same to produce any desired tone of the color in any desired gradation or intensity; insensibly growing or lessening or brought in as willed. Additionally, this lighting may be in the nature of flood lighting in which the performer may be placed, or any limited zone or portion directly surrounding the performer or performers, or disposed at any other parts of the circumambient space and within hearing of the musical tones, as may be desired, and controlled from any point to give the desired unity of impression through unity of design over the space desired simultaneously; reaching the individual in three dimensional manner as sound reaches him.

I claim:

1. The combination with means, for producing musical notes, of lighting means, means for gradually effecting changes in light produced by said lighting means, and means for varying the intensity of said light, both of said means being timed with the musical notes produced.

2. The combination with means for producing musical notes of a source of illumination, means for gradually effecting changes in the light produced by said source, means for varying the intensity of the said light and means for timing both of said means with the musical notes produced.

3. The combination with a musical instrument, of lighting means, means controlled by said instrument for gradually effecting changes in said lighting means, means for varying the intensities of said lighting means, and means for timing the intensities with the musical notes produced.

4. The combination with light producing means and sound producing means, of means for gradually effecting changes in the light, and other means for effecting changes in the light intensities, both of said means operating in timed relation with the sounds produced.

5. The combination with a musical instrument, a perforated sheet, and means whereby said perforated sheet automatically effects the production of music by said instrument, of a lighting circuit, means whereby said perforated sheet controls said circuit, and means for varying the intensity of the light produced by the lighting circuit.

6. The combination with a musical instrument, of colored lamps, means whereby said instrument selectively illuminates said lamps, and manually controlled means for varying the intensities of the light produced by the said lamps in timed relation to the musical tones produced by the said instrument.

7. The method of associating musical sounds with accompanying illumination, which consists in providing a source of light, automatically effecting changes in the color of said light, and varying the intensity of the light produced in timed relation to the musical tones produced.

8. The method of combining sound and light for æsthetic expression which consists in producing sounds in a rhythmic relationship and simultaneously producing lighting effects within the area of audibility of the sounds by varying the intensity of the light in timed relationship with the sounds.

9. The method of combining sound and light for æsthetic expression, consisting in producing audible sounds in timed, rhythmic relationship, flooding with light an area within the area of audibility of the sound and simultaneously producing gradual variations in the light in timed relationship with the emotional or æsthetic content of a succession of such sounds.

10. The method of combining sound and light for æsthetic expression, consisting in producing audible sounds in timed, rhythmic relationship, flooding with light an area within the area of audibility of the sound and simultaneously producing gradual variations in the color and intensity of the light in timed relationship with the emotional or æsthetic content of a succession of such sounds.

11. The method of combining sound and light for æsthetic expression, consisting in producing audible sounds in timed, rhythmic relationship, flooding with light an area within the area of audibility of the sound, and simultaneously producing gradual variations in the light in timed relationship with the musical effect produced by a succession of such sounds.

12. The method of combining sound and light for æsthetic expression consisting in producing audible sounds in timed rhythmic relationship, producing a light in an area within the area of audibility of the sound, maintaining said light during a succession of such sounds, and producing gradual variations in the light without extinguishing it in timed relationship with such succession of sounds.

13. The method of combining light and rhythmic sound for æsthetic expression which consists in merging in sympathy with the successive emotional values of rhythmic sound the intensity or color of lights from a source of light without interrupting the light for a substantial length of time.

14. The method of combining light and sound for æsthetic expression, consisting in producing music and producing a flood lighting within the range of audibility of the said music and varying while maintaining for a substantial length of time the emotional values of the light in sympathy with or complemental to the successive emotional values of the music.

15. The method of combining light and sound for æsthetic expression which consists in producing rhythmic sound having successive emotional values and producing light within a range of audibility of said sound, and in variably merging color of the light in sympathy with the successive emotional values of the sound.

16. The method of combining sound and light for æsthetic expression which consists in producing rhythmic sound and producing a flood lighting within the range of audibility of said sound, and varying while maintaining said light in sympathy or con-

trast with successive emotional values of said sound.

17. The method of combining sound and light for æsthetic expression, which consists in producing rhythmic sound, producing a flood lighting within the range of audibility of said sound, and varying said light by insensible gradations in sympathy with or contrast to the successive emotional values of said rhythmic sound.

In testimony of which invention, I have hereunto set my hand, at Philadelphia, Pennsylvania, on this 13th day of October, 1924.

MARY HALLOCK GREENEWALT.

DISCLAIMER

Re. 16,825.—*Mary Hallock Greenewalt*, Philadelphia, Pa. METHOD OF AND MEANS FOR ASSOCIATING LIGHT AND MUSIC. Patent dated December 20, 1927. Disclaimer filed December 23, 1933, by the patentee.

Hereby enters the following disclaimer, the aforesaid claims numbers 1 to 4 inclusive, and 7 to 17 inclusive, as follows:

I disclaim the use of stereoptically focussed images such as are known as painted pictures and the like, projected between lenses as distinguished from the use of substantially shapeless flood of light.

[*Official Gazette January 16, 1934.*]

MAUDE MAPLE MILES

Appliance for Displaying Colors (1919)

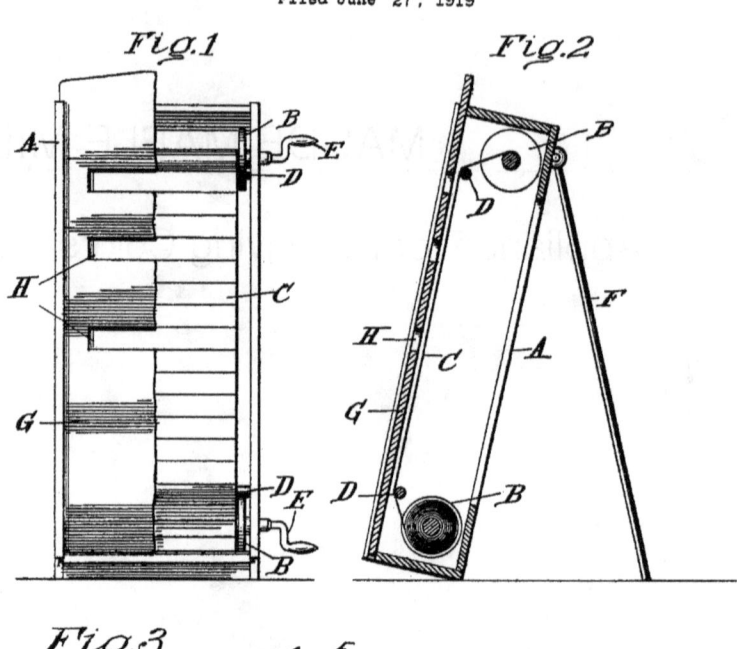

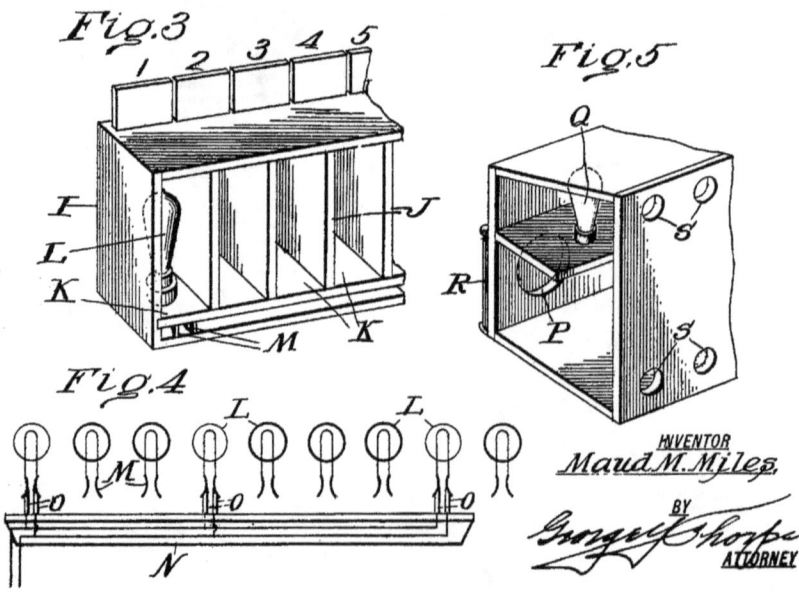

Patented June 26, 1923.

1,460,264

UNITED STATES PATENT OFFICE.

MAUD MAPLE MILES, OF LOMBARD, ILLINOIS.

APPLIANCE FOR DISPLAYING COLORS.

Application filed June 27, 1919. Serial No. 307,177.

To all whom it may concern:

Be it known that I, MAUD MAPLE MILES, a citizen of the United States, residing at Lombard, in the county of Du Page and State of Illinois, have invented certain new and useful Improvements in Appliances for Displaying Colors, of which the following is a specification.

This invention relates to color display appliances and my object is to produce an appliance capable of embodiment in different forms, by which colors may be displayed in related hues which are believed to suggest to the spectator related tone values, for the purpose of visualizing and aiding in the memorizing of the notes in music and also for enabling artists, modistes, milliners, interior decorators, etc., to quickly and effectively display such a large number of combinations in two or more harmonizing colors that the esthetic taste of the most critical customers may be satisfied.

In the above connection it is pointed out that it is also a distinctive feature of the invention to provide a carrier for the colors which may be in the form of a ribbon or tape, the said colors being arranged on the ribbon in the form of a color scale wherein the colors are related to each other in the same manner as the notes or harmonies of a musical scale are related.

To this end the invention consists in certain novel and useful features of construction and combinations of parts as hereinafter described and claimed; and in order that it may be fully understood reference is to be had to the accompanying drawing, in which:

Figure 1, is a front view of a combination color display appliance equipped with a device for masking all the colors except a particular combination of them; the mask being shown broken away.

Figure 2, is a central vertical section of the appliance.

Figure 3, is a perspective view of a different form of the appliance.

Figure 4, is a diagrammatic plan of the appliance shown in Figure 3.

Figure 5, is a fragmentary perspective view of a third type of the appliance.

Referring to the appliance illustrated by Figures 1 and 2, A indicates a frame wherein are journaled winding drums B connected by a ribbon C, which may be of either opaque or transparent material, and preferably of sufficient length to contain seven and one-third octaves of color—twelve semi-tones to the octave—each of such twelve semi-tones being numbered consecutively from 1 to 12 inclusive, with the maximum wave length of each color in certain ratio to the preceding color.

The colors or shades of color of each of the different octaves will each contain twelve half tones of color. The lightest octave shows a pure yellow and eleven tints of other colors, all twelve high light in value (high light being a tint slightly distinguishable from white) but preferably growing slightly lighter in value as they progress toward the upper end of the octave. The next octave below will contain as its purest colors, a pure yellow green and a pure orange yellow, also the first shade of yellow and nine tints of other colors, all twelve of a light value ("light value" being the value that is slightly distinguishable as being darker than "high light value") but preferably growing somewhat lighter as they progress toward the top of the octave. The same sequence of color effect is carried out in the succeeding octaves and in the partial octave mentioned.

The ribbon for practically the full distance between the drums or reels runs over the guide rolls D in order that the part of the ribbon between the guide rolls, which part is preferably of sufficient length to display an octave of twelve colors, shall be substantially parallel with the face of the frame A. The ribbon may be wound from one drum to the other by means of handles E which may be detachable or not as desired, and there will preferably be sufficient friction to hold the ribbon stretched fairly taut and to guard against accidental turning of either of the drums. For convenience in displaying the device to a class or to a customer, it will be found convenient to make it in the form of an easel, that is with a hinged back F which when opened will brace the frame in an inclined position without other support.

For use in conjunction with the construction thus far described, there will be a large number of masks, each of which will have a plurality of display openings relatively arranged to show only colors which will harmonize.

The masks G are in the form of removable covers which can be easily and quickly fitted over the face of the frame A, and, as above stated, each mask will be provided at predetermined points with two or more openings. For two color combinations there will be several masks each containing openings for exposing two colors at a time, which will harmonize because of the measured interval between the rate of their major vibrations. One of these masks will show two colors which are a major third of an octave apart. The other two-color masks will show the openings at prescribed distances apart so that two colors of the ribbon simultaneously appearing through said openings will always harmonize. To change the combinations, the ribbon, of course, will be moved by turning one of the drums or reels, the other turning under the pull of the ribbon. It will be seen that six masks of the two-opening type may be utilized to show six times twelve times seven and one-third schemes of color in pairs which can be depended upon to harmonize.

There will be a set of masks containing groups of three openings in different positions, a set containing four openings, and other sets containing different numbers of openings, the distance between the openings in the different masks being determined by the harmonic relation in music between notes spaced to correspond with the said openings.

With a device of this character a salesman entirely ignorant of either music or color can display two-color combinations, three-color combinations, four-color combinations, etc., and know that these colors harmonize.

In Figure 3, the appliance is in the form of a box I, open at the back and having a front composed of colored glass, non-inflammable film or other transparent material, arranged in series of twelve different colors as described with respect to the said ribbon, the box being divided by partitions J into compartments K, each containing an incandescent lamp L. The lamps will contain contacts M and be independent of each other. In place of masks there will be a series of contact combs N. The three-color combination combs for example, will have their teeth O spaced in relation to the colored face plates of frame I, and said three-contact comb will be wired in multiple and be adapted for connection by a cord to a wall socket or the like, not shown, so that when the switch is operated and the comb is slipped with its teeth between the contacts M of the correspondingly located lamps such lamps will be lighted and thus illuminate and display their respective color plates.

It will thus be seen that by simply slipping these comb contacts in position, a very large number of combinations of color may be displayed.

In Figure 5, a box is shown having a display opening P through which rays of light may pass from a lamp Q through a transparent ribbon R composed of colors like ribbon C, and adapted to be moved by hand or otherwise, for the purpose of displaying different colors in melodic relation. To avoid danger of fire, with this closed box type, and especially if the ribbon should be in the form of an inflammable film, it is desired to provide the box with openings S through which the air may circulate. If it is desired to throw the colors upon a screen or otherwise display them in succession, singly or in groups, usually but one light need be turned on, the succession of colors being produced by the movement of the ribbon or film. If it is desired only to show certain colors and to omit others, by this system of moving the ribbon or film, special ribbons or film may be used in which the colors not wanted may be omitted, only those desired to be shown being on the ribbon or film. By this plan colors may be shown in melodic arrangement as well as harmonic, similar in their color relationship to each other as is the sound relationship of musical notes that are shown in melodic or harmonic relationship. In both cases it is because of their relative vibration as will hereinafter more fully appear. Colors arranged in melodic form may be employed in arranging borders or putting colors in long narrow rows as on counters or shelves. That is to say, the present invention resides particularly in the formation of a color scale which bears a numerical relation of colors similar to the musical scale which enables the operator to obtain color harmonies which are related as are the harmonies of a musical scale.

As certain colors are believed to bear a fixed relationship to certain tones, I contemplate the use of ribbons or films for showing directly or projecting on a screen, colors in such relationship and of such relative length—tempo—that the travel of the ribbon or film past the opening shall record on the mind of the observer capable of distinguishing between harmony and discord in music, the melody represented by such arrangement of colors, so that the deaf may enjoy music as well as those whose hearing is unimpaired.

In the above connection it is pointed out that it is proposed to relate color to color in exactly the same manner that scientific musicians relate tone to tone.

That is to say, beginning on any color designated by the vibration of its dominant wave length I build both the diatonic scale, the untempered chromatic scale and the tempered chromatic scale in exactly the same manner that musicians build these scales of sound. On this basis a scale of musically related hues would be produced, except for the physical difference in the sense perception of the eye and the ear.

1,460,264

It is well known that the mathematical science of music is based on the laws of physics, but that the sense perception of music is psychologically different. However, the sense perception and mathematical science of music are in accord because the ear measures music with the same result that the scientist obtains when he measures the rates of vibration of the musical tones.

But, the eye does not measure color with the same result that the scientist obtains when he measures the vibration of light. Hence, the scales built in the purely physical way as mentioned above needs further modification, based upon the retinal sensibility of the eye.

Therefore, it will be seen that the color scales formed according to the present invention are made by utilizing the dominant wave length of the colors as far as such colors are found in the spectrum and assembling them in the scale in the same way that the musical scales are made, but modifying the tempered or untempered chromatic scale of color built on the purely musical laws by a suitable table of retinal sensibility of the eye, thereby giving a color scale that will produce results similar to the results obtained in the use of the musical scale.

By way of example red may be assumed to be "middle C", because some hypothesis must be made, and there are, so far, more reasons for this assumption than any other.

For purposes of the present illustration the wave length of red may be assumed to be 760 millicrons because on this basis the colors derived by the musical system are of the hues commonly accepted under the names used. Thus, a scale built under the present system with red at 760 would work out as follows:

Diatonic scale (purely physical).

Red=760 millicrons in wave lengths.
Orange=8/9 of red or 675.
Yellow=4/5 of red or 608.
Yellow-Green (half step)=3/4 of red or 570 millicrons, etc.

To get the (purely physical) untempered chromatic scale use the figures of the physical diatonic scale and find the half steps by finding 24/25 of preceding color.

For instance:

Wave lengths of red-orange=24/25 of 760 or 729.

Wave lengths of orange-yellow=24/25 of 675 or 648.

To get the purely physical tempered chromatic scale divide the wave lengths of any color by 1.05646 to get the following half-step in color for instance:
760=red.
760÷1.05646=718 or red-orange.
718÷1.05646=678 or orange, etc.

But the scales thus derived serve only as a basis for the derivation of color scales for the eye does not measure color with the same results that science obtains when it measures the wave lengths; while the ear does measure sound with the same results that science obtains in measuring musical notes. For this reason these purely physical scales must be modified by a table of the retinal sensibility of the eye.

The unit of measurement of the retinal sensibility of the eye is usually called a step-limen. By using one table of retinal sensibility and assuming the lacking numerals in some instances, the given tempered and untempered limen-scales of color are obtained based on the purely physical scales below using their relative intervals in ratio to the accepted step-limen.

Tempered chromatic scale of color, purely physical.	Interval in wave length.	Untempered scale of color, purely physical.	Interval in wave length.
760		760	
	42		31
718		729	
	40		54
678		675	
	38		27
640		648	
	36		40
604		608	
	34		38
570		570	
	32		23
538		547	
	30		40
508		507	
	29		23
479		484	
	27		28
452		456	
	26		20
426		436	
	24		31
402		405	
	22		25
380		380	

In both the tempered and untempered scale the second color is assumed to be true for the first step-limen in the scale as it is a barely perceptible step. If any difference between these figures were to be made it would preferably consist in increasing the interval by moving the first figure from 760 toward a possible 780.

The resultant chromatic scales, limen (both tempered and untempered) follow:

Tempered limen scale of color (chromatic).	Untempered limen scale of color (chromatic).
760	760
718	729
620	608
591.8	595
573.7	570.1
543	533.2
508	510.6
492.6	489.4
478.2	476.5
454.4	452.1
433.3	437.2
405.8	405.8
380	380

The diatonic limen scale may be derived from the untempered scale by beginning on the first (760) color selecting the colors according to the wish to derive a major or a minor scale. The steps in any chromatic scale are termed 1/2 steps or 1/2 tones. The scale of C (red) major would be as follows: 760—608—579.1—533.2—489.4—452.1—405.8—380. Were the last two colors found in the spectrum this would be a scientific scale but not the best adapted to a change of key. In the tempered scale begin on any color and build the chromatic scale according to the intervals of the desired scale—for instance use 620—as the first color for a major scale: 620—573.7—508.—492.6—454.4—(405.8—not found in any spectrum as a psychologically true hue) 718—620. These figures refer only to the hue.

In this connection, it should be borne in mind that the term "hue" refers to that extremely narrow portion of the spectrum which corresponds to a definite wave length, "tint" is a hue diluted with white, while "shade" is the hue altered by the addition of black. A hue is always specified by the wave length of the monochromatic light used (wave length of the dominant hue). It has been demonstrated experimentally that any color can be made by the mixture in proper proportions of white light with monochromatic spectral light of the proper wave length. The amount of saturation of a color determines its proximity to monochromatism. In building up any color scale, therefore, the saturation of the colors must be taken into consideration, that is, their tone-value.

Thus, by recapitulation, the following color scales are obtained which are not absolute perhaps but which are sufficiently accurate to prove the psychologically derived scales.

The scales.

Note.	Music (frequency).		Color (wave length).				
	Inter.	Scientif.	Color.	Temper.	Untemper.	Tem. L.S.	Unt. L.S.
	Pitch.	Pitch.					
1. C	258.6	256	1. Red.	760	760	760	760
2. C#	274	271	2. R. O.	718	729	718	729
3. D	290.3	287.3	3. Orange.	678	675	620	608
4. D#	307.5	304.4	4. O. Y.	640	648	591.8	595
5. E	325.8	322.5	5. Yellow.	604	608	573.7	570.1
6. F	345.2	341.7	6. Y. G.	570	570	543	533.2
7. F#	365.3	362	7. Green.	538	547	508	510.6
8. G	387.5	383.6	8. G. B.	508	507	492.6	489.4
9. G#	410.6	406.4	9. Blue.	479	484	478.2	476.5
10. A	435	430.4	10. B. V.	452	456	454.4	452.1
11. A#	460.9	456.1	11. Vio.	426	436	433.3	437.2
12. B	488.3	483.2	12. R. V.	402	405	405.8	405.8
Octave C	517.3	512	1. Red.	380	380	380	380

From the foregoing it will be apparent that the ribbon C is provided with a color scale in which the colors are definitely related in psychologically the same manner as the notes of a musical scale, and the forms of apparatus described herein may be used to display the colors in the various ways suggested. As a matter of fact other forms of apparatus may be used and the forms shown herein are simply illustrative of different types that may be employed to advantage.

I claim:

1. A ribbon having a color scale thereon, comprising a series of hues the wave lengths of which bear substantially the same relation to each other as the wave lengths of a series of notes which comprise a musical scale.

2. A ribbon having a color scale thereon, comprising a plurality of series of colors, each series consisting of a sequence of colors, the wave lengths of which bear substantially the same relation to each other as the notes in a sequence which comprise a musical octave.

3. A ribbon having a color scale thereon, comprising a plurality of series of colors, each series consisting of a sequence of colors, the wave lengths of which bear substantially the same relation to each other as the notes in a sequence which comprise a musical octave, and means for displaying certain of the colors in musically harmonious relations.

4. A ribbon having a color scale thereon, comprising a plurality of series of colors, one of the series consisting of a sequence of hues, the other series consisting of sequences of tints and shades of these hues, each member of a sequence being related to the other members in the same manner that the members of a musical scale are related to each other.

5. A ribbon having a color scale thereon, comprising a plurality of series of colors, one of the series consisting of a sequence of hues, the wave lengths of which are related to each other in substantially the same manner as the sequence of notes which comprise a musical octave, the corresponding colors in another sequence being of a different degree of saturation, all of the colors in one sequence being of substantially the same degree of saturation.

In testimony whereof I affix my signature.

MAUD MAPLE MILES.

ARTHUR C. VINAGERAS

Chromopiano (1921)

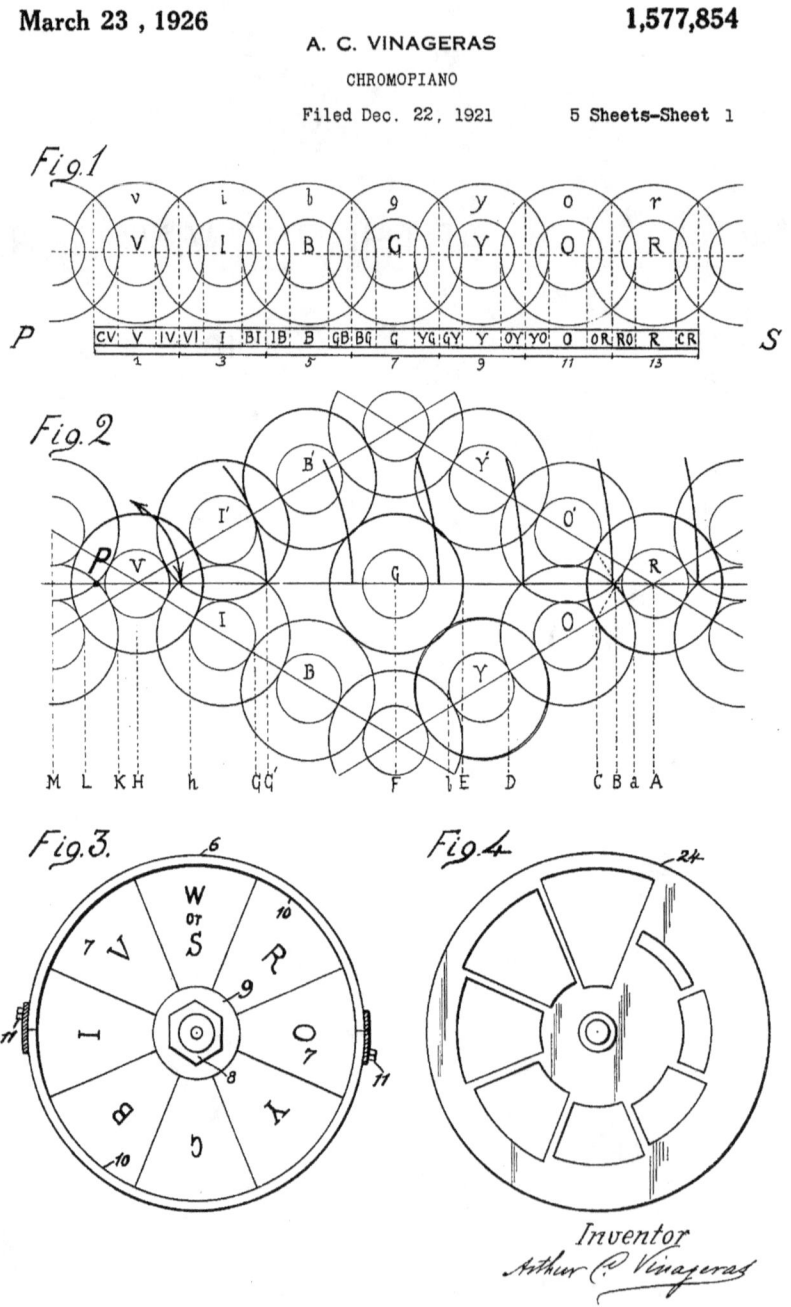

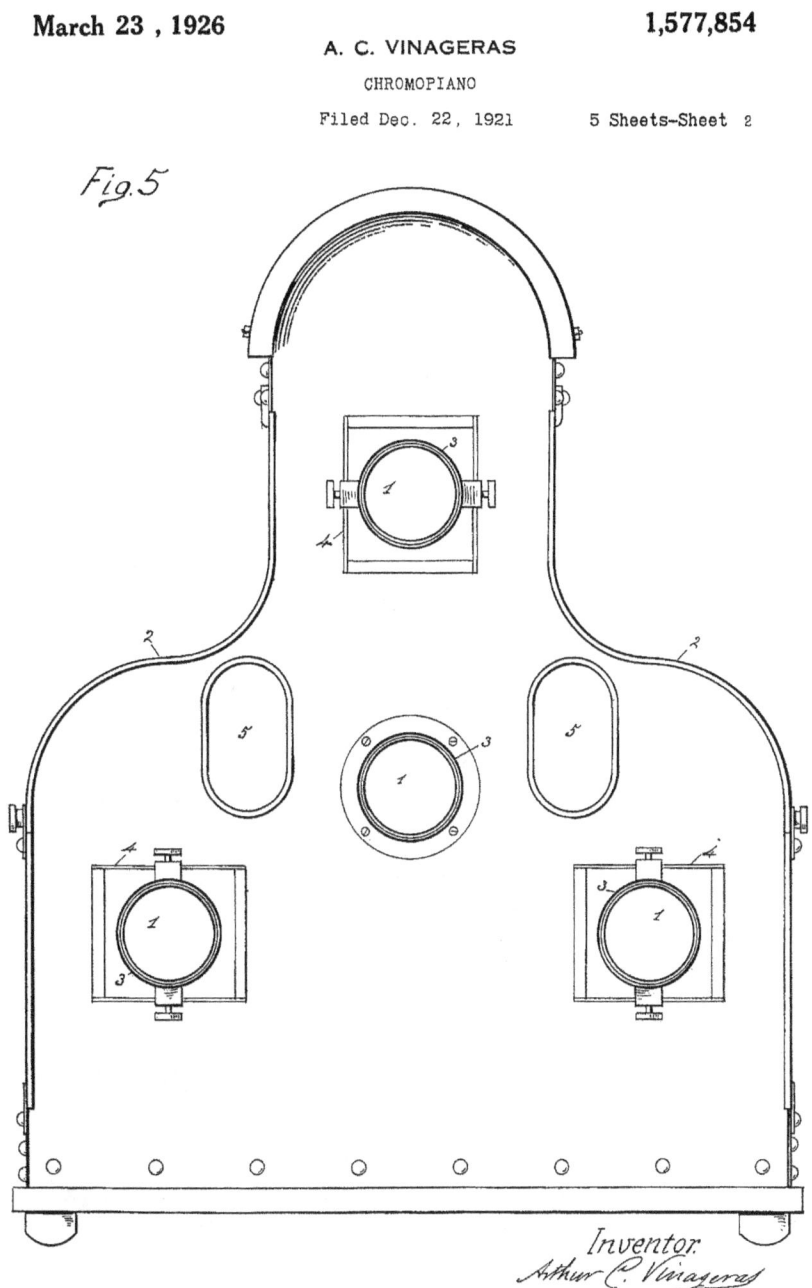

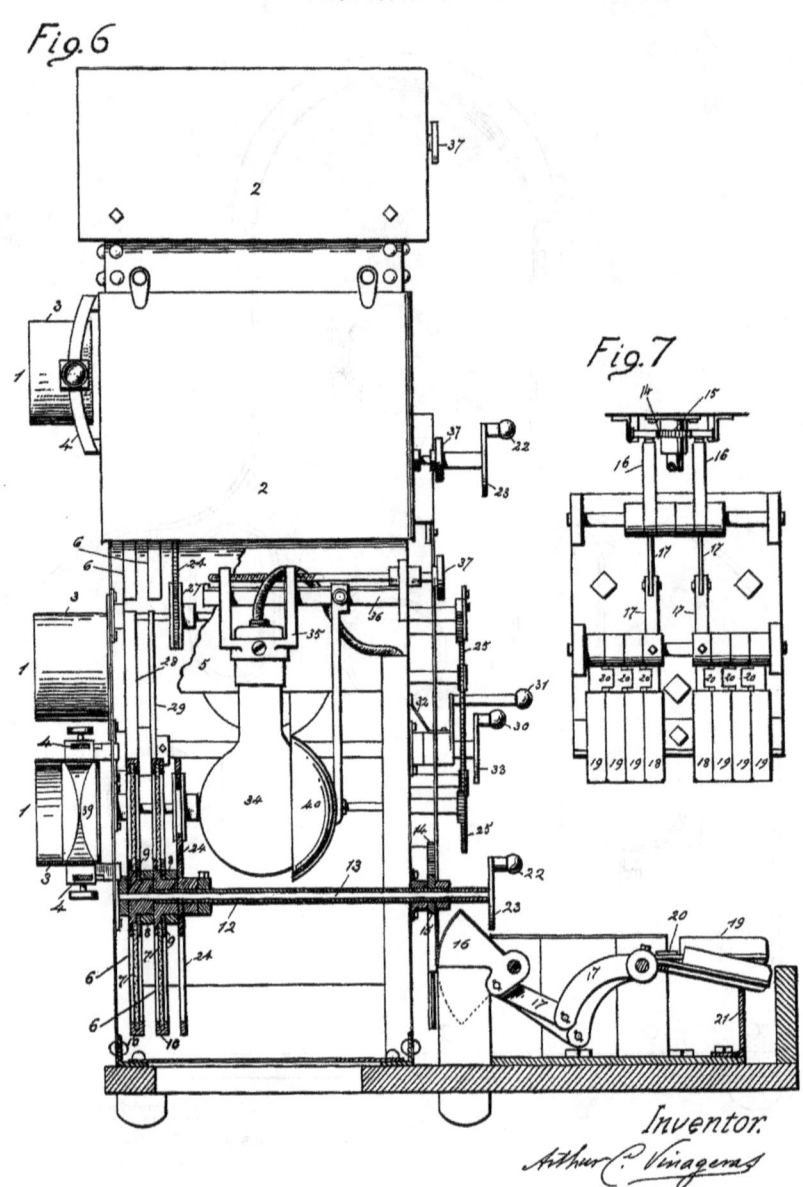

VISUAL MUSIC INSTRUMENT PATENTS (I)

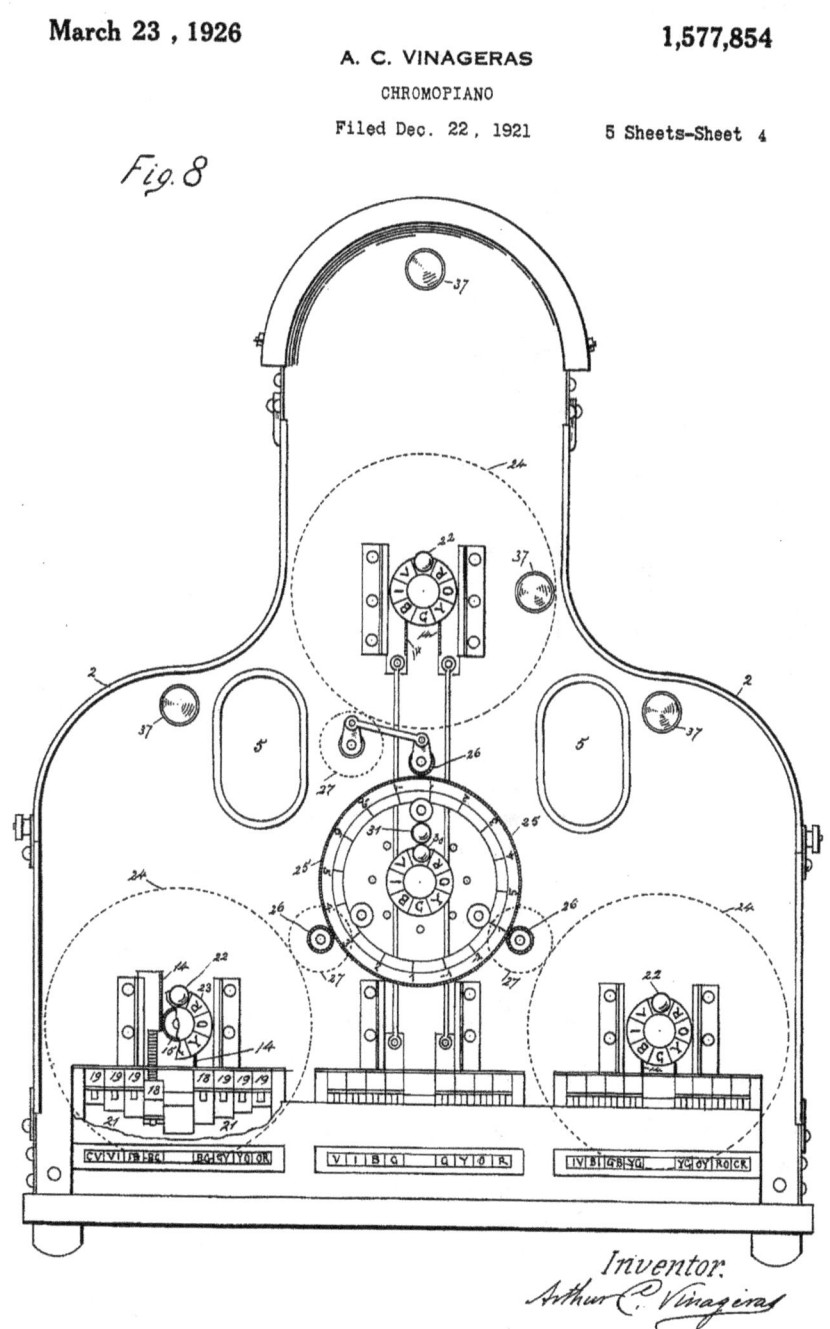

March 23, 1926
A. C. VINAGERAS
CHROMOPIANO
Filed Dec. 22, 1921
1,577,854
5 Sheets-Sheet 4

Fig. 8

Inventor.
Arthur C. Vinageras

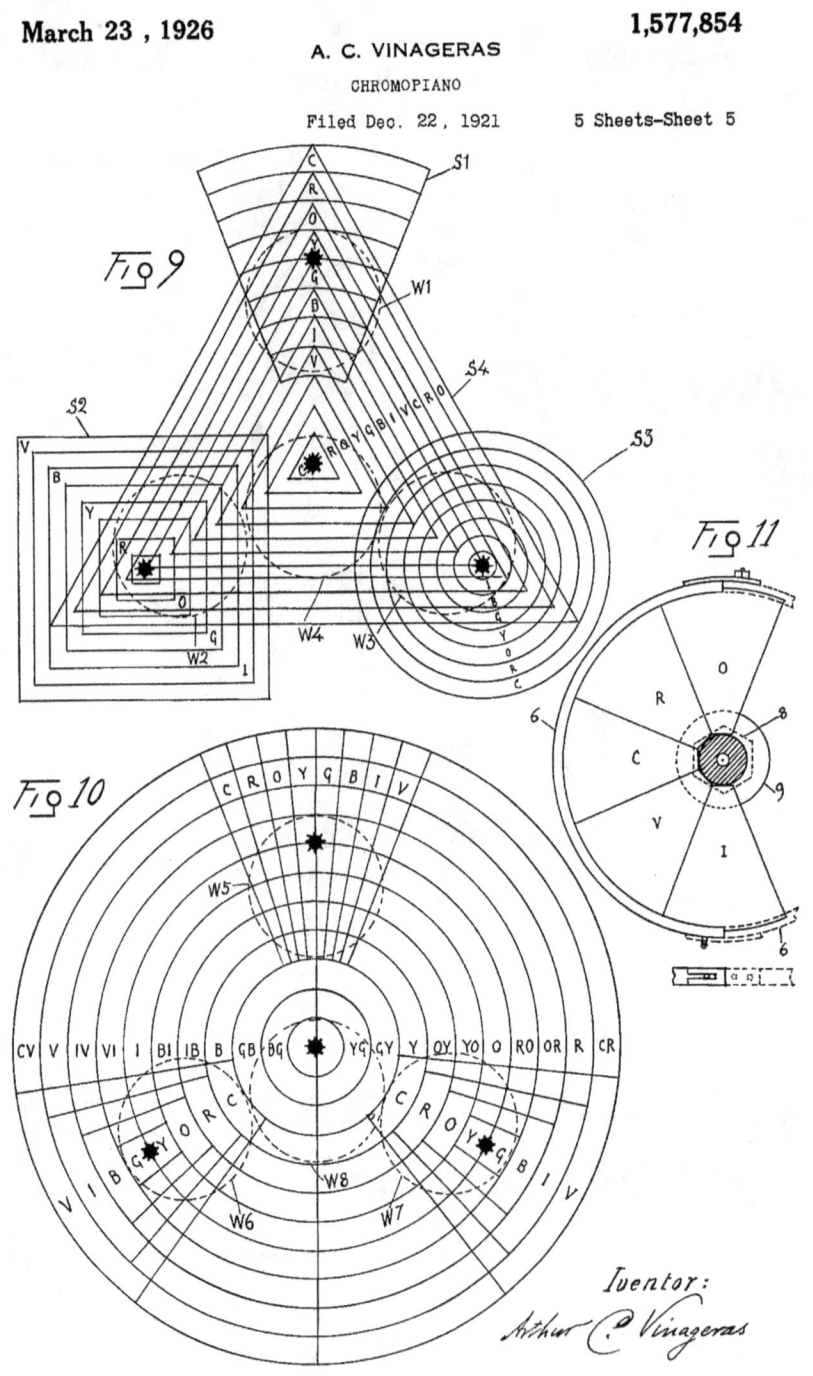

Patented Mar. 23, 1926.

1,577,854

UNITED STATES PATENT OFFICE.

ARTHUR C. VINAGERAS, OF LAWRENCE, MASSACHUSETTS.

CHROMOPIANO.

Application filed December 22, 1921. Serial No. 524,207.

To all whom it may concern:

Be it known that I, ARTHUR CODEZO VINAGERAS, a Cuban citizen, residing at Number 3½ Jackson Terrace, city of Lawrence, State of Massachusetts, United States of America, have invented a Light-Projecting Instrument Designated with the Name of the Chromopiano.

With this instrument or apparatus successions, juxtapositions and superpositions of spots of colored light are harmonized in tone as musical notes. Therefore the chromopiano can be tuned to unison with musical instruments. I describe my invention for the first time in this specification to which four sheets of drawings are attached. Similar numerals refer to similar parts throughout the several views.

The invention of the chromopiano includes in reality the invention of an absolutely original art to which I have given the name of chromomusic or music of colors. It is evident that without the discovery of the physical significance of tone quality in natural combinations of colors, such as those observed in, spectra, soap bubbles, mother of pearl, feathers, etc., it would have been impossible to me to invent chromomusic and the chromopiano. The object of chromomusic is to illuminate stages, halls, buildings and other things, with spots of colored light rhythmically changing in tone and duration as a musical composition and constituting sequences and chords of color notes composed and written in a manner analogous to that in which sequences and chords of musical notes are composed and written.

It is useful to remind that till Helmholtz discovered the physical significance of tone quality in music little or nothing was known concerning the physico-mathematical basis of music, notwithstanding that the habit of picking out some harmonious combinations of sounds is, undoubtedly, as ancient as the human race. Therefore it is not a rare thing that, though the art of making harmonious combinations of colors may be as old as music, few persons have believed in the possibility of harmoniously and methodically combining colors and musical notes.

In the same manner that music is the art of speaking without gestures and words, or an idealization of the arts of expression, chromomusic is an idealization of the art of painting. It is the art of painting not only in space but also in time, that is, the art of making harmonious combinations of incessantly changing colors, dividing them in regular metrical portions, and furnishing them with accent and cadence. In fact, all musical terms can be used in chromomusic without altering their artistic meaning.

Physical observations tend to prove that colors are the relative speeds of oscillation of atomic electromagnets. These kinetic variations are transmitted through the ether to the retina and are subject to a law of physico-mathematical harmony which I have discovered and which I further explain. In consequence, in chromomusic colors are considered in perpetual motion.

The invention of chromomusic and the chromopiano will increase the beneficent subjective influence of color and music. It uncovers a new field of the art of lighting and illumination. It makes possible to play melodies and harmonies of color notes in accordance with the geometric and kinetic principles of the iridescent plays of light; to harmonize chromomusical and musical compositions, and to play chromopianos tuned to unison with the instruments of an orchestra; to synchronize the movement of a chromopiano with the movement of a player piano, an organ or a phonograph, and make them play together automatically; to accompany on a chromopiano the rhythmic movements of dancers; besides that the chromopiano will facilitate in technical schools the artistic study of light and the teaching of polychromatic ornamentation.

In this specification I use geometrical drawings to explain the physico-mathematical law that governs the harmony of spectral colors. In Fig. 1 I divide the line VR into six equal parts VI, IB, BG, GY, YO, OR, and taking as centers the points V, I, B, G, Y, O, R, I describe the seven pairs of concentric circles $Vv, Ii, Bb, Gg, Yy, Oo, Rr$. I suppose that the distance between two consecutive intersections of the large circles represents the width of the colored regions of a solar spectrum PS, and the diameter of the small circles represents the diameter of the electrons of atomic electromagnets oscillating around the line of propagation of light. In Fig. 2 I display in a tangential order several pairs of concentric circles to obtain the representation of an electromagnet of light with its atomic nucleus G and its electrons V, I, I', B, B', Y, Y', O, O', R. Now supposing that an infinite number of these electromagnets oscillate around the line of propagation P (Fig. 2) in the direction of the arrows passing through V, it is easy to conceive that the tones of spectral colors are geometrically represented by the relative areas of seven concentric and consecutive circular rings of equal width, and arithmetically represented by seven consecutive terms of a progression beginning with one and having as difference two. This kinetic conception of light is confirmed by the geometrical coincidence existing between the Fraunhofer lines A, a, B, C, D, E, b, F, G', G, h, H, K, L, M, (see Fig. 2), and some centers and points of tangency or intersection of the pairs of concentric circles displayed in a tangential order in Fig. 2. In short, the harmony of a sequence of color notes is independent of the absolute areas of the color notes, and depends essentially of the area ratios of the color notes in terms of violet or any other color note taken as keynote. These area ratios are between them as seven consecutive terms of a progression beginning with one and having as difference two, the terms 15, 17, 19, 21, 23, 25, 27, 29, of this progression, being, evidently, the more approximate to the relative vibration numbers of a natural and fundamental scale of musical notes.

In the following table I compare the notes of a musical major diatonic scale with the color notes of my fundamental chromomusical scale:

Musical notes—do re mi fa sol la si do'
Relative vibration numbers—24 27 30 32 36 40 45 48
Vibration ratios in terms of do—1 9/8 5/4 4/3 3/2 5/3 15/8 2
Equivalent ratios—15/15 135/120 75/60 20/15 45/30 5/3 75/40 30/15
Mean difference between vibration ratios—1/7
Color notes—violet indigo blue green yellow orange red violet'
Relative area numbers—15 17 19 21 23 25 27 29
Area ratios in terms of violet—1 17/15 19/15 7/5 23/15 5/3 9/5 29/15
Equivalent ratios—15/15 136/120 76/60 21/15 46/30 5/3 72/40 29/15
Mean difference between area ratios—2/15

In accordance with the facts explained I enunciate the physico-mathematical law of the natural harmony of spectral colors as follows: the tones of the seven pure spectral colors are geometrically represented by the relative areas of seven concentric and consecutive circular rings of equal width; they are arithmetically represented by seven consecutive terms of a progression beginning with one and having as difference two; the area ratios thus obtained in terms of violet can be made practically equal to the vibration ratios in terms of do of a musical major diatonic scale.

Now let the spectral scale of colornotes shown in Fig. 1 be again examined. The meaning of the capital letters indicating the pure spectral colors and their intermediate hues is as follows: CV (V flat, crimson violet), V (violet), IV (V sharp, indigo violet), VI (I flat, violet indigo), I (indigo), BI (I sharp, bluish indigo), IB (B flat, indigo blue), B (blue), GB (B sharp, greenish blue), BG (G flat, bluish green), G (green), YG (G sharp, yellowish green). GY (Y flat, greenish yellow), Y (yellow), OY (Y sharp, orange yellow), YO (O flat, yellowish orange), O (orange), RO (O sharp, reddish orange), OR (R flat, orange red), R (red), CR (R sharp, crimson red). It is easily seen that the twenty one divisions of this scale (see Fig. 1) comprise, like a complete octave of musical notes, seven flats, seven notes and seven sharps.

Figure 5 is a vertical front view of a chromopiano having a circular row of three projection holes or outlets for rays of light 1, 1, 1 and a central projection hole 1. Figure 6 is a vertical side view of the same instrument with part of the sheet iron hood or casing 2, 2 removed and several interior mechanical combinations shown in section. Figure 8 is a vertical view of the back of the same instrument. Each projection hole 1, 1 . . . (Figs. 5 and 6) is provided with a metal mounting or frame 3 to be used with any convenient system of projecting lenses. Each mounting can be moved along a vertical or horizontal circular arc 4, 4 the center of which coincides with the center of the electric light or other light-producing device used in connection with the mounting. By means of these circular arcs 4, 4 the spots of colored light can be projected in any desired position. The instrument has two looking tubes 5, 5 through which the performer can see the result of his work. Behind each projection hole 1 of the row there is a pair of color wheels 6, 6. I use glass sectors 7, 7 . . . (Fig. 3) with the radial edges in close contact. These glass sectors 7, 7 . . . are kept in place by means of the nut 8, the washer 9 and the grooved rim 10 made of two detachable parts joined by means of the bolts 11, 11. Therefore the glass sectors of each color wheel 6, 6 are easily interchanged or substituted. Each color wheel 6, 6 (Fig. 6) has a space W or S (Fig. 3) without any glass sector or with an opaque sector, the remaining seven spaces having colored glass sectors imitating the seven pure colors, the seven flats or the seven sharps of the solar spectrum (see Fig. 1). With a pair of color wheels arranged in the above explained manner, a color note as well as a complete or partial superposition of color notes can be projected. To execute the precedent operations the two color wheels 6, 6 are mounted on independent concentric axles 12, 13 (Fig. 6). One of the wheels 6, 6 is operated by means of the two parallel racks 14, 14 either of which drives the pinion 15. The racks 14, 14 are driven by other racks moved by the sectors 16, 16 (Fig. 7). The main keys 18, 18 move the levers 17, 17 which drive the sectors 16, 16. The keys 19, 19 ... have projecting parts 20, 20 ... (Fig. 7) by means of which the main keys 18, 18 can be lowered more or less, these movements being limited by stopping blocks 21, 21 ... (see Figs. 6 and 8).

The other of the two color wheels 6, 6 (Fig. 6) is operated by means of the crank 22 (Fig. 8), the position of the color wheel being constantly known by means of the circular plate 23 which is divided in eight equal sectors corresponding to the eight divisions of the color wheel shown in Fig. 3.

Besides the pair of color wheels 6, 6 (Fig. 6) already described I use behind each projection hole of the circular row a shutting diaphragm disk 24 (Fig. 4) having eight holes in the shape of circular ring sectors of different area. This shutting disk 24 is loosely mounted on the axle 12 (Fig. 6). Three shutting disks 24, 24, 24 corresponding to the circular row of three projection holes are simultaneously operated by means of the toothed ring 25, the pinions 26, 26, 26 and the pinions 27, 27, 27, these latter driving the shutting disks 24, 24, 24. (Figs. 6 and 8).

The central projection hole is combined with a color wheel 28 and a shutting disk 29 mounted on concentric axles and respectively operated by means of the cranks 30 and 31. The shutting disk 29 is kept in place by the friction spring 32 (Fig. 6). The position of the color wheel 28 is constantly known by means of the circular plate 33 which is divided in eight equal sectors corresponding to the divisions of the color wheel shown in Fig. 3.

The source of light of the chromopiano can be an incandescent electric light or lamp or an arc lamp. There are in the chromopiano as many lamps as projection holes. The incandescent lamp 34 (Fig. 6) is sustained by the sliding piece 35, this piece being supported by the round guiding bar 36. A thumb screw 37 is used to change the distance between the center of the lamp 34 and the condensing lens 39. A reflector 40, hanged from the bar 36, is used with the lamp.

With the chromopiano described in this specification several thousands of different three color note chords can be produced. When chromomusical chords with more than three color notes are desired the chromopiano is provided with more projection holes and more keys, but the essential working principles of the instrument remain the same. There is no difficulty to transform a musical composition into a chromomusical composition. It suffices to substitute the notes of the musical composition by the necessary color notes taken among the twenty-one divisions of the spectral scale shown in Fig. 1. It is only a matter of exercise and taste to make this substitution simple and beautiful keeping in mind that one color note can substitute, when desired, a chord of musical notes. When playing chromomusic the change and duration of color notes are determined by fingering the keys of the chromopiano in accord with any convenient musical rhythm. Keynote effects are produced by means of the color wheel and shutting disk of the central hole. An infinite number of complex color tones are produced by simultaneously projecting two of the colored glass sectors of a pair of color wheels belonging to a projection hole.

I claim:

1. In a light projecting apparatus, the combination of light-producing devices, a central outlet surrounded by a row of outlets, a central frame surrounded by a row of frames, for lenses, said frames being provided with means for changing and fixing the relative directions of the optical axes of the lenses without suppressing the coincidence of said optical axes with the luminous centers of the light-producing devices, wheels carrying interchangeable opaque or transparent sectors of various colors, for shutting, coloring or changing the intensity of color of rays of light, means for controlling the relative areas of colors projected in juxtaposition or superposition within the area of a spot of light, and means for controlling the duration of projection of spots of light.

2. In a light-projecting apparatus, the combination of light-producing devices, groups of parallel and concentric wheels carrying interchangeable opaque or transparent sectors of various colors, means for changing step by step the relative positions in their respective plans of rotation of the wheels of a group, means for conjoint or independent rotation of the wheels of a group, means for controlling the duration of projection of spots of light.

3. In a light-projecting apparatus, the combination of groups of wheels provided with interchangeable opaque or transparent sectors of various colors, rotary diaphragm-disks, each diaphragm-disk being provided with a circular row of openings of different areas for changing one by one or together the relative areas of spots of light, pinions for driving said diaphragm-disks, and means for driving said pinions.

4. In a light-projecting apparatus, the combination of light-producing devices, groups of parallel and concentric wheels carrying interchangeable opaque and transparent sectors of various colors, of the wheels of a group being rigidly mounted on loose sleeves provided with pinions driven by racks, keys controlling the movement of said racks, means to know the sector correspond-

ing to each key, the remaining wheels of the group being rigidly mounted on the shaft supporting the sleeves, said shaft being rotatable step by step and provided with means for knowing the relative positions of the wheels of a group in their respective plans of rotation.

5. In a light-projecting apparatus, the combination of light-producing devices, groups of parallel and concentric wheels carrying interchangeable sectors, rotary diaphragm-disks loosely mounted on the shaft of each group of wheels, each diaphragm-disk being provided with a circular row of openings of different areas, means for independently rotating step by step each diaphragm-disk, means for rotating together and step by step all the diaphragm-disks, and means for knowing the relative positions in their respective plans of rotation of the diaphragm-disks.

6. In a light-projecting apparatus of the character described, the combination with rotary color-wheels, of one driving pinion for each color-wheel, each pinion being driven by a rack the course of which is controlled by a key.

7. In a light-projecting apparatus of the character described, the combination with rotary color-wheels, of main keys for controlling the movements of the color-wheels, several auxiliary keys provided with means for controlling the main keys, and means for controlling the movements of the auxiliary keys.

8. In a light-projecting apparatus of the character described, the combination with outlets for rays of light, of lenses or combinations of lenses, each of the frames supporting the lenses or combinations of lenses being revolvable around the optical axis of its lens or lenses, and movable along a guiding arc having its center in the luminous center of a light-producing device, and means for securely fixing each optical axis in any desired direction.

9. In a light-projecting apparatus of the character described, the combination with frames for lenses, of means for making the directions of the optical axes of said frames convergent, parallel or divergent, means for making the luminous centers of lamps to coincide with the optical axes of said frames, and means for moving the reflectors of the lamps toward and from their corresponding lamps.

ARTHUR C. VINAGERAS.

Certificate of Correction.

It is hereby certified that in Letters Patent No. 1,577,854, granted March 23, 1926, upon the application of Arthur C. Vinageras, of Lawrence, Massachusetts, for an improvement in " Chromopianos," an error appears in the printed specification, requiring correction as follows: Page 3, line 126, claim 4, after the comma following the word " colors " insert the word *some;* and that the said Letters Patent should be read with this correction therein that the same may conform to the record of the case in the Patent Office.

Signed and sealed this 4th day of May, A. D. 1926.

[SEAL.]   M. J. MOORE,
Acting Commissioner of Patents.

HAZEL H. ADLER

Device for Selecting Colors (1923)

Dec. 6, 1927.
H. H. ADLER
1,651,860
DEVICE FOR SELECTING COLORS
Filed April 10, 1923 2 Sheets-Sheet 1

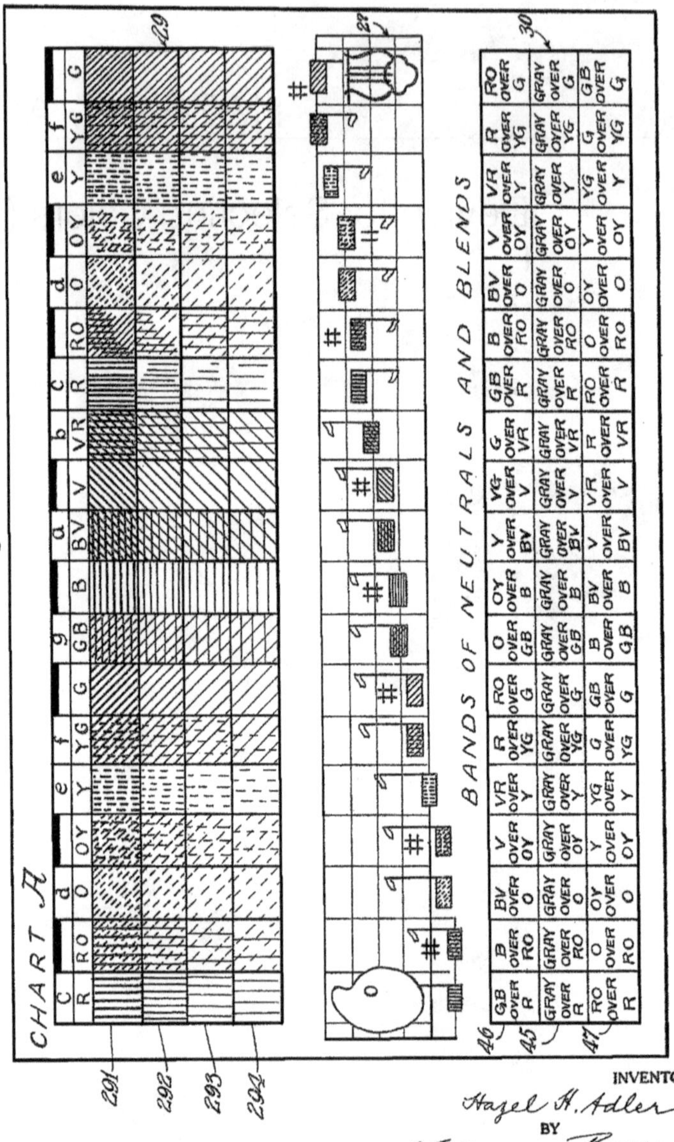

INVENTOR
Hazel H. Adler
BY Williams & Pritchard
ATTORNEYS

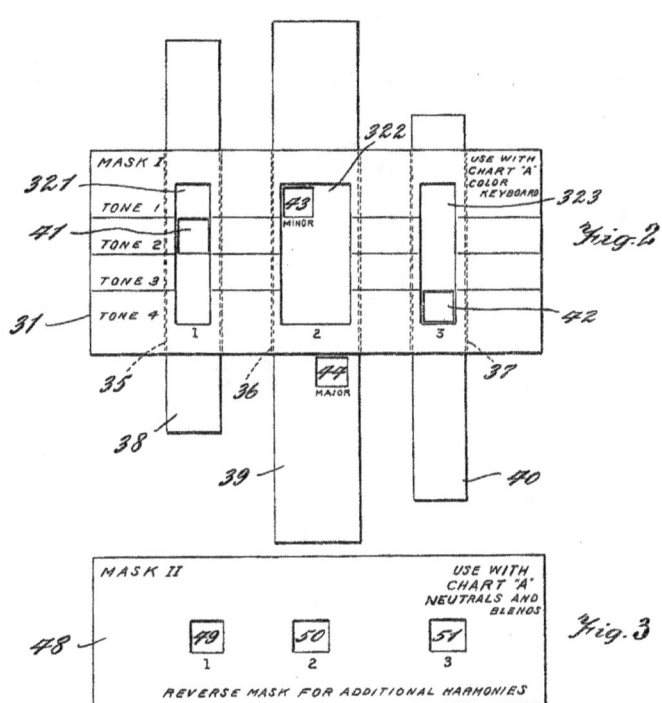

Patented Dec. 6, 1927.

1,651,860

UNITED STATES PATENT OFFICE.

HAZEL H. ADLER, OF NEW YORK, N. Y.

DEVICE FOR SELECTING COLORS.

Application filed April 10, 1923. Serial No. 631,065.

While my invention is not limited thereto, it is particularly useful in color printing. The printer usually is a person unskilled in the art of selecting and preparing harmonious color combinations, and it has usually been necessary as a preliminary to a color printing job, to have a person skilled in color effects select and prepare the colors and the printer then carry out the printing operation with the colors so selected and prepared.

In accordance with my invention, a color device is provided with a plurality of color indications from which the printer or other person, no matter how unskilled in the art of colors, may select harmonious color combinations. While I have shown my invention embodied in a device that is particularly applicable for color printing, it will be understood that it is not limited thereto.

The following is a description of a device embodying my invention in the form at present preferred by me, but it will be understood that various modifications and changes may be made therein without departing from the spirit of my invention and without exceeding the scope of my claims.

My invention will best be understood by reference to the accompanying drawings, in which Fig. 1 is a face view of a chart made in accordance with my invention; Fig. 2 is a face view of a mask for use in connection with the colors illustrated in the upper portion of the chart shown in Fig. 1; Fig. 3 is a face view of a mask for use in connection with the bands of neutrals and blends shown in the lower portion of the chart illustrated in Fig. 1.

Like reference characters indicate like parts throughout the drawings.

The chart illustrated in Figure 1 has two parts, 29 and 30, each an assemblage of color areas, and between these two parts a representation of a musical chromatic scale 27, with colored rectangular notes corresponding in color with the vertically aligned colors in the part 29 above it. At the upper line of the part 29 are the musical designations of the notes of the chromatic musical scale, including one octave and a portion of another octave, commencing with "C" followed by a space indicating C-sharp, then "D", then a space indicating D-sharp, then "E", then "F", then a space indicating F-sharp, and so on, the last space to the right indicating F-sharp of the second scale. These indications of musical notes are in vertical alignment with the pictures of the musical notes shown in the illustration 27 of the chromatic scale.

Beneath the line indicating the notes is another line indicating the corresponding colors, which appear in the row of spaces immediately below, "R" indicating red, "R O" indicating red-orange, "O" indicating orange, etc., the colors shown being harmonically selected and arranged as in the patent to Taylor No. 1,308,512, July 1, 1919, and therefore being red, red-orange, orange, orange-yellow, yellow, yellow-green, green, green-blue, blue, blue-violet, violet, violet-red, and then in the repetition thereof red, red-orange, orange, orange-yellow, yellow, yellow-green, and green, these constituting a full range of the normal spectrum followed by a considerable part of a second identical range in the same order, so that the whole series is harmonically arranged. In this specification and the appended claims the word "harmonically" is used to indicate that the relations between the colors are those originally suggested by the numerical relations between the vibrations of the musical harmonies. These colors are shown as arranged in four rows, 291, 292, 293 and 294, the successive rows showing different tones. For example the first color in each of the rows is red, but the four red colors differ in tone, being successively lighter and preferably so made by admixture of white. This tone variation is followed throughout the series, so that each horizontal row shows the same colors in the same order but the successive rows are of lighter tones.

A mask is provided for selecting from the part 29 harmonious color combinations of triads of the same or different tones. This mask 31 is shown in Figure 2. It is provided with openings 321, 322 and 323, the middle opening 322 being substantially twice as wide as the other two openings and spaced from each by the width of two full columns of colors. The mask is also provided with transverse guides 35, 36 and 37 in which are received strips 38, 39 and 40 formed of cardboard or the like. The strip 38 is provided with an opening 41. The strip 40 is provided with an opening 42 and the strip 39 is preferably provided with two openings 43 and 44, the one located on the left side of the strip and the other on the right side of the strip and spaced apart longitudinally of the strip or vertically a distance greater than the vertical width of the rows 291, 292, 293, 294. It will be understood that the color areas on the part 29 of Fig. 1 are the same size as the openings 41, 42, 43 and 44 of the mask. By suitably positioning the strips 38, 39 and 40, the same or different tone color combinations which are in harmony, may be exhibited. For example, with the strips positioned as indicated in Fig. 2, when the mask is placed over the part 29, with the opening 41 exposing the first color, red, at the left of the second rod 292, representing the second row of tone colors, then the color exposed through the opening 43 will be orange-yellow of row 291, or the first tone, and the color exposed through the opening 42 will be green blue of row 294 representing tone four, the red, orange-yellow and green-blue forming a harmonious color combination in correspondence with a minor chord of the musical scale. By bringing the opening 44, instead of the opening 43, over the colors, harmonious color combinations corresponding to major chords of the musical scale may be selected in a manner which will be obvious without further explanation. The foregoing are given only as illustrations. It will, of course, be understood that any desired color combination of the same tones or of different tones may be secured.

The upper part 29 of the chart and the corresponding mask 31, above described, form the subject of my Patent No. 1,630,247, May 31, 1927, and are not separately claimed herein.

At the bottom of the chart shown in Fig. 1, the part 30 represents a plurality of bands or rows of neutrals, gray neutrals and blends. The middle row 45 is preferably formed by printing gray over the vertically corresponding color of the top row 291 of the part 29; that is, the first color at the left of the middle row 45 would be formed by printing gray over red. The top row 46 is preferably formed by printing the eighth color to the right in the top row 291 of the part 29 over the vertically corresponding color of said top row 291; that is to say, the first blend would be formed by printing green-blue over red. The bottom row 47 is preferably formed by printing over the vertically aligned color in the top row 291 of the part 29, the succeeding color in said top row 291 in the part 29. For example, the first blend would be formed by printing red-orange over red. Each band or row 45, 46, 47, thus consists of a series of color areas aligned with the corresponding color areas in the rows 291, 292, 293 on which they are respectively based. Each row or band therefore is composed of a single color systematically modified from the approximately normal colors of the spectrum followed by a considerable part of a second identical range, the whole of each row forming a series of such systematically modified colors. The simple mask 48 shown in Fig. 3 is for use with the part 30, illustrating the neutrals and blends, and will be understood without further description, it being understood that the color areas in the part 30 are of the same size as the openings 49, 50 and 51 of the mask shown in Fig. 3.

For example, if darker tones than those of row 291 are desired the mask 48 is placed upon row 45, 46 or 47 with its openings directly below the corresponding openings in the mask 31 upon the chart 29, reversing the mask 48, if necessary, to bring the opening 50 under the opening 43 or 44, as the case may be. The darker tones appearing at the openings 49, 50 and 51 of the mask 48 may be either substituted for the color tones then appearing at the openings in the mask 31, or may be used in combination therewith as parts of harmonies containing more than three colors. Thus by the simultaneous use of the two masks, four-color, five-color, and six-color harmonies may be mechanically obtained.

It will be apparent that one unskilled in color effects may select from the whole chart a wide range of harmonious color combinations either of pure spectrum colors or of modified spectrum colors or of combinations of the two.

I claim:

1. A device for selecting harmonizing colors containing a color chart showing the principal colors of the solar spectrum harmonically arranged in series in a straight line, said series including one range of the spectrum colors systematically modified to show a darker tone followed by a considerable part of a second identical range in the same order so that the whole series is harmonically arranged, and a mask adjustable to any color of the series so as to mechanically select and exhibit a color harmonizing with a color to which it is adjusted.

2. A device for selecting harmonizing colors containing a color chart showing the principle colors of the solar spectrum harmonically arranged in series in a straight line, said series including one range of the spectrum colors systematically modified by over-printing to show a darker tone followed by a considerable part of a second identical range in the same order so that the whole series is harmonically arranged, and a mask adjustable to any color of the series so as to mechanically select and exhibit a color harmonizing with a color to which it is adjusted.

3. A device for selecting harmonizing colors containing a color chart showing the principal colors of the solar spectrum har-

monically arranged in series in a straight line, said series including one range of the spectrum colors systematically modified to show a darker tone followed by a considerable part of a second identical range in the same order so that the whole series is harmonically arranged, a second aligned series of spectrum colors systematically but differently modified, and a mask adjustable to any color of either series so as to mechanically select and exhibit a color harmonizing with the color to which it is adjusted.

4. A device for selecting harmonizing colors containing a color chart showing the principal colors of the solar spectrum harmonically arranged in series in a straight line, said series including one range of the spectrum colors modified by overprinting with a neutral, followed by a considerable part of a second identical range in the same order so that the whole series is harmonically arranged, a second aligned series of spectrum colors systematically modified by overprinting with a color varying with the under color, and a mask adjustable to any color of either series so as to mechanically select and exhibit a color harmonizing with the color to which it is adjusted.

5. A device for selecting harmonizing colors containing a color chart showing the principal colors of the solar spectrum harmonically arranged in series in a straight line, said series including one range of the spectrum colors followed by a considerable part of a second identical range in the same order, so that the whole is harmonically arranged, a second aligned series of spectrum colors systematically modified by overprinting, and means settable to different colors to mechanically select and exhibit colors harmonizing therewith in both series.

6. A device for selecting harmonizing colors containing a color chart showing the principal colors of the solar spectrum harmonically arranged in series in a straight line, said series including one range of the spectrum followed by a considerable part of a second identical range in the same order so that the whole series is harmonically arranged, a second aligned series of spectrum colors systematically modified to show a lighter tone also including one range and a considerable part of a second identical range, a third aligned series of spectrum colors systematically modified to show a darker tone also including one range and a considerable part of a second identical range, and means for mechanically selecting from all said series two colors which harmonize with any desired one of the colors.

7. A device for selecting harmonizing colors containing a color chart showing the principal colors of the solar spectrum harmonically arranged in series in a straight line, said series including one range of the spectrum followed by a considerable part of a second identical range so that the whole is harmonically arranged, two series of spectrum colors aligned therewith, each systematically but differently modified to show a lighter tone, each including one range of the spectrum followed by a considerable part of a second identical range, two other series of spectrum colors aligned therewith, each systematically but differently modified to show a darker tone, each including one range of the spectrum followed by a considerable part of a second identical range, and means for mechanically selecting from all said series two colors which harmonize with any desired one of the colors.

8. A device for selecting harmonious colors containing a color chart showing the principal colors of the solar spectrum systematically modified and arranged in series, said series including one range of the spectrum followed by a considerable part of a second identical range so that the whole is harmonically arranged, and means for mechanically selecting a color about two-thirds the length of a spectrum from any given color together with a color about half way between said two colors, but nearer one than the other, so that the three colors together form a tri-color harmony.

9. A device for selecting harmonious colors containing a color chart showing the principal colors of the solar spectrum systematically modified and arranged in series, said series including one range of the spectrum followed by a considerable part of a second identical range so that the whole is harmonically arranged, a second series of spectrum colors systematically but differently modified and aligned with the first series, and means for mechanically selecting a color about two-thirds the length of a spectrum from any given color together with a color about half way between said two colors, but nearer one than the other, so that the three colors together form a tri-color harmony.

10. A device including a color chart showing colors harmonically arranged in series in a straight line, said series including one entire range of colors based on the spectrum colors overprinted with gray followed by a considerable part of an identical range in the same order, so that the whole series is harmonically arranged, and a mask adjustable to any color of the series so as to exhibit a color harmonizing with the color to which it is adjusted.

11. A device including a color chart showing colors harmonically arranged in series in a straight line, said series including one entire range of colors based on the spectrum colors overprinted with gray followed by a considerable part of an identical range in the same order, so that the whole series is harmonically arranged, and a mask adjustable

to any color of the series so as to exhibit colors harmonizing with the color to which it is adjusted and making a three color harmony.

12. A device including a color chart showing colors harmonically arranged in series, said series including one entire range of colors based on the spectrum colors but systematically modified from the approximately normal spectrum colors by printing another systematically selected color over each approximately normal spectrum color followed by a considerable part of an identical range in the same order so that the whole series is harmonically arranged, and a mask adjustable to any color of the series so as to exhibit a color harmonizing with the color to which it is adjusted.

13. A device including a color chart showing colors harmonically arranged in series, said series including one entire range of colors based on the spectrum colors but systematically modified from the approximately normal spectrum colors by printing another systematically selected color over each approximately normal spectrum color followed by a considerable part of an identical range in the same order so that the whole series is harmonically arranged, and a mask adjustable to any color of the series so as to exhibit colors harmonizing with the color to which it is adjusted and making a three color harmony.

14. A device including a color chart showing colors harmonically arranged in series, said series including one entire range of colors based on the spectrum colors but systematically modified from the approximately normal spectrum colors by printing over each color a color of the spectrum range considerably removed therefrom, followed by a considerable part of an identical range in the same order so that the whole series is harmonically arranged, and a mask adjustable to any color of the series so as to exhibit colors harmonizing with the color to which it is adjusted and making a three color harmony.

15. A device including a color chart showing colors harmonically arranged in series, said series including one entire range of colors based on the spectrum colors but systematically modified from the approximately normal spectrum colors to show a darker tone by printing over each color an adjacent color, followed by a considerable part of an identical range in the same order so that the whole series is harmonically arranged, and a mask adjustable to any color of the series so as to exhibit a color harmonizing with the color to which it is adjusted.

16. A device including a color chart showing colors harmonically arranged in series, said series including one entire range of colors based on the spectrum colors but systematically modified from the approximately normal spectrum colors to show a darker tone by printing over each color an adjacent color followed by a considerable part of an identical range in the same order so that the whole series is harmonically arranged, and a mask adjustable to any color of the series so as to exhibit colors harmonizing with the color to which it is adjusted and making a three color harmony.

17. A device including a color chart showing a plurality of rows of colors harmonically arranged in series in each row, each series including one entire range of colors based on the spectrum colors but systematically modified in a form individual to the series from the approximately normal spectrum colors, each range followed by a considerable part of an identical range in the same order so that each series is harmonically arranged, and a mask adjustable to any color of any series so as to exhibit a color harmonizing with the color to which it is adjusted.

18. A device including a color chart showing a plurality of rows of colors harmonically arranged in series in each row, each series including one entire range of colors based on the spectrum colors but systematically modified in a form individual to the series from the approximately normal spectrum colors, each range followed by a considerable part of an identical range in the same order so that each series is harmonically arranged, and a mask adjustable to any color in any series so as to exhibit colors harmonizing with the color to which it is adjusted and making a three color harmony

HAZEL H. ADLER.

ALEXANDER E. O. MUNSELL

Color Piano (1923)

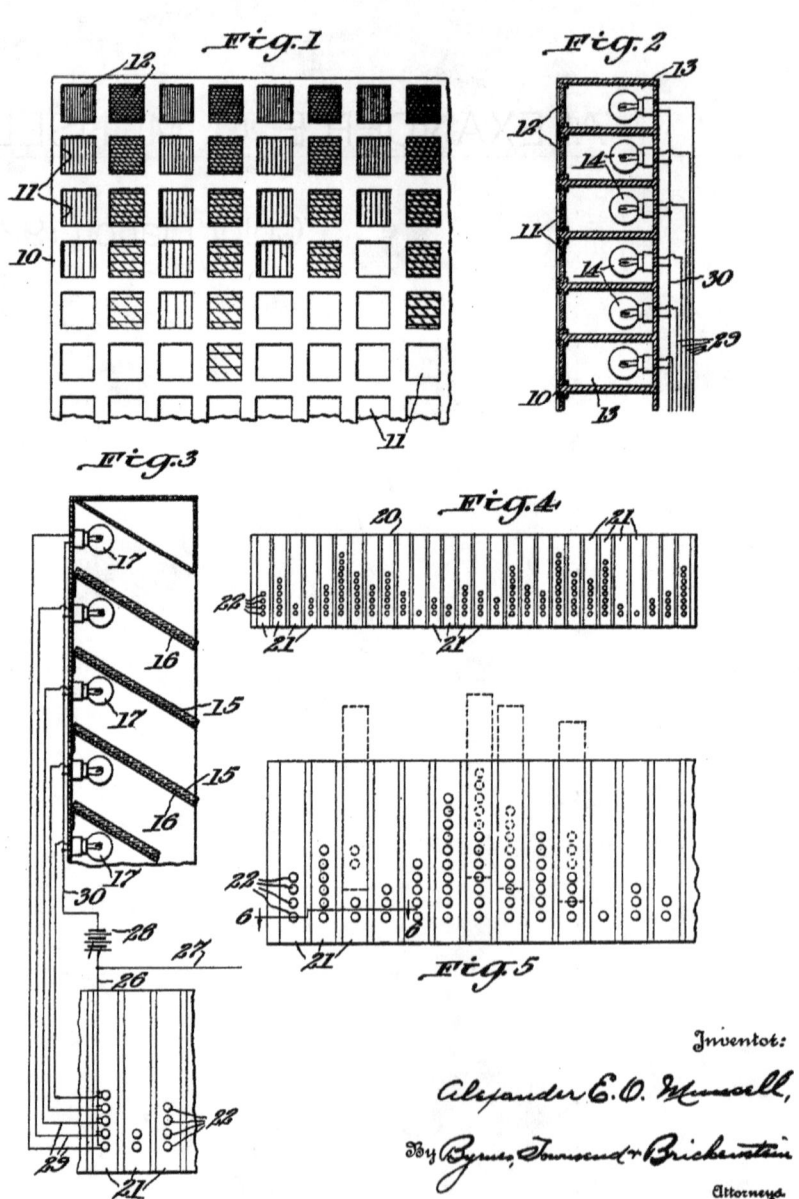

Feb. 26, 1924

A. E. O. MUNSELL
COLOR PIANO
Filed March 24, 1923

1,484,795

2 Sheets-Sheet 2

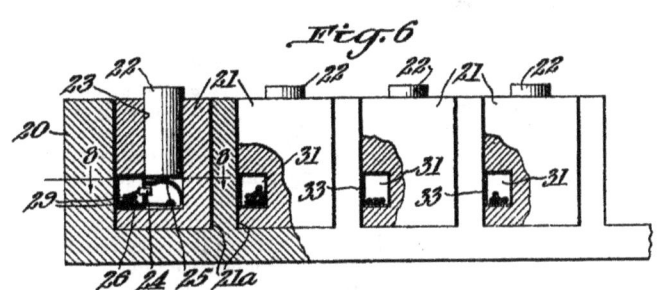

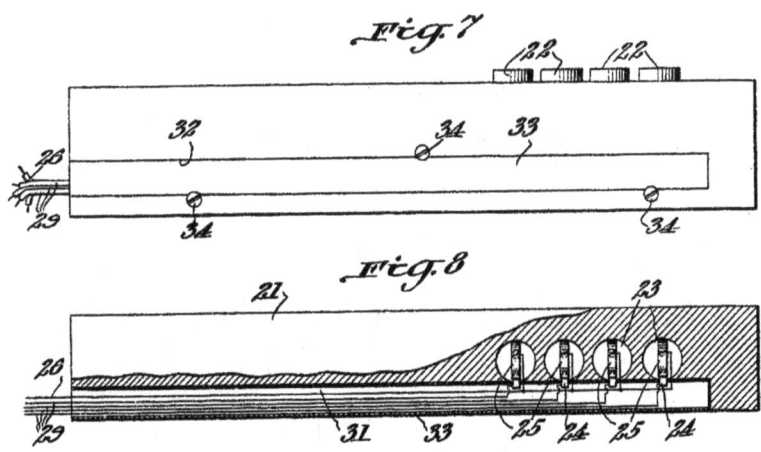

Inventor:
Alexander E. O. Munsell,
By Byrnes Townsend & Bricks
Attorneys

Patented Feb. 26, 1924.

1,484,795

UNITED STATES PATENT OFFICE.

ALEXANDER E. O. MUNSELL, OF NEW YORK, N. Y.

COLOR PIANO.

Application filed March 24, 1923. Serial No. 627,506.

To all whom it may concern:

Be it known that I, ALEXANDER E. O. MUNSELL, a citizen of the United States, residing at New York, in the county of New York and State of New York, have invented certain new and useful Improvements in Color Pianos, of which the following is a specification.

This invention relates generally to apparatus for facilitating the comparison of colors.

Various devices have been proposed for comparative color studies, but their scope is usually limited to small groups of colors. For color comparison and color study the intermediate shades or tints are just as important as the pure pigments and their principal derivatives.

In accordance with the Munsell system of classification described in the patent to Munsell No. 824,374 each color has three characteristics: hue, chroma and value. The hue determines dominant wave length i. e. its approximate position in the spectrum of sunlight. The chroma indicates the purity of the wave length. The value signifies the total reflection of white light. The number of distinct colors that can be formed or are conceivable is very large.

It is the general object of the invention to provide an apparatus for selectively exhibiting any single color or group of colors.

It is a more specific invention to provide an apparatus for rapidly and directly bringing before an observer any desired color or group of colors.

The most specific object is an apparatus which in analogy to the piano may be called a color piano.

For a full understanding of the invention and the principles of operation on which it is based, I refer to the accompanying drawings in which—

Fig. 1 is an elevation of a color board;

Fig. 2 is a fragmentary section therethrough;

Fig. 3 is a fragmentary section through a modification thereof;

Fig. 4 is a plan view of a key board embodying the invention;

Fig. 5 is a fragmentary plan view of a keyboard according to Fig. 4, but on a larger scale;

Fig. 6 is a fragmentary cross-section through the key board;

Fig. 7 is a side view of key; and

Fig. 8 is a sectional view on line 18—8, Fig. 6.

In Figs. 1 and 2, 10 represents a board containing a large number of openings 11 which are occupied by colored glass panes 12. Behind the board 10 are as many compartments 13 as there are panes and each compartment contains an electric light bulb 14. The electric wires for lighting the lamps may be separately controlled so that each bulb or any group of bulbs may be energized at will, as will be more fully pointed out. In practice I prefer to apply means for diffusing the light which may be accomplished, as is well understood by applying a thin sheet of white paper or a ground glass screen behind the colored panes or using a diffusing light bulb, as is well understood. As an alternative the glass panes may consist of ground glass and the bulbs may be colored. Instead of using colored bulbs or colored glass panes, colored paper may be pasted on the glass panes. In either case it is advisable to use a light diffusing medium to thoroughly diffuse the light to make the light emission to the observer uniform.

Instead of transmitting light through glass panes as shown in Figs. 1 and 2, I may cause light to be reflected from colored surfaces. To this end I may form the compartments with inclined bottoms and tops, the angle of inclination being preferably 45° relatively to the horizontal or vertical. The bottoms may be covered by color samples 15 and the top may be provided with reflecting surfaces 16. The arrangement of the light bulbs 17 may be the same as in Figs. 1 and 2. The light from the bulbs 17 falls on the color sample and is reflected therefrom through the openings 18 to the observer. By using reflecting surfaces 16, the light distribution over the color samples 15, is more substantially uniform and the diffuse reflection from the color samples provides a uniform light emission.

So far as the production of the desired color effects is concerned there is considerable latitude within the scope of the invention. I contemplate the use of any means by which all conceivable color effects may be separately exhibited from a color board or frame.

The principal point of novelty is a means for selectively exhibiting any plurality of colors in a very short time.

In analogy to the key board of a piano I propose the use of a key board or a series of such key boards. As generally indicated in Fig. 4, a keyboard 20 may contain a plurality of elements 21 which are slidably disposed in channels 21^a. Each element 21 contains a plurality of small electric push button switches 22.

As indicated in Fig. 6 the buttons are loosely mounted in bores 23 of the element 21. At the bottom of the bore is a contact piece 24 and a contact spring 25. When the push button is depressed it bears upon the spring 25 and forces the latter into contact with the contact piece 24. When the pressure upon the button is released, the spring will return to its normal position thereby breaking contact with the contact piece 24 and lifting the push button to its normal position.

The springs are connected to a common conductor 26 and the conductors 26 of all the keys are connected to a common bus-bar 27 which leads to one terminal of an electric source which for the sake of convenience is indicated as a battery 28.

The contact pieces 24 are separately connected to individual wires 29 which lead to the individual light bulbs on the color board. From all light bulbs a common return 30 leads back to the other terminal of the source 28. By depressing any one button, current passes from the battery through the connection established by the push button and through the particular wire 29 to one particular light bulb and back to the battery. The mode of connection is merely illustrative and may be changed in various ways as is well understood.

The important feature is any arrangement by which any desired color may be quickly exhibited and by which any plurality of colors may be quickly exhibited for comparison. The relative disposition of the colors on the board and of the connections on the key board is largely a matter of choice.

For the sake of convenience and in accordance with the disclosure of the patent to A. H. Munsell No. 824,374, I have divided the colors according to hue into ten principal groups: Red (R), yellow-red (YR), yellow (Y), green-yellow (GY), green (G), blue-green (BG), blue (B), purple-blue (PB), purple (P), and red-purple (RP).

It is particularly advantageous to have complementary colors in juxtaposition because from the standpoint of color harmony complementary colors blend better than other colors and by having them grouped closely together, a more reliable comparison is afforded. For this reason it may be desirable to place opposite hues adjacent each other. Thus on the board all the colors of one principal hue may be placed adjacent the group containing all colors of the opposite hue.

The colors may be arranged according to their order in the spectrum or in any other orderly fashion and the elements 21 may be likewise arranged.

The colors in each principal group are subdivided according to value and chroma. It has been found sufficient and practical so far to subdivide chroma into no more than ten degrees and value into seven degrees in order to cover all distinguishable color sensations obtainable by the available pigments, in contradistinction to white, black and neutral gray.

The colors on the board may thus be graduated in vertical rows according to chroma and in horizontal rows according to value or vice versa. The rows may alternately bear colors of opposite hue so that complementary colors of like chroma and like value may be directly adjacent each other.

The elements 21 are slidable in the channels 21^a as indicated in Fig. 5 so that the button of one element 21 may be brought into juxtaposition to any of the buttons of another element 21 or generally into alinement with certain buttons of other elements 21.

The elements 21 may be disposed on a single key board or distributed over a plurality of key boards in superposition as desired. In any case the manipulation of the elements 21 and separate push buttons for selectively exhibiting colors, simultaneously or successively is rapid.

The practical utility of the apparatus lies in the ease and rapidity of exhibition of all available colors for comparison, to artists, commercial artists and color composers and also for educational purposes.

The apparatus may be operated in the dark so as to make all colors not illuminated invisible, in daylight or subdued light, as desired.

In the foregoing, for the sake of simplicity, only fragments of the color board and of the key board have been illustrated. The mode of connection, however, is the same throughout, and what applies to one part applies to the whole construction. Fig. 3 is thus representative of all the connections between the color board and the key board.

The detail arrangement of the electric connections is of no particular importance and may be modified in various ways as is well understood. The arrangement shown in Figs. 6, 7 and 8, however, in which the wires 26 and 29 are contained in a trough

31 which in turn may be placed into and removed from a corresponding channel 32 in the side of the element 21 is simple and expeditious. The cover 33 of a trough may be separately secured by screws 34 or the like.

In the claims the term "push button" is intended to mean every kind of element adapted to be pressed to establish a current flow in a circuit.

I claim:—

1. The combination of a color board containing color samples graduated according to hue, value and chroma, electric light bulbs for individually illuminating the color samples and means for controlling the illumination, said means including a key board containing a plurality of parallel rows of switches, a source of electricity and connections for establishing a plurality of circuits including each the source, a switch and a bulb.

2. The combination of a color board containing samples differing as to three characteristics of hue, chroma or value and means for selectively illuminating said samples, said means including a plurality of parallel rows of switches, a source of electricity, an incandescent bulb for each sample and separate circuits each including one of the switches and one of the bulbs.

3. Arrangement according to claim 2 in which all samples controlled by switches in alignment across the series of rows represent an orderly color sequence according to said three characteristics.

4. Arrangement according to claim 2 in which the samples controlled by successively adjacent rows represent an orderly color sequence according to said three characteristics.

5. Arrangement according to claim 2 in which the samples controlled by different rows represent different hues.

6. Arrangement according to claim 5 in which complementary hues are displayed by pairs of adjacent rows of samples on the color board and are controlled by pairs of adjacent rows of switches.

7. Arrangement according to claim 2 in which the samples controlled by the switches of each row of switches represent an orderly color sequence according to said three characteristics.

8. Arrangement according to claim 2 in which each row of switches is mounted upon an element slidable in the direction of the row.

In testimony whereof, I affix my signature.

ALEXANDER E. O. MUNSELL.

WILHELM SCHMEER

Color Harmonium (1924)

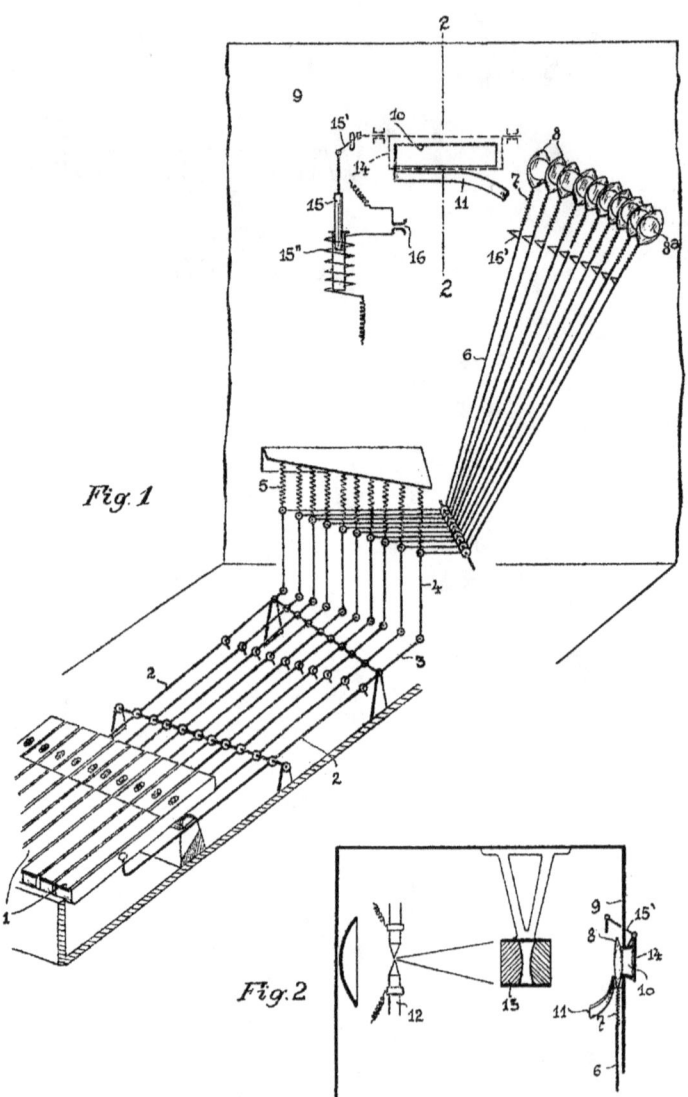

Patented Mar. 30, 1926.

1,578,373

UNITED STATES PATENT OFFICE.

WILHELM SCHMEER, OF NUREMBERG, GERMANY.

KEY INSTRUMENT FOR EXECUTING COLOR MUSIC.

Application filed October 27, 1924. Serial No. 746,229.

To all whom it may concern:

Be it known that I, WILHELM SCHMEER, a citizen of the German Republic, and a resident of Nuremberg, Germany, have invented certain new and useful Improvements in Key Instruments for Executing Color Music, of which the following is a specification.

My invention relates to a key-instrument by means of which color-music may be executed in an improved manner.

Musical tones are, as is known, in a certain so-to-say parallel ratio to colors or color-tones or tints. I have succeeded in determining and ascertaining arithmetically quite a distinct ratio between the number of vibrations of a musical tone and the length of the color-vibrations, this ratio being such that the sensations and sentiments caused are equal to one another throughout all octaves.

The previously known key-instruments intended for the execution of color-music suffer from the deficiency that the color-tones, or tints respectively, do not appear in a closed succession, joining one another without gaps, but appear separated from one another according to the unvarying position of their color-fields or color-bodies so that a closed accord consisting of a continuous succession of color-effects, or of groups of such ones respectively, cannot be executed whereby the reception and the sensational capacity of the spectators is impaired.

The present invention does away with that deficiency, and for this purpose the color-disks or equivalent color-bodies are arranged to be movable, and their movements are controlled in such a manner that the disks, etc., appear alternately, without any consideration to the position of the motion transmitting members actuating them, or to the keys actuated respectively, singly or in groups behind an aperture or a projection-opening provided for this purpose. The colors concerned appear, therefore, at the same place before the eyes of the spectators, and pass along singly or in groups, as the case may be, the spectators receiving in this way closed total impression and their enjoyment being thus, greatly enhanced.

It is a matter of course that the tempo of the play must be comparatively slow, corresponding to the particularity of the color-music, the proper tempo is about that used when playing on a harmonium.

My invention is illustrated by way of example in the accompanying drawing in which Figure 1 is a perspective illustration of a combination and arrangement of parts by which the invention can be turned into practice, and Figure 2 is a vertical section through the upper part of a box enclosing certain of said parts, the section being taken in the line 2—2 of Fig. 1.

The keys 1 of the instrument act singly on oscillating arms 6 by the intermediary of double-armed levers 2 and 3, and transmission-rods 4. Small frames 8, preferably of oval shape, are attached to the upper ends of the arms 6, one frame, or oval frame respectively, to each arm. Each of said frames carries a small transparent color-disk 8^a, the color of which corresponds to the tone pertaining to the position of the key in the series of the octaves of the instrument.

Figure 1 shows only one group of the color-disks in order to obviate complicatedness of the figure, but I wish it to be understood that the arrangement is the same for all keys.

Each rod 4 is subjected to the action of a retraction spring 5 by which the parts are moved back into their position of rest.

The arrangement of the frames 8 with their color-disks 8^a is such that they can cover one another, and in order to permit easily this change of their relative position each frame 8 is attached to its appertaining arm 6 by the intermediary of a flexible or pliable member, as for instance a helical spring 7.

9 denotes a box and 10 an oblong slot in the front-wall thereof. The arrangement of this slot and the frames 8 with their color-disks relatively to the slot 10 is such that said frames can be swung behind the slot and said disks can become visible through it. 11 denotes an elastic guide-member, such as a flat spring or the like, by which the frames 8 with their color-disks 8^a are brought into and maintained in, proper position with respect to the slot when being caused to appear behind it by means of the keys and the motion-transmitting members described.

The color disks can appear behind the slot 10 singly or in a multitude of arrangements and combinations, one behind the other or others or side by side. In this latter case, in which two or more colors are caused to appear side by side, the frames 8 are so located with respect to one another that no gap remains between them. The frames with their color disks form then what may be termed a "closed group or set", in which every frame lies immediately at the side of, or immediately between, the adjacent frame or frames, as the case may be.

The slot 10 can be closed at its outside by a flap 14, the axle of which (shown in Fig. 1, in dotted lines) is connected by a bell-crank lever 15' with the core 15 of a solenoid 15'', the circuit of which is interrupted at the point 16 where there are two contact-springs which can be connected conductively with one another by metallic lugs 16' projecting forth from the arms 6 in the direction towards said contact-springs 16.

The solenoid-circuit can be closed by any of the lugs or projections 16', and the core 15 will then be attracted, down into the solenoid-coil, whereby the bell-crank lever 15' will be so turned that the flap 14 will be opened, the respective color-disk or disks becoming then visible through the slot 10. The projections 16' cannot be retained by the contact-springs 16, but will leave them as soon as the respective key is, or keys are, disengaged, when the current will be interrupted, the core 15 will be raised by the weight of the dropping flap 14, and the respective arm or arms 6 will be caused to reassume its, or their, initial position by the respective retraction spring 5.

The color-disks arriving and appearing behind the slot 10 are illuminated by a source of light, for instance an arc-lamp 12 (Fig. 2), preferably with the aid of a condenser 13, and the colors are thrown upon a suitable screen (not shown) on which they appear singly or in groups, corresponding to the key or keys depressed.

I claim:

A key-instrument for the execution of color-music, comprising, in combination, a wall and a slot therein; means for closing said slot; transparent colored bodies arranged to appear singly or in groups behind said slot; means for transmitting motion from the depressed key or keys to the appertaining color-bodies, and means for opening the slot automatically when a color-body arrives behind it, these means being actuated by the respective color-body carrier or carriers.

In testimony whereof I affix my signature.

WILHELM SCHMEER.

THOMAS WILFRED

Clavilux (1924)

Clavilux, Jr. (1927)

Stereo Clavilux (1930)

Home Clavilux (1931)

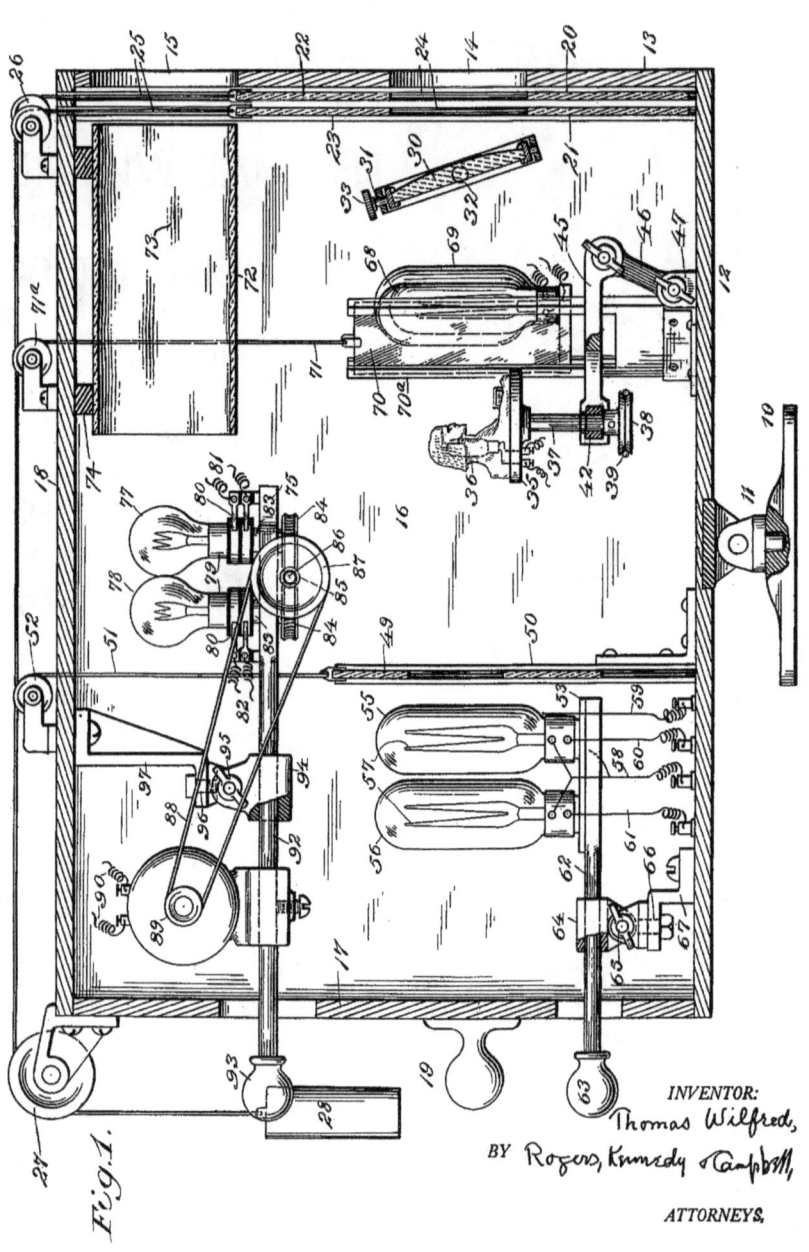

Fig.1.

March 4, 1930.   T. WILFRED   1,749,011
                        LIGHT PROJECTION DISPLAY
                   Filed Aug. 30, 1924   3 Sheets-Sheet 2

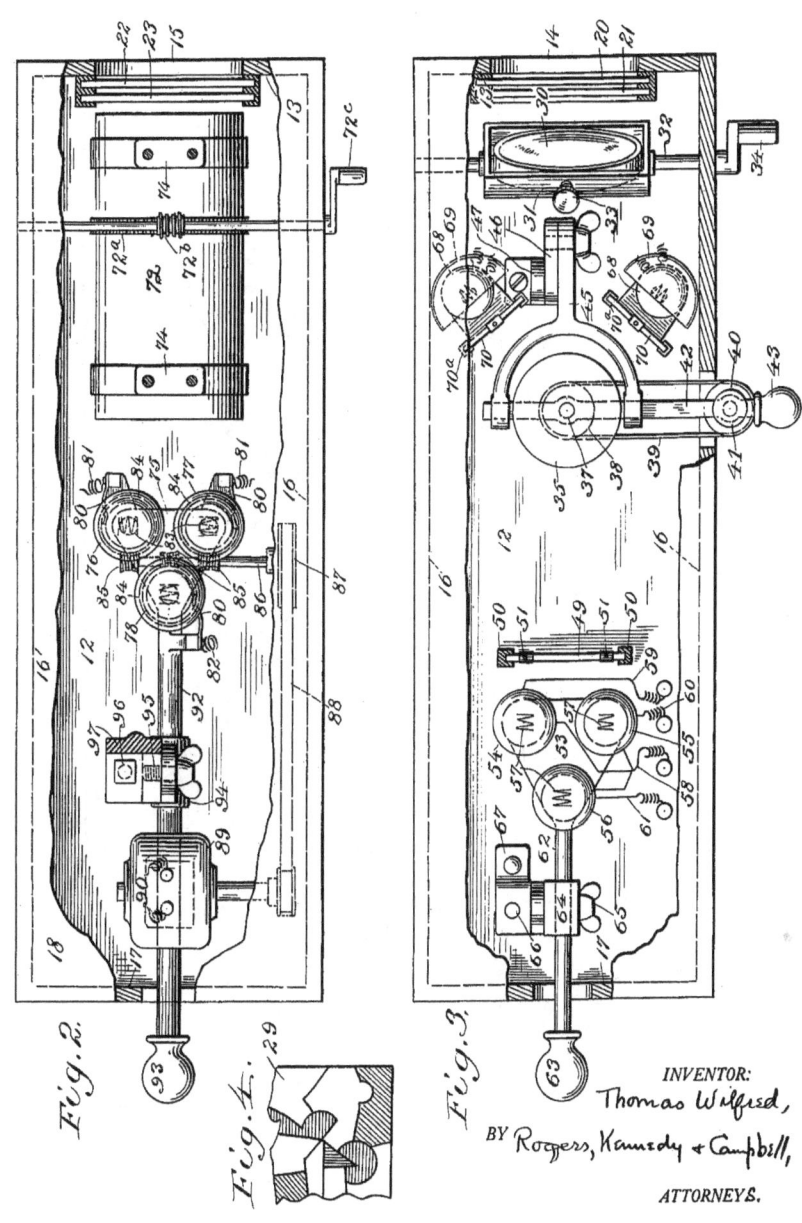

Fig.2.   Fig.4.   Fig.3.

INVENTOR:
Thomas Wilfred,
BY Rogers, Kennedy & Campbell,
ATTORNEYS.

March 4, 1930. T. WILFRED 1,749,011
LIGHT PROJECTION DISPLAY
Filed Aug. 30, 1924 3 Sheets-Sheet 3

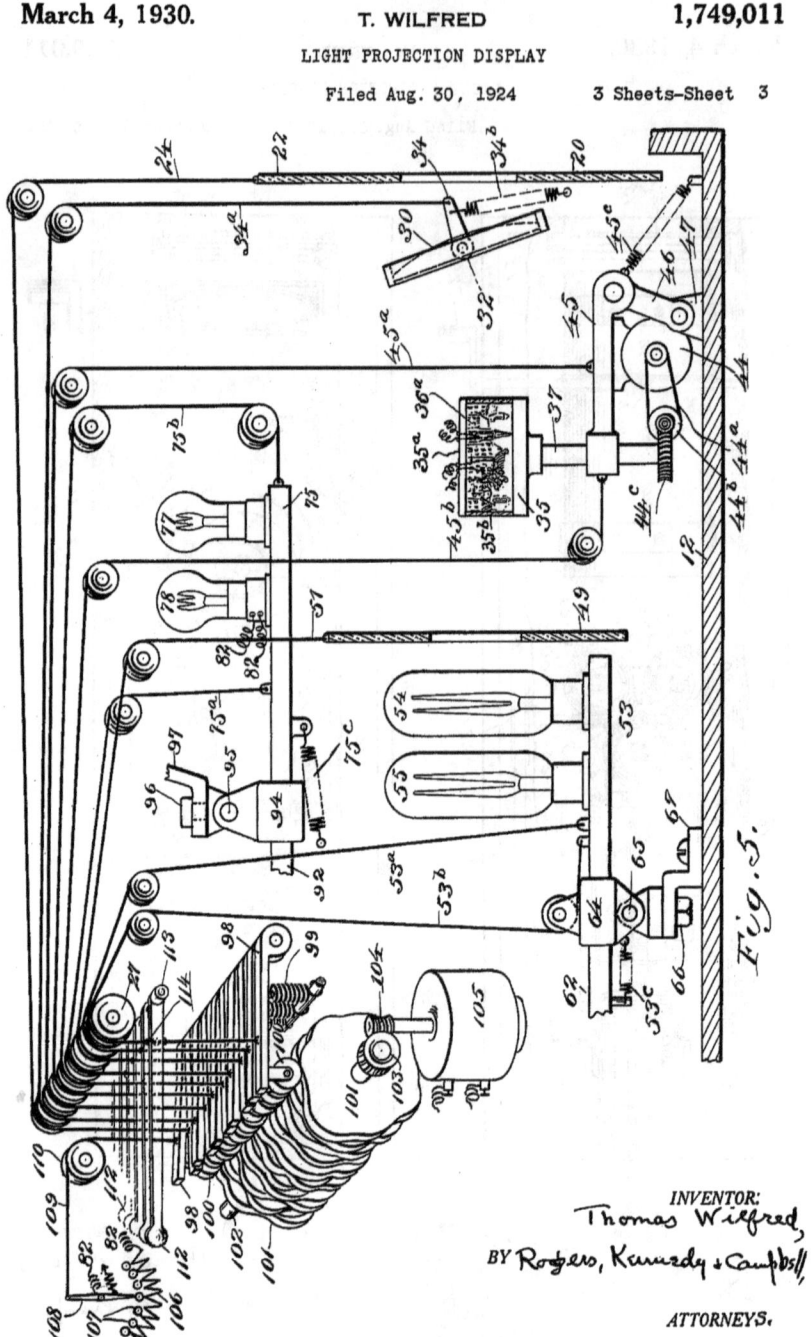

Fig. 5.

INVENTOR:
Thomas Wilfred,
BY Rogers, Kennedy & Campbell
ATTORNEYS.

Patented Mar. 4, 1930

1,749,011

UNITED STATES PATENT OFFICE

THOMAS WILFRED, OF HUNTINGTON, NEW YORK

LIGHT-PROJECTION DISPLAY

Application filed August 30, 1924. Serial No. 735,168.

This invention relates to the art of light projection display for example the projection of effects in light or color upon a curtain, for exhibition. A novel method or system is involved and also a novel apparatus or machine for carrying out the same. The utility of the invention is broad as it may be used not only for entertainment but for interpretive purposes, for psychical study, for treatment of the mind or eye, and other uses.

The main object of the present invention is to enable the projection upon a suitable curtain or other background of effects in lights and shadows, or colors, adapted to please the mind or stir the imagination or emotions, and with the production of extensive variations in tone, pattern, motion and evolution of effect. A particular object of the present invention is to afford new and interesting types of projected effects. The further and more detailed objects and advantages of the present invention will be elucidated in the hereinafter following description or will be apparent to those conversant with the subject.

To the attainment of the objects and advantages referred to, the present invention consists in the novel art, system or method and the novel apparatus or machine herein described or illustrated, as well as the novel features of combination, arrangement, operation, construction and detail.

In the accompanying drawings Fig. 1 is a right hand elevation of an apparatus illustrating the present invention, with the right hand wall broken away or sectioned to show more fully the interior mechanism. What I term the forward side of the machine is at the right hand of Fig. 1, this side being provided with the aperture which is directed toward the curtain, and the operator or performer stands at the rear or left side of Fig. 1.

Fig. 2 is a plan view of the apparatus, with the top wall broken away to show the interior, but with all the parts in the lower half of the apparatus omitted.

Fig. 3 is a view similar to Fig. 2, but with all the parts in the upper half of the apparatus omitted.

Fig. 4 shows a modified color screen; and Fig. 5 is a diagram showing coordinated or automatic timing and operation.

A base plate 10 is shown, which may be attached upon any support, and by a universal joint 11 the box or casing of this invention is supported, in a manner so that it can be tilted longitudinally or swung to right and left. The box or casing constitutes the frame of the apparatus, giving support to the interior parts, and it is shown consisting of a bottom wall or floor 12, a front wall 13 having a lower optical opening 14 and an upper optical opening 15, opposite side walls 16, a rear wall 17 and a top wall 18. A handle or knob 19 may be provided, for example on the rear wall, for the purpose of swinging or tilting the apparatus as a whole.

In order that the projected light may be colored a system of color screens adjacent to the optical openings 14 and 15 is provided, the same movable vertically into and out of projecting position. For purposes of illustration there are shown a lower color screen 20 and to the rear of that a second lower screen 21, also upper color screens front and rear 22 and 23. These screens may be suitably guided in their shifting movements and operated by connectors or cords 24 for the lower screens and 25 for the upper screens, the cords all passing over a series of pulleys 26 mounted at the front of the top wall 18. The operation of the lower screens may be independent of the upper ones, through wholly separate cords, or the cords 24 may simply connect the lower screens to the upper ones so that they will move in unison. In either case the optical opening 14 may be partly or wholly covered by a lower screen or an upper screen or both. For example, the upper front color screen 22 might be of red color and dropped a third way down over the optical opening, and the lower rear screen 21 of a blue color lifted a third way up into the optical opening, thus giving a red, white and blue projection. The several cords passing around the several pulleys 26 may all extend to the rear and there pass around a series of pulleys 27 and downwardly into a series of counterweights 28, one for each cord. The screens may be manipulated by lifting and lowering the counterweights or otherwise moving the cords.

To the rear of the lower optical opening 14 is shown a lens 30, which may be of various types, and for convenience is shown as a plano-convex lens, which is adapted to be set obliquely, at an adjustable slant, for the purpose of altering or distorting the projection and thus giving characteristic effects on the curtain. The lens is shown mounted to turn about a vertical axle 31 and a horizontal axle 32, with a knob 33 on the former and a handle 34 on the latter, permitting ready adjustment of the lens in any manner desired.

One feature of improvement in the present invention is the interposing of an object in the path of the light rays, adapted to cast a shadow in respect to illumination from the rear, or to project its own image through illumination from the front, or both; rendering possible many unique and weird figures of projection. For such purposes a platform 35 may be employed on which an object 36 may be positioned in the path of the light rays, and to the rear of the lens 30. There is no limit to the character of object that may be placed upon the platform 35. It may be a still figure, an animated object, or even a live object. It may be opaque or translucent, or even luminous; or a combination of these. Specific objects that may be used to advantage are the following: a flower, a piece of mechanism or clockwork, still or in motion, a statuette, such as the sphinx which is indicated in the drawings, or a luminous article or tube formed or bent to any desired shape, the sphinx being shown as containing a lamp, which may be illuminated or extinguished. It is proposed to move bodily the platform and object during the projection and suitable means for giving universal movement thereto may be as follows. The platform 35 is mounted on a vertical shaft 37 which has a pulley 38 at its lower end engaged by a belt 39 which extends through an aperture in the right hand wall 16 to an exterior pulley 40, the shaft of which is provided with a knob 41 which may be manipulated to rotate the platform as desired. The elements 37 to 41 are mounted on a cross bar 42 which is provided with a knob 43 at its exterior end by which the operator may bodily lift or lower the platform, or shift it toward left or right. This shifting movement is permitted by reason of the cross bar 42 being arranged slidingly in the two arms of a yoke lever 45, this lever extending forwardly and being pivotally connected to a link 46, the lower end of which is mounted on a lug 47 on the bottom wall of the apparatus. The various movements of the object 36 are reproduced on the curtain. The elements 45 and 46 permit front and back motion, changing the condition of focus.

It may be desirable to silhouette the object 36 through colored illumination from the rear, and for this purpose a color screen device 49 is shown, analogous to the color screens at the front, with guides 50 therefor, and a cord 51 passing over a pulley 52 at the top and extending to a counterweight 28, to enable control at will.

The main projecting lamps for the described system may be enclosed in the rear portion of the casing. A lamp support or carriage 53 is shown supporting three lamps, two front lamps 54 and 55 and a rear lamp 56, symmetrically arranged. The lamps are preferably incandescent filamentary lamps, and the filaments 57 may be of any desired configuration, it being possible with this invention to project images of the filaments upon the curtain through the lens 30, these images undergoing various movements and evolutions during the performance, and the lamps may be arranged to be rotated during the performance. Electric current may be communicated to the three lamps by the four wires 58, 59, 60 and 61, controlled by suitable switches, so that any one or more or all of the lamps may be illuminated; and rheostats may be provided in each circuit to permit the gradual dimming or strengthening of the illumination from each lamp.

The lamp platform 53 is shown supported at the forward end of a rod 62 which is universally mounted so as to permit universal manipulation of the lamps, through a knob 63 at the exterior end of the rod. The rod may rotate and slide within a bearing or slideway 64, which may tilt about a horizontal axle 65 and swivel about a vertical axle 66, these parts carried on a base lug 67.

The apparatus thus far described is capable of projecting extremely interesting and curious effects, even with the still object illustrated or a similar one such as a vase or a crystal, and with a small bit of machinery such as the works of a clock very weird effects can be made to loom up on the curtain. The object 36 may be replaced by a vacuum tube illuminated by high frequency electricity, this both throwing a shadow, and throwing illumination of its own particular color, depending on the character of the gases present in small quantities in the tube. Very interesting and useful effects in the projection of stage scenery can be effected, the instrument located either in front of or behind the curtain on which the projection is made; for example a landscape can be projected, to form the background of a stage setting, and the background of the landscape may consist of light from the rear of the apparatus, which may be changed in hue and intensity to represent natural changes during the day or seasons, while the projected scenery itself can be brightened or darkened to correspond.

When an opaque or non-luminous object is interposed in the path of the light rays this may be caused to project its own image in natural colors by illumination from the front, or rather at an incline. For this purpose a pair of lamps 68 is shown combined with reflectors 69, arranged to illuminate strongly the front and sides of the object. These lamps are set at a diagonal position, and either or both may be illuminated, dimmed or extinguished, through separate electric connections, so that the effect of light and shadow, and relief may be universally altered at will. When a white light is so projected on the object it will project itself in natural colors upon the curtain, and its details of form and color will appear. The effect may be varied by coloring the illumination of the object and for this purpose each lamp is shown provided with a color screen 70 which may slide up and down in guides 70^a through cords 71, passing over pulleys 71^a at the top, controlled by counterweights 28. It will be understood that the lens 30 can be set in true position for normal projection of the image, or slanted at will to give effects of distortion. As already suggested the object 36 may have front illumination for the purpose of projecting its own image, in white or in colors, such image to be surrounded by a field or background projected from the rear lamps 54, 55, 56, the filaments of which may produce striking effects of form and motion covering the curtain, with the image of the object superposed in the middle of the field, in white or in color, and with any desired changes of illumination and position. In effect one is enabled to project a silhouette which itself discloses details of color and form. The revolving of an object on the platform 35 is found to give a most realistic effect of depth, which is more or less lost when the object is stationary. This projection itself is of great interest, and is the more interesting with the accompaniment of the rear lamp filament projection as described.

The projecting means in the upper part of the casing may be used alone if desired, but in conjunction with the arrangements in the lower part of the casing combined effects are producible, which are much more than the sum of the two effects. Various degrees of light, with various shades and hues of color, thrown upon the curtain in a manner to overlap partially, give additive effects which are sometimes extremely surprising and beautiful; and an artist skilled in the practice of the invention can compose harmonious combinations or performances, which can be recorded and repeated at will. Indeed the different elements of the present invention may be controlled by a systematic means, such as a keyboard, rather than the detached control means employed in the drawings for purposes of illustration. The various lamps and the various motions of the various moving parts can all be connected with a controlling key-board, enabling written notation to be made for the guidance of the operator in repeating performances; and if found desirable automatic control by a preforated control sheet or other record would be available.

The characteristic thing about the projecting means in the upper part of the illustrated apparatus is what may be termed the internal reflector, or reflecting tube 72, located behind the upper optical opening 15 in the front wall of the apparatus. This tube may be of various forms, cylindrical, conical, polygonal, or any other arrangement of reflecting surfaces facing inwardly and surrounding the path of projection. A cylindrical tube 72 is shown, and it reflects and directs to the curtain the filamentary illumination from the rear, without the need of a projecting lens. The tube may consist of internally polished metal, silvered glass or the like and means may be provided for maintaining it in rotary or tilting motion during the performance. Instead of a regular surface the tube 72 may be formed with rifling or corrugations or other irregularities such as the slight protuberances 73 illustrated. The tubular reflector 72 is shown held in place by clamping means 74.

On a supporting block 75 are mounted two front lamps 76, 77 and a rear lamp 78, these being filamentary lamps, in line with the axis of the projecting tube 73. Each lamp may be mounted in a rotatable socket 79 having a commutator device 80 for delivering current thereto. Conducting wires 81 supply current to the front lamps and wires 82 to the rear lamp. Each socket is formed with a short axle 83 passing through the support 75, and each axle may have a worm wheel 84, all of which are driven from worms 85 on a shaft 86, so that by revolving the shaft the lamps are maintained in rotation during the performance. It will be understood that each lamp may have its own switch and rheostat for the purpose of complete control of illumination. Each filament projects its own image, which is highly multiplied by the reflecting tube, giving geometrical effects, which may be distorted by the irregularities in the tube.

The action of any of the movable devices may be performed automatically or by power. For example the rotation of the lamps 76, 77 and 78 may be effected as follows. The worm shaft 86 is provided with a pulley 87 connected by a belt 88 with an electric motor 89 supplied with current by wires 90 with which may be associated a switch and a rheostat to control action and speed.

The described elements 75 to 90 may be supported upon a carrying rod 92 which has an exterior knob 93 for manual control. The rod may slide forwardly and rearwardly in a slideway 94, and may rotate therein, imparting corresponding movements to the lamps. The slideway 94 is shown as tiltable about a horizontal axle 95 and swingable about a vertical axle 96, all carried by a bracket 97 standing downwardly from the top wall. The three lamps thereby may be given universal bodily movements in addition to their rotation during projection.

The light projected through the tube 72 may be colored by interposing one of the screens 22 or 23, which may be of different colors.

It was above stated that the cylindrical reflector 72 could be kept in motion during the performance, and for this purpose is shown a gear 72^a surrounding the cylinder, engaged by a worm 72^b, the shaft of which is provided with an external handle 72^c, that can be turned to give slow rotation to the mirror, by hand or power, steadily or intermittently.

The platform 35 carrying the object 36 is shown rotatable by hand in Figs. 1 and 3; but such rotation may be by motor, and Fig. 5 shows a motor 44 adapted for this purpose, being connected by a belt 44^a with a worm 44^b turning a gear or worm wheel 44^c on the upright spindle or shaft 37 of the platform.

The various screens 20—24, 49, 50, and 70, may be plain color screens or may be patterned screens having designs of various sorts such as stripes, or irregular designs, for example of the character shown at 29 in Fig. 4, such screens introducing weird variations in the performance.

It was stated that the various elements could be actuated automatically, and this can be done with any desired coordination, for example by a control means such as a perforated sheet record, system of cams, or the like. A convenient way to convey automatic movement to the different elements is through cords such as the cords 24 and 51 already mentioned. The diagram Fig. 5 shows one manner in which the variations may be coordinated in an automatic manner. The counterweights 28 shown in Fig. 1 are omitted in Fig. 5 and replaced by a system of horizontal levers 98, to which the various cords are attached. These levers are pulled down by strong springs 99. Each lever has a cam roller 100 at its free end, and the several rollers ride upon cams 101 mounted on a cam shaft 102. This system of cams may be considered as constituting the playing record of a given performance, and the same may be replaced by a substitute system at will. The cam shaft 102 is shown having a worm wheel 103 at one end, engaged by a worm 104 on the shaft of a driving motor 105, which thereby gives slow rotation to the cams. The cams acting through the cam rollers and levers operate to let out or draw down the various cords extending to the different movable elements.

It has been stated that various operations or illuminations may be controlled by rheostats and the diagram shows such a rheostat consisting of a resistance coil 106, the contacts 107 of which are contacted by a swinging arm 108 connected by a cord 109 passing over a pulley 110 to one of the levers 98.

It may be desirable sometimes to modify the cam action and for this purpose a series of hand levers 112 may be employed, located above the cam levers 98. The levers 112 are fulcrumed at 113 and are attached at points 114 to the various cords, so that the performer may readily either elevate or depress any lever 112 to modify correspondingly the movement of the connected element. The bank of levers 112 constitutes substantially a keyboard.

Various of the elements already described may be controlled by the cam mechanism, for example the following. The color screens 20, 22, et cetera, connected by cords 24 to levers 98, are automatically lifted and lowered by the corresponding cams. The lens 30, through its handle 34, may be slowly tilted during a performance, namely by cord 34^a, a spring 34^b pulling oppositely on the handle, in opposition to the pull on the cord. The platform 35 may be lifted and lowered through the cord 45^a similarly connected and operated. The platform 35 may be moved forwardly or rearwardly through cord 45^b, opposed by spring 45^c. The color screen 49, connected by its cord 51, may be moved automatically, as already described. The lamp platform 53 may be lifted and lowered by cord 53^a. The lamp platform may be moved rearwardly by cord 53^b, and returned forwardly by spring 53^c. The lamp platform 75 may be lifted and lowered by cord 75^a and may be moved forwardly by cord 75^b, opposed by spring 75^c.

Any of the lamps may be illuminated or dimmed in coordination with the other movements; for example the conducting wires 82 of lamp 78 may extend to rheostat 106—108, for automatic regulation.

It will be understood that Fig. 5 is only diagrammatic; and illustrates the principles of automatic coordination of movements. It is not endeavored to illustrate the cams 101 with the exact or preferred contours that would be used in practise, as indeed it would be preferred in the case of many of the described connections to give the elements a greater throw or movement than is actually provided in the form shown in the diagram. It will be understood that where an extended movement is desired, for example to lift or drop one of the color screens the full distance permitted, a mechanical departure from the diagrammatic illustration could readily be made, either by redesigning the cam or by introducing special pulleys, levers, or other mechanism to multiply the delivered motion.

The silhouetted object 36 is shown in Fig. 1 as a figure resting on the platform 35 to the rear of the distorting lens 30 and with the filamentary lamps 55, 56, 57 to the rear, and appropriate color screens interposed in the path of the light, the object having practically universal movability, including rotation. There is no limitation to the nature of the object that may be placed on the platform 35. With a lens such as illustrated, there will be distortion when the lens is tilted as shown, although the distortion can be eliminated by righting the lens; and the projected image will be inverted unless supplemental inverting reflectors are provided. In Fig. 1 therefore it will be understood that the figure 36 will be projected in an inverted position, unless it is inverted on the platform 35, or unless inverting means are employed. The simplest plan would be to invert the object on the platform, as illustrated by the object 36^a in the diagram Fig. 5. This object represents an outdoor scene such as a village, which is preferably not a mere pictorial representation, but an actual miniature village in three dimensions. This is shown mounted at the underside of an inverted support 35^a which in turn is carried above the support 35 by a transparent support or wall 35^b. Being inverted this object is projected on the screen in natural position, and when the lens is in its correct position the village is thrown on the curtain in silhouette. Under these conditions the gradual rotation or other progressive movement of the object will cause progressive changes on the curtain with very interesting and realistic effect. Thus when used as a stage scene, a group of persons can be arranged to walk apparently in one direction, while the village scenery on the curtain can be operated to move in the other direction, thus fully carrying out the illusion.

The effect with this or other objects is greatly enhanced by having the object not merely silhouetted but illuminated. This refers both to exterior illumination, for example by the lamps 68 and color screen 70, already mentioned, and to interior illumination as indicated by the electric lamp and wiring, which in the case of the village may represent illuminated windows. The scene thrown on the curtain can be gradually changed from a representation of the village in the dark of a night, through the varying changes representing dawn, sunrise and full daylight. The rear lamps 54 and 55 throw the illumination representing the sky, which can be gradually changed from dull tones and colors through the colors representing dawn and sunrise, the village itself being at first a pure silhouette but being gradually illuminated from the front so as to bring out the colors and details of the houses and other portions of the scene; the interior illumination being maintained until terminated after dawn to represent the extinguishing of lamps within the house. Manifestly the effects can be varied greatly within the principles described and the objects shown in the drawings are merely instances representative of the principles employed.

It will thus be seen that I have described an art or method or light projection display and apparatus therefor embodying the principles and attaining the purposes of the present invention. Since many matters of method, operation, effect, arrangement, combination and detail may be variously modified without departing from the inventive principles it is not intended to limit the invention to such matters except so far as specified in the appended claims.

What is claimed is:

1. The art of light projection display comprising throwing changing forms upon a curtain through a lens from a moving filamentary source of light arranged to cast images of its own filaments by progressively moving such source of light relatively to the axis of projection, and varying the effect by interposing in the light path between the light source and lens a relatively movable three dimension object and bodily rotating the object in the light path during projection about an axis transverse to the axis of projection to superpose a changing silhouette upon the projected light.

2. The art of light projection display comprising projecting light from a glowing filament through a lens upon a curtain and representing by shadow a moving scene by interposing in the light path between the filament and lens a miniature scene in three dimensions and progressively moving the same during projection by rotation about an upright axis in the light path.

3. Light projection display apparatus comprising a front projecting lens, a filamentary source of light to the rear of the lens, and a three dimension object interposed in the light path between the light source and lens adapted to throw a shadow on a curtain, said object having means for progressively bodily rotating it in the light path during projection, and a second source of light arranged to illuminate the front of the object to cast a reflected image thereof.

4. Light projection display apparatus comprising a projecting lens, a rear source of light, and an object interposed in the light path adapted to throw a shadow on a curtain, said object being a scene in three dimensions, with means for progressively rotating it in the light path during projection to produce the effect of three dimensions in the projected shadow, and a second source of light

arranged to illuminate the front of the scene to cast a reflected image thereof.

5. Light projection display apparatus comprising a front projecting lens, a source of light to the rear of the lens, and means for holding in the light path between the light source and lens a three dimension object to be silhouetted on a curtain, said holder being rotatable about an axis extending through the object and transverse to the light path, and means causing predetermined rotation of the holder and object in the light path during projection.

6. The art of light projection display comprising projecting upon a curtain through a lens a beam of light and interposing a three dimension object in the light path between the lens and light source to cast its shadow while at the same time independently illuminating the object to develop reflected details of the object on the projected shadow, and rotating it in the light path to develop depth of projection.

7. The art of light projection display comprising throwing upon a curtain a beam of light and interposing a three dimension object in the light path to cast its shadow while at the same time illuminating the object to develop details of the object on the projected shadow and rotating it in the light path to develop depth of projection; the illumination of the object being by light thrown upon the front of the object to be reflected to the curtain, said light being of a different color from the beam of light thrown upon the curtain.

8. The art of light projection display comprising projecting upon a curtain through a lens a beam of light and interposing an object in the light path behind the lens to cast its shadow while at the same time independently illuminating the object to develop details of the object on the projected shadow, namely by maintaining within the object an interior source of light separate from the beam of light projected upon the curtain, and the object having light transmitting walls.

9. The art of light projection display comprising projecting upon a curtain through a lens a beam of light and interposing a scene in the light path behind the lens to cast its shadow while at the same time independently illuminating the scene to develop reflected details of the scene on the projected shadow, while the projected light represents sky or background.

10. Light projection display apparatus comprising a front lens, a filamentary source of light to the rear of the lens, means for holding a three dimensional object in the light path between the light source and lens to throw its shadow, means for rotating the holding means about an axis crossing the light path between the light source and lens, means for simultaneously illuminating the front of the rotating object, and means for cooperatively operating the rotating means and progressively moving the light source during projection.

11. Light projection display apparatus comprising a front lens, a source of light to the rear of the lens, means for holding a three dimensional object in the light path between the light source and lens to throw its shadow, means for rotating the holding means about an axis crossing the light path between the light source and lens, and means for simultaneously illuminating the front of the rotating object.

12. Light projection display apparatus comprising a front lens, a filamentary source of light to the rear of the lens, means for holding an object in the light path between the light source and lens to throw its shadow, means for simultaneously illuminating the front of the object, and means for progressively and cooperatively moving the object and the filamentary light source during projection.

13. Light projection display apparatus comprising a front lens, a source of light to the rear of the lens, means for holding an object representing a scene in three dimensions in the light path between the light source and lens to throw its shadow, means for simultaneously illuminating the front of the scene, and means for progressively rotating the holding means and thereby rotating the scene in the light path during projection.

14. Light projection display apparatus comprising a front lens, a source of light to the rear of the lens, means for supporting an object representing a scene in the light path between the light source and lens to throw its shadow, means for simultaneously illuminating the front of the object by light of a different color from the light projected from the rear of the object, and means for progressively moving the object during projection.

15. Light projection display apparatus comprising a front lens, a source of light to the rear of the lens, means for supporting an object in the light path between the light source and lens to throw its shadow, means for simultaneously illuminating the front of the object, means for progressively moving the object during projection, and means for varying the relative intensity of the rear source of light and the front illuminating means during projection.

16. Light projection display apparatus comprising a front lens, a source of light to the rear of the lens, means for supporting an object in the light path between the light source and lens to throw its shadow, means for simultaneously illuminating the front of the object, means for progressively moving the object during projection, and a patterned

screen interposed in the light path between the light source and object, having means for moving it during projection.

17. Light projection display apparatus comprising a plurality of projection means arranged to superpose simultaneous and mutually modifying effects upon a curtain; one means comprising an internal reflector of tubular form with a filamentary source of light behind it arranged and movable for the lensless projection of representations of its filaments on the curtain, and the other a lens with a filamentary source of light behind it arranged and movable for the projection of moving images of its filaments on the curtain, and means for differently coloring the superposed projections.

18. Light projection display apparatus comprising a front lens a holder behind the lens for a three dimension object to be silhouetted, means for progressively rotating said holder during projection, a filamentary source of illumination to the rear of the holder, and means for progressively shifting said source during projection, in combination with a timing mechanism and connections controlled therefrom for giving predetermined cooperative movements to said holder and source of illumination.

19. Light projection display apparatus comprising a tiltable lens, means for progressively changing the tilt of the lens during projection, a holder behind the lens for a three dimension object to be silhouetted, means for progressively rotating said holder during projection, a source of illumination to the rear of the holder, in combination with a timing mechanism and connections controlled therefrom for giving predetermined cooperative movements to said lens tilting means and said holder.

20. Apparatus as in claim 18 and wherein is means controlled by said timing mechanism for varying the intensity of light.

21. Apparatus as in claim 18 and wherein is a color screen moved progressively in the path of light by control of said timing mechanism.

22. Apparatus as in claim 11 and wherein is means for progressively moving the supporting means and object during projection, means for changing the relative intensity of the rear light and front illumination, timing mechanism, and means controlled thereby for giving predetermined actions to said object moving means and said intensity changing means.

23. A lensless light projection display apparatus, comprising a filamentary light source, and adjacently in front of the light source an internal reflector of hollow form arranged to enclose the beam of light rays passing from the light source to the curtain and to deflect part of such rays to the curtain, and means for effecting progressive relative movement between the filamentary light source and the internal reflector during projection, whereby a changing projected effect is afforded.

24. Apparatus as in claim 23 and wherein the reflector surface is substantially cylindrical but with portions departing from a true cylinder, and the filament is progressively moved about an axis other than the axis of the light path.

25. Light projection display apparatus comprising a filamentary light source, and adjacently in front of it an internal reflector of hollow form arranged to enclose the light beam between the light source and curtain, and to modify the beam of light and thence deliver it without subsequent distortion to the curtain, and means for effecting bodily movement of the filamentary light source during projection.

26. Apparatus as in claim 25 and wherein the internal reflector is of tubular form, adapted to pass the center of the beam without deflection but to deflect the outer light rays to the curtain.

27. Apparatus as in claim 25 and wherein the reflector is tubular, with departures from circular cross section, and has means for rotating it during projection.

28. Light projection display apparatus comprising a filamentary light source, and adjacently in front of the light source an internal reflector of hollow form arranged to enclose the light path at a point in front of the light source and arranged to deliver direct to the curtain, and means for bodily moving the filamentary light source relatively to the axis during projection.

In testimony whereof, I have affixed my signature hereto.

THOMAS WILFRED.

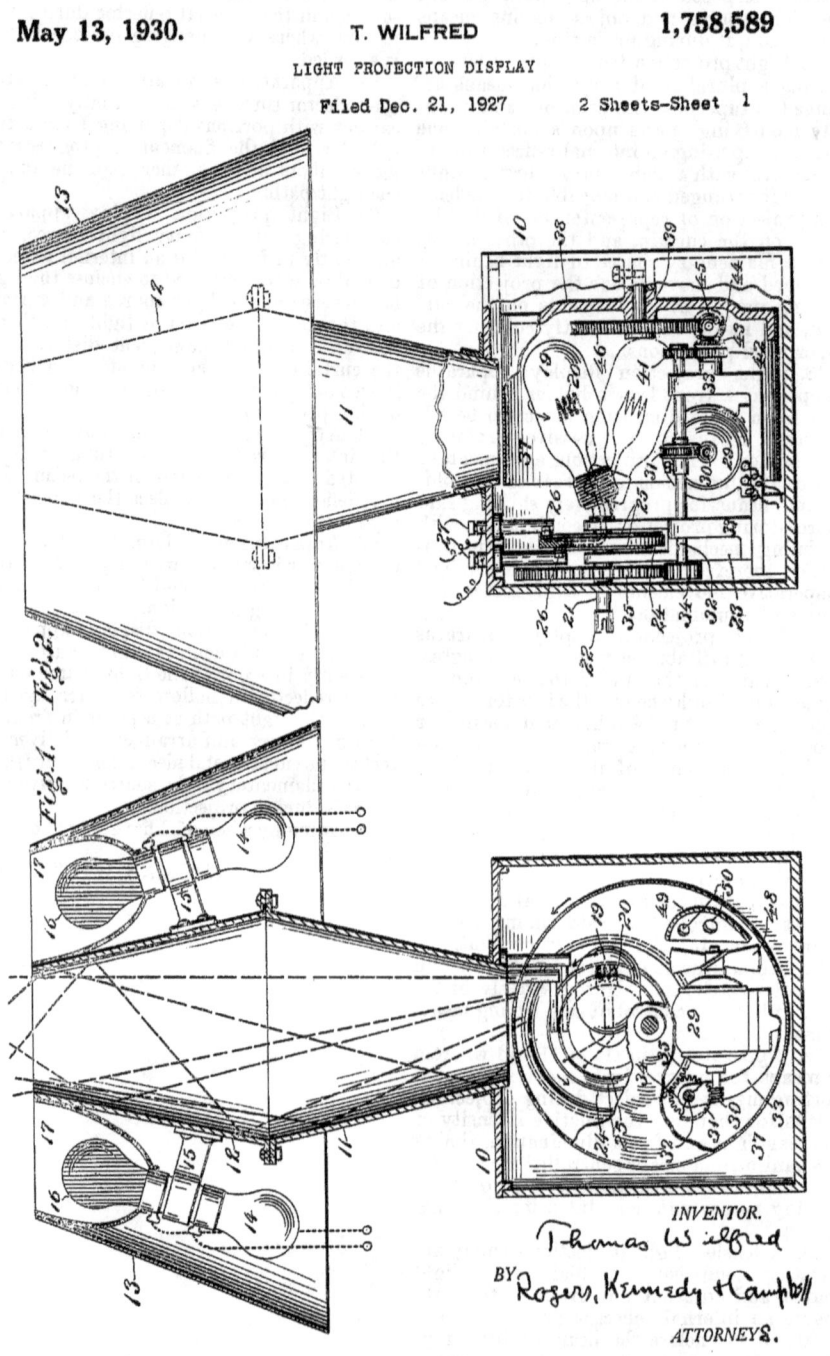

VISUAL MUSIC INSTRUMENT PATENTS (I) 153

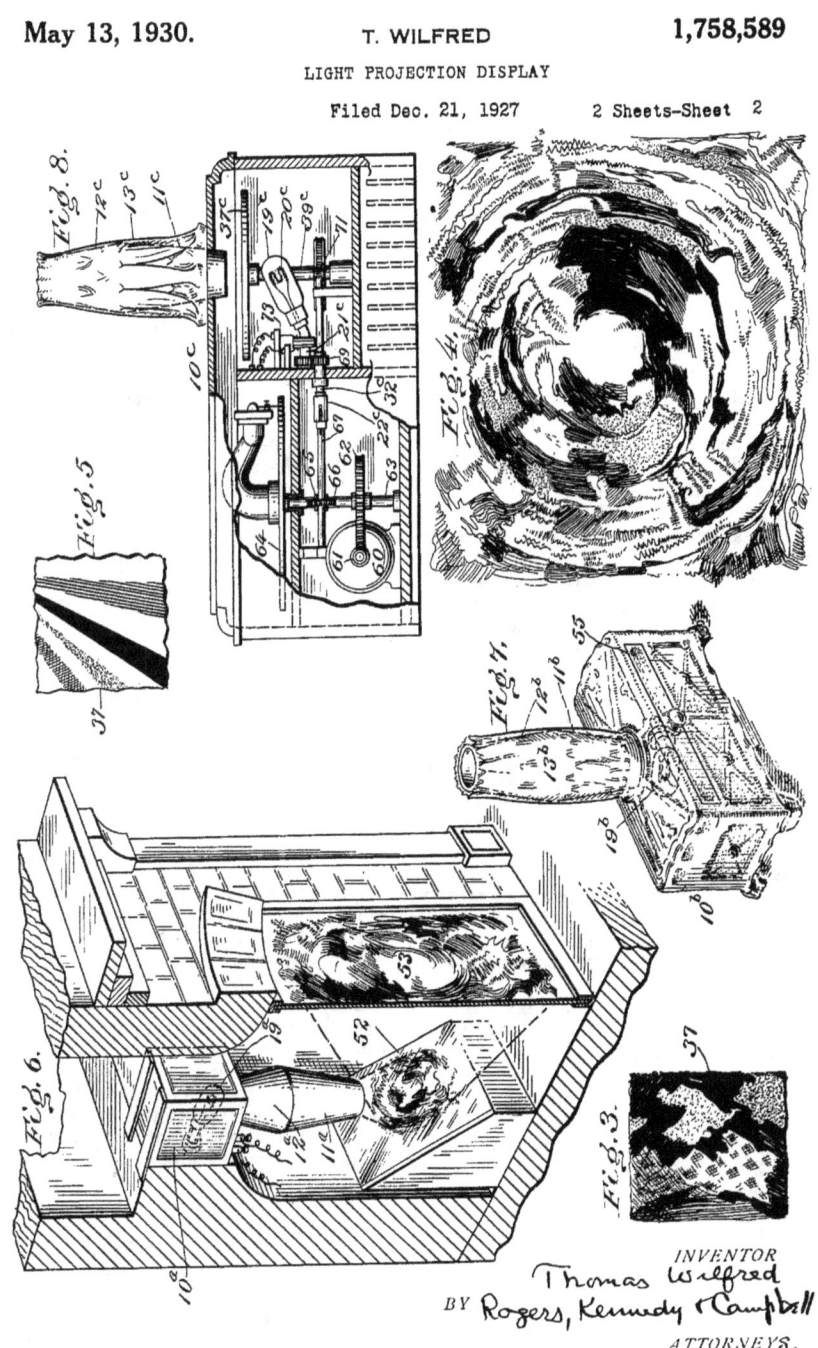

UNITED STATES PATENT OFFICE

THOMAS WILFRED, OF FOREST HILLS, NEW YORK

LIGHT-PROJECTION DISPLAY

Application filed December 21, 1927. Serial No. 241,577.

This invention relates to the art of light projection display, for example in the projection of effects in light or color upon a curtain or other surface for exhibition, entertainment, interpretation, eye treatment or other purposes. A novel method or system is involved as well as a novel apparatus or machine for carrying it out.

The general object of the present invention is to afford a system of projection upon a suitable receiving surface of effects in lights and shadows or colors adapted to please the mind or stir the imagination or emotions, the effects including infinite and continuous variations in tone, pattern, motion and evolution of effect. A particular object of the present invention is to afford certain new, interesting and entertaining types of projected effects as will be herein described. Other and further objects and advantages will be pointed out in the following specification or will be apparent to those conversant with the subject.

To the attainment of the objects and advantages referred to the present invention consists in the novel art, system or method, and the novel apparatus or machine, herein described or illustrated, as well as the novel features of operation, interaction, combination, arrangement and structure.

In the accompanying drawings Fig. 1 is a vertical substantially central section view of a projecting apparatus embodying the principles of the present invention.

Fig. 2 is a similar view taken however in section at right angles to Fig. 1 and with the upper part of the figure in elevation.

Fig. 3 is a developed or face view of the patterned or multicolor screen constituting one of the elements shown in Figs. 1 and 2.

Fig. 4 in a rough way shows the character of one of the infinite number of projected effects producible with the apparatus of Figs. 1, 2 and 3.

Fig. 5 is a view similar to Fig. 3 showing one of the many forms of patterned screen which may be employed for the purposes hereof.

Fig. 6 is a perspective elevation, partly in section of a modified form of apparatus in which the projected effect is bent by a mirror from vertical to horizontal and thrown against an upright translucent receiving screen.

Fig. 7 in perspective shows a further modification wherein the apparatus is embodied in an ornamental form.

Fig. 8 partially in elevation and partially in central section shows the combination of an automatic sound or music producing machine with an apparatus embodying the present invention, the two connected to be driven in unison.

First will be described the apparatus shown in Figs. 1 to 3 inclusive, the mode of action and effects to be described subsequently. A box or housing 10 encloses the mechanism and light source. In this embodiment the projected effects are intended to be thrown upwardly to be received, for example upon the ceiling of a living room, auditorium or other place. The optical devices exterior to the box 10 therefore are located at the top side of the box, although obviously the entire structure could be turned and directed in any desired manner. The exterior optical devices are shown as including a novel reflecting system, the principal element of which is a flaring cone 11, connected to the box top, and with its interior surface silvered or polished, and either geometrically true or with any desired variations or irregularities in order to alter or heighten the effects. The reflector therefore may be broadly considered as a hollow flaring interior reflector or mirror. The combination of this with the other elements, later to be described, is capable of certain novel effects, but the full embodiment of the present invention comprises, in combination with the flaring internal reflector 11 a succeeding tapered internal reflector 12, which in this embodiment is shown also of conical form, or rather that of a truncated cone, the extreme or upper end being open for the passage of the light and color effects as will be more fully described.

With the vertical or upright type of apparatus the double cone reflector 11, 12 may be partly concealed and made to simulate a lamp by providing an enclosing shade 13. The effect of a table lamp can be further carried out by providing between the reflector and the shade a number of ordinary electric lamps or bulbs 14, which may be extinguished if desirable during the performance of an optical effect. The lamps 14 are shown supported on brackets 15 which also support upwardly directed lamps or bulbs 16 which may be of some rich color, as red, to throw a background on the ceiling for the reception of the moving effects of this invention. The several colored bulbs 16 are shown enclosed in upwardly directed reflectors 17.

The source of illumination for the present invention consists preferably of a filamentary lamp 19 which may be an ordinary, or a specially designed, incandescent lamp, having a filament 20 which may be given a contour consonant with the effect desired, since the present invention operates by the projection of light from the particular form of incandescent filament used. Moreover the invention preferably involves the continuous or evolutionary movement of the lamp 19, which may, for example, be given a rotary movement and at the same time a movement of revolution, these combined movements being conveniently obtained by mounting the lamp eccentrically upon a shaft 21, so that as the shaft is turned the lamp passes through what may be described as wobbling movements, substantially indicated by the full line and dotted line positions in Fig. 2. It will be noticed that the filament 20, in each of its positions, is substantially within the theoretical continuation of the surface of the flaring reflector 11. In its lowest position the filament reaches almost to the apex of the flaring cone, the revolutionary movement of the filament carrying it both inwardly, from and toward the apex, and laterally from side to side.

The lamp shaft 21 is shown as having an exterior coupling 22 by which it may be coupled to a music box or other musical instrument arranged to perform simultaneously with the present invention. The lamp shaft is shown mounted in a bearing bracket 23 and as provided with a commutator disk 24 having opposite rings 25 connected respectively to the terminals of the filaments 20, while brushes 26 contacting upon the rings are mounted on terminal posts 27 by which electric current can be delivered to the lamp.

The mode of drive may next conveniently be described. An electric motor 29 is shown, its shaft carrying a worm 30 driving a worm wheel 31 mounted on what may be termed the main shaft 32, supported in bearing brackets 33. A pinion 34 on the main shaft drives a gear 35 on the lamp shaft, thus maintaining the lamp in continuous motion.

While interesting effects can be obtained with the apparatus thus far described there is herein shown a screen 37 which cooperates in producing unusual and novel effects. This screen is preferably formed with regular or irregular patterns, an example being shown in Fig. 3, producing the effect shown in Fig. 4, and another example being shown in Fig. 5; and the various area portions preferably being colored or tinted with varying colors. The pattern screen 37 is shown in the form of an endless band or drum, arranged to surround the lamp and certain mechanism, thus giving an endless moving screen which is at the same time compact and easily operated. The drum or screen 37 is shown mounted on a web or disk 38 which is keyed to a shaft 39 parallel to the shafts 21 and 33 already mentioned.

The driving connections for the pattern drum may comprise a pinion 41 on the main shaft driving a pinion 42 to which is attached a bevel pinion 43 engaging a bevel pinion 44 which in turn carries a worm 45 engaging a worm wheel 46 mounted on the screen shaft 39.

The various described gearing may be so proportioned as to give substantially the following rates of movement. Assuming a motor running at 1200 R. P. M. the gearing 30, 31 may be such as to drive the main shaft 32 at the rate of 12 R. P. M. The gearing 34, 35 may be such as to turn the lamp shaft one rotation per minute. The gearing 41—46 between the main shaft and the color screen however preferably contains a greater degree of reduction, such that the screen will make one complete rotation in twelve minutes. The complete cycle of the machine in such case will occur in a period of twelve minutes during which the screen patterns are producing constantly varying effects while the projecting filament is passing twelve times through its individual cycle of movement.

In order to minimize overheating within the housing there is shown a fan 48 attached on the motor shaft and opposite to this a concave baffle or wall 49 at the ends of which are ventilating apertures 50, so that the air within the housing is constantly renewed, being ejected through the cone reflector.

The screen may be comprised of glass, mica or other transparent material, and the pattern applied by painting or attachment of areas of transparent or translucent color or capacity. It may be removable for replacement by a substitute screen, or the effect may be altered by axially shifting the drum to a new zone, giving latitude in operation so that the effect may be changed with changes in mood of accompanying music, acting, etc. Instead of an endless drum the screen may be wound from spool to spool.

The modification shown in Fig. 6 embodies the same principles. A domestic fireplace is shown. Within this is mounted the box or housing 10ª and extending downwardly below it the flaring and tapered reflectors 11ª and 12ª. The filamentary lamp 19ª within the housing thereby casts light downwardly through the double cone, the beam being received upon a preferably flat mirror 52 set at 45° so that the projection is thrown forwardly to illuminate with the effects of this invention a translucent or ground glass surface 53 occupying the fire-place opening, forming an attractive mode of exhibiting the invention.

In the form shown in Fig. 7 the housing 10^b is designed as an ornamental or treasure chest. Above it are the cones 11^b and 12^b concealed by a cover designed as a vase 13^b resting upon the chest. The lamp 19^b is within the housing, and between it and the conical reflectors is a drawer or slide 55 which may carry one or more shiftable or rotary disk screens, for example such as that shown in Fig. 8, which may thus be readily replaced at will.

In any case there may be a plural number of projectors in cooperating relation; for example to the several walls of a room or sections of a dome ceiling.

The modification of Fig. 8 shows a musical instrument mechanically combined with the present invention. The housing 10^c has superposed on it the flaring and tapered cones 11^c and 12^c concealed in a vase 13^c. The lamp 19^c contains the filament 20^c and is mounted eccentrically on the lamp shaft 21^c giving the wobbling movement as in Fig. 2. The main shaft 32^c may be analogous to the shaft 32 in the other figures, driving the lamp and the pattern screen 37^c which in this case is in the form of a flat disk supported upon an upright screen shaft 39^c.

The remainder of the apparatus may be described beginning with the motor 60, which is connected by worm 61 and wheel 62 with the upright shaft 63 of a phonograph 64. The upright shaft through worm 65 and gear 66 drives a shaft 67 which is coupled to the main shaft 32^c, by coupling 22^c.

The gearing 69 between the main shaft and the lamp shaft may be analogous to the already described figures, and the gearing 71 from the main shaft to the screen shaft may be analogous, and such as to give a much slower rate of rotation to the screen than the rotation of the lamp. The electrical connection 73 may be analogous to the other figures.

One of the characteristic features hereof is the flared internal reflector between the filamentary lamp and curtain, and especially the flared reflector followed by a non-flared or tapered one. The evolving effect comprises a central nucleus or vortex, as seen in Fig. 4, of maximum brilliance, and a surrounding field of designs produced by the combination of the incandescent filament, the patterned screen when used, and the internal reflector. Rays of light pass in many ways from the lamp to the curtain, some paths being indicated in Fig. 1, these intersecting and overlapping at many points, as they weave back and forth with the oscillation of the filament. The vortex itself shifts progressively around an orbit on the curtain, returning at intervals to the same position, while the pattern changes progressively through its complete cycle at a creeping speed through a much longer interval. It is a multiple pattern in light and shadow, form and color, tending toward circular shapes, each of exquisite texture due to the interlacing paths of the rays reflecting from the internal mirrors, and further complicated by any irregularity of reflector surface. The pattern and color of the screen may change along predetermined lines, and these are introduced into the curving, weaving effect of the projected filament, affording a visual composition of great beauty, or of grotesque or entertaining character, at the heart of which is the bright area or center formed by rays received direct, without reflection, from the lamp. The complete effect is unique and of a character rendering it available as a mobile mural decoration for various purposes and places. By removing the second or converging reflector a different effect is obtainable with the diverging or flared one; with an alternating motion of expansion and contraction of the entire color design while displaying within itself exquisite progressions of pattern, texture and depth.

In the case of coordination of projection with automatic music production, the two can be coordinated and synchronized throughout the performance in appropriate relation.

To the extent that this application contains subject matter of claim in common with the disclosure of my copending application, Serial No. 735,168, filed August 30, 1924, this application is a continuation of the earlier one.

There have thus been described an art or method or light projection display and apparatus therefore embodying the principles and attaining the purposes of the present invention. Since many matters of operation, interaction, combination, arrangement and structure may be variously modified without departing from the inventive principles it is not intended to limit the invention to such matters except so far as specified in the appended claims.

What is claimed is:

1. Lensless light projection display apparatus comprising a filamentary lamp, and adjacently in front of it a truncated conical internal reflector arranged to enclose the beam of light between the lamp and curtain and deliver it without subsequent distortion to the curtain, and means for effecting progressive relative movement between the lamp and conical reflector during projection.

2. Light projection display apparatus com-

prising a filamentary lamp, and adjacently in front of it an internal reflector of flared-tapered form arranged to enclose the beam of light between the light source and curtain, the same being centrally open to pass the central rays direct to the curtain, and means for effecting progressive relative movement between the light source and reflector during projection.

3. Light projection display apparatus comprising a filamentary lamp, a flared internal reflector in front of the lamp, the lamp being within the angle of flare of the reflector, whereby the reflector passes central rays and deflects outer rays direct to the curtain, without distortion, and mechanism for methodically shifting the lamp during projection.

4. Apparatus as in claim 3 and wherein the filamentary lamp is shifted bodily towards and from the apex of the flare angle during projection.

5. Apparatus as in claim 3 and wherein the reflector stands upright with the lamp beneath, a housing shaped to represent the base of a table lamp surrounding the lamp, and a shade surrounding the upper part of the reflector.

6. Light projection display apparatus comprising a filamentary lamp, a base housing around it, a flared-tapered internal reflector above the lamp and housing, supplemental lamps exterior to the reflector, a shade enclosing the supplemental lamps, and mechanism for methodically shifting the lamp during projection.

7. Lensless light projection display apparatus comprising a filamentary lamp, and adjacently in front of it an internal reflector of hollow truncated double conical form arranged to enclose the light beam between the lamp and curtain and deliver it without subsequent distortion to the curtain, and means for effecting progressive relative movement between the lamp and hollow reflector during projection.

8. Light projection display apparatus comprising a filamentary lamp, a flared and tapered internal reflector in front of the lamp, arranged to deliver the beam without subsequent distortion to the curtain and centrally open to pass the center of the beam to form a projected nucleus on the curtain, and mechanism for methodically shifting the lamp during projection, relatively to the axis of the reflector, whereby to cause changing projected effects including progressive displacement of the projected nucleus.

9. Light projection display apparatus comprising a filamentary lamp, and adjacently in front of it an internal reflector of hollow truncated conical form, flared from the lamp, and in front of that a hollow truncated conical reflector tapered from the lamp, and means for effecting progressive movements of the lamp during projection, including both rotation of the lamp and bodily movement relative to the axis of the reflector.

10. Light projection display apparatus comprising a filamentary lamp, an internal reflector in front of the lamp delivering without subsequent distortion to the curtain, the lamp and reflector being relatively arranged so that the center of the beam may pass undeflected to the curtain, a movable colored pattern screen, and a common mechanism for methodically shifting the lamp during projection, relatively to the reflector, and shifting the screen relatively to both the reflector and lamp.

11. Apparatus as in claim 10 and wherein the mechanism comprises connections for advancing the color screen at a speed slower than that of the lamp.

12. Light projection display apparatus comprising a filamentary lamp, and adjacently in front of it an internal reflector of hollow form arranged to enclose the beam of light between the lamp and curtain and deliver it without subsequent distortion to the curtain, mechanism for effecting progressive relative movement between the light source and reflector during projection, an endless pattern screen mounted to travel gradually around the lamp and between it and the reflector, and drive means for effecting progressive movements of the elements during projection.

13. Apparatus as in claim 12 and wherein is a single power source for driving both the screen and lamp, with connections for moving the lamp through a plurality of cycles for a single complete cycle of the screen.

14. Light projection display apparatus comprising a filamentary lamp, and adjacently in front of it an internal reflector of flared conical form arranged to enclose the beam of light between the light source and curtain and deliver it without subsequent distortion to the curtain, mechanism for effecting progressive movement of the lamp during projection, a mechanical musical instrument, and a common actuating drive operating the mechanism and instrument in synchronism.

15. Light projection display apparatus comprising a filamentary source of light, and adjacently in front of it an internal reflector of flared-tapered form arranged to enclose the beam of light between the light source and curtain, the same being centrally open to pass the central rays direct to the curtain, and the source of light being arranged to project light to the interior surface of the reflector, and means for effective progressive relative movement between the light source and reflector during projection.

16. Light projection display apparatus comprising a filamentary lamp, a flared internal reflector in front of the lamp, arranged to deliver the beam to the curtain and cen-

trally open to pass the center of the beam to form a projected nucleus on the curtain, and the source of light being arranged to project light to the interior surface of the reflector, and mechanism for methodically shifting the lamp during projection, relatively to the axis of the reflector, whereby to cause changing projected effects including progressive displacement of the projected nucleus.

In testimony whereof, I have affixed my signature hereto.

THOMAS WILFRED.

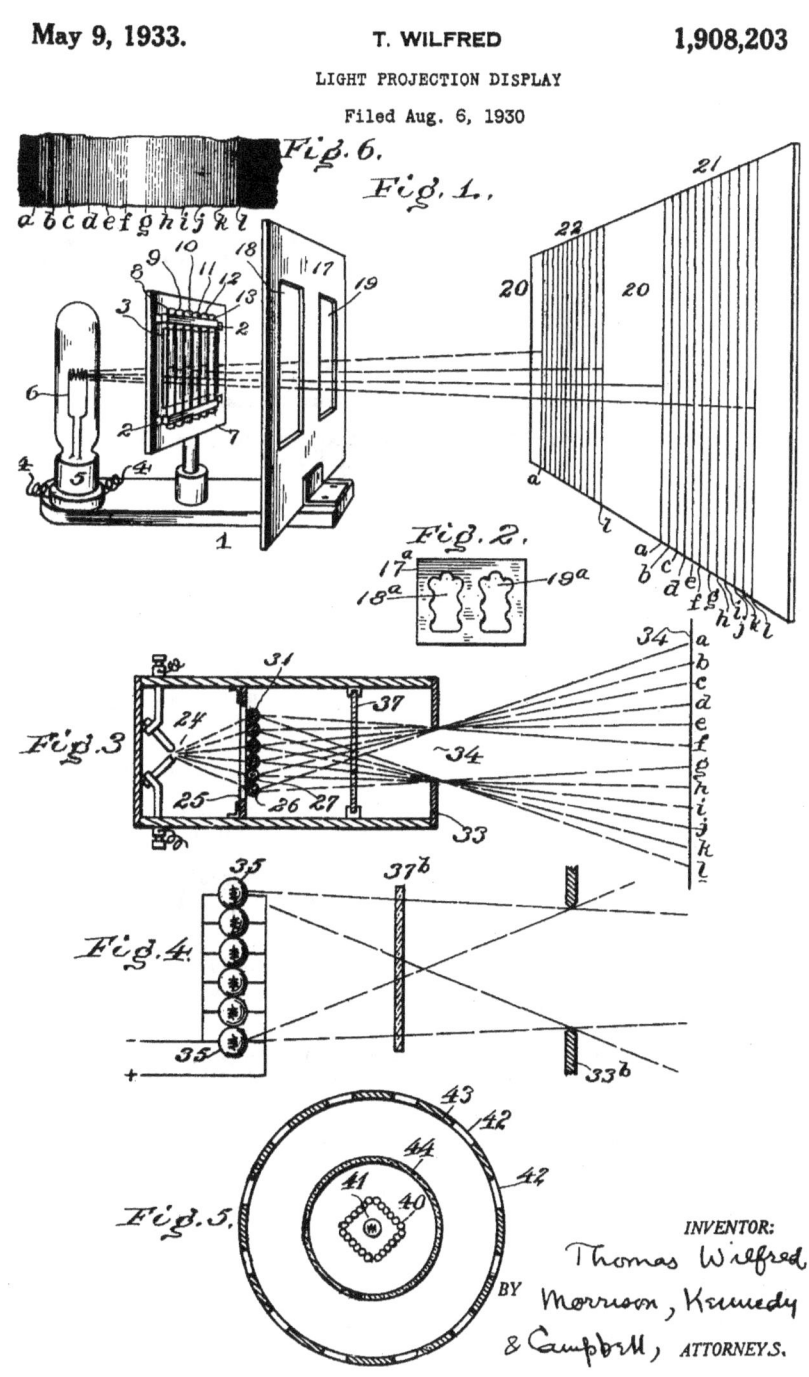

Patented May 9, 1933

1,908,203

UNITED STATES PATENT OFFICE

THOMAS WILFRED, OF FOREST HILLS, NEW YORK

LIGHT PROJECTION DISPLAY

Application filed August 6, 1930. Serial No. 473,495.

This invention relates to the art of light projection display, and more particularly to method and apparatus for the projection of effects in light or color on a wall or curtain for exhibition.

The main object of the present invention is to enable the projection upon a suitable surface of effects simulating architectural and other forms, such as columns, the projected effect having repeated elements which diminish in intensity toward the final edge or outline, thereby creating an effective optical illusion of the projected effect having three dimensions, such as the convex roundness of a column or other form.

A further object is to afford a relatively simple projection apparatus adapted to produce effects of the kind set forth.

A further object is to supplement the basic idea and effect by additional combinable features or effects for the purpose of lending greater scope or variety.

The invention may be practically applied for many different purposes, for example for the decoration of the interior or exterior wall and ceiling surfaces of a building or room with projected columns, arches or other designs, these having the advantage over painted or sculptured forms of being instantly interchangeable or removable.

In the accompanying drawing Fig. 1 is a perspective side view in diagram showing the principles of the invention. Fig. 2 shows a modified intercepting screen or mask. Fig. 3 is a diagrammatic top view illustrating the manner in which the light rays are produced and projected to give the desired effects. Fig. 4 is a partial diagrammatic top view of a modification. Fig. 5 is a top view of a modified projector from which images are producible in many directions from the same source. Fig. 6 shows one type of projected effect.

The drawing, showing several embodiments of the apparatus, may be specifically described in detail as follows. Referring first to Fig. 1, upon a base plate 1 is shown mounted a support or socket 5, holding a filamentary lamp 6, constituting the source of light, energized by conductors 4. In front of the light source is a bracket supporting a frame 7 having an opening 3, in front of which is a series of cylindrical glass rods 8, 9, 10, 11, 12 and 13 constituting lenses. These are held by means of straps 2.

On the extreme front of base plate 1 is mounted an opaque wall 17 having a series of, for example two, vertical slits 18 and 19 through which the light rays from lamp 6, after having passed through the cylindrical lenses 8 to 13, can travel to curtain or wall 20.

The cylindrical glass rods, placed vertically in front of the light source each distribute the light from said source over an area having considerable horizontal width. The entire series of such glass rods, placed side by side, will produce a plurality of overlapping areas. I have found that if an opaque screen, having one or more slits, is placed between the rods and the curtain upon which the light is projected, a plurality of images of each slit will appear on the projection curtain, overlapping in such a way as to present to the eye a composite image of each slit, this image composed of a plurality of elements or areas which present the maximum intensity near the middle and diminish in intensity toward the extreme right and left edges. This phenomenon affords an interesting and beautiful effect creating an optical illusion of roundness or of an image or column having three dimensions.

Each rod or cylindrical glass bar is a cylindrical lens, and to prevent aberration each lens may have its side edges opaquely coated. The projected effect from each slit or window is a complete convex column, or may be in some cases, a concave form, in three dimensions. Thus the aperture 18 gives the column

21 and the aperture 19 the column 22. The space on the curtain or wall 20 between the column effects, will usually be black, but is left blank for simplicity of showing, but might have background effects projected upon it, combining with the columns. Fig. 6 shows a column effect so projected, having a fluted appearance, and representing the columns 21 and 22 of Fig. 1.

The slits 18 and 19 may each be rectangular and so narrow that the central area of the wall image, illuminated by the light beams from all the rods, is of the same horizontal width as the distance from each of the successive projected areas to the next, on either side, the image on the screen will give a striking resemblance to a round fluted column of great beauty. Due to the substantial horizontal spread of each of the light beams, a number of such column images can be produced from the same projector by merely having more slits or apertures in the opaque mask or screen interposed between the glass rods and the projection screen. In fact, the entire wall surface of a hall or room can have projected upon it a series of such column or other images. For example, as shown in Fig. 5 a plurality of series of glass rods 40 are placed so as to completely surround the lamp 41, this combination being in turn surrounded by a cylindrical or polygonal mask 43 with a plurality of apertures or slits 42. Varying colors are here producible in the images by means of a cylindrical or polygonal transparent color screen 44. The type of projector shown in Fig. 5 can conveniently be built resembling an ornamental chandelier and suspended from the ceiling.

By the use of masks or partitions having slits of irregular or ornamental shape, for example such as shown in Fig. 2 a multitude of fantastic images can be produced. Also, by using glass rods of different colors or by interposing transparent color screens, between the glass rods and the slitted mask, these images can be colored in any way desired, the colors generally appearing in soft gradations which change in intensity with the various outlines.

In Fig. 2 the partition 17^a has apertures 18^a, 19^a of arbitrary shape, varying the projected form but on the same principles.

The preferred way in which a multiple area projection, for instance overlapping projections to afford a column image, is produced, is shown in Fig. 3.

The light source 24, which in this case is shown as an electric arc, passes through six vertical glass rods or cylindrical lenses 26 to 31, mounted on a frame 25. The six individual beams of light 26^{a-z}, 27^{b-h}, etc., are partially intercepted by slitted partition 33, before passing on to the projection surface 34, and may be colored by a screen 37. The beam of light issuing from glass rod 26 can thus illuminate the surface 34 from point a to point g only, from rod 27 area b to h only, etc., until rod 31 covers area f to h. Area f to g thus receives light from all six rods and consequently constitutes a vertical stripe of the brightest area in the projection. Each subsequent field or stripe to either side of area $f—g$ receives light from one less rod, or five, and so on, until areas $a—b$ and $k—l$ at the extreme sides receive light from only one rod and are the darkest areas. This progressive reduction in intensity, being effected from the center outward in both directions, gives a startling illusion simulating the lights and shadows of the roundness of a cylindrical column or other form.

For the decoration of large surfaces, such as the exterior wall of an entire building, or where the distance or great intensity of light is desirable, the single light source and the series of glass rods can be replaced by a series of individual light sources, such as incandescent bulbs or arc lights 35, such an arrangement being shown in Fig. 4. Six individual lamps are shown producing six individual beams of light which are intercepted substantially as above described by slitted screen 33^b.

The apertured partition 17, 17^a, 33 or 33^b in each case must be so spaced from the row of lenses or lamps that the image stripes will overlap and give progressive decrease of brightness from a middle stripe outward. The relation between the series of beam sources, and the apertures and the receiving curtain is such that the bright stripe or area $f—g$ will be of suitable width to carry out the effect desired, as indicated in Figs. 1, 3 and 6.

While the invention has been particularly shown as employed in the production of the effect of vertical columns either straight or with irregular contours, it is clear that the principles could be used for giving the effect of other architectural form, for example horizontal forms, with convex rounding toward the upper and lower edges, or for that matter forms that are spherical or rounded in all directions from a general center, namely by means of a solid bank of lamps or lenses and apertures limited in dimension both horizontally and vertically.

While in each embodiment there has been shown a row or bank of light beam sources, either lenses or lamps, spaced slightly apart, and giving the effect of fluting on the column, the embodiment could be altered by increasing the closeness or continuity of the light sources, or even replacing the series thereof by a continuous source of light such as luminiscent tubes, thus affording the effect of a true cylindrical column or figure without the effect of fluting produced by the spaced sources.

While the partition 17 or 33 or 33^b or 43

has been referred to as preferably opaque with apertures or slits in the nature of windows cut therein to give passage to the light beams, I contemplate an arrangement wherein the partition is composed of a sheet of glass in which case the glass partition as a whole may be coated with a suitable coloring matter, such as dark blue, of transparent character, so as to permit the passage of rays to form a colored background on the distant wall, with however clear spaces left in the places designated for the apertures 18, 19, 34 and 42 respectively, these clear spaces permitting the passage of white or relatively strong light to afford the illusion of described columns, appearing upon a background of the darker color transmitted through the remainder of the partition.

There have thus been described a method and apparatus for projection of effects in light or color embodying the principles and attaining the objects of the present invention. Since many matters of arrangement, combination and detail may be variously modified without departing from the principles it is not intended to limit the invention except so far as set forth in the appended claims.

What is claimed is:

1. Light projection display apparatus comprising a light source, a bank of beam producing lenses in front of the light source, and a partition in front of the bank of lenses and having one or more apertures, a receiving wall, the partition so spaced between the bank of lenses and receiving wall that each aperture passes a series of overlapping beams, thereby giving a progressively graded projected effect with maximum intensity at the middle and minimum at the edges thereof.

2. Apparatus as in claim 1 and wherein the lenses are vertical cylindrical lenses and the apertures are vertical oblong apertures, giving the effect of columns in three dimensions.

3. Apparatus as in claim 1 and wherein the light source is at the center, the lenses are arranged in successive series around all sides of the light source, and the partition surrounds the lenses on all sides and has a large number of apertures directed in various directions from the center.

4. Light projection display apparatus comprising a bank of at least four light beam sources of substantially the same color of illumination, arranged transverse to the direction of projection, a projection receiving surface, and a partition having a fixed relation to the bank of sources and formed with one or more relatively narrow vertical slots and arranged transverse to the direction of projection, in front of the bank of sources; the partition being arranged between the light sources and the receiving surfaces and spaced substantially nearer to the sources than to the receiving surface and each slot having such width as to pass a series of beams from the respective sources, causing them to overlap on the distant receiving surface; thereby giving a progressively graded projected effect of at least seven stripes with maximum intensity near the middle and minimum near the edges thereof, affording the projected effect of a round fluted column.

In testimony whereof, this specification has been duly signed by:

THOMAS WILFRED.

VISUAL MUSIC INSTRUMENT PATENTS (I)

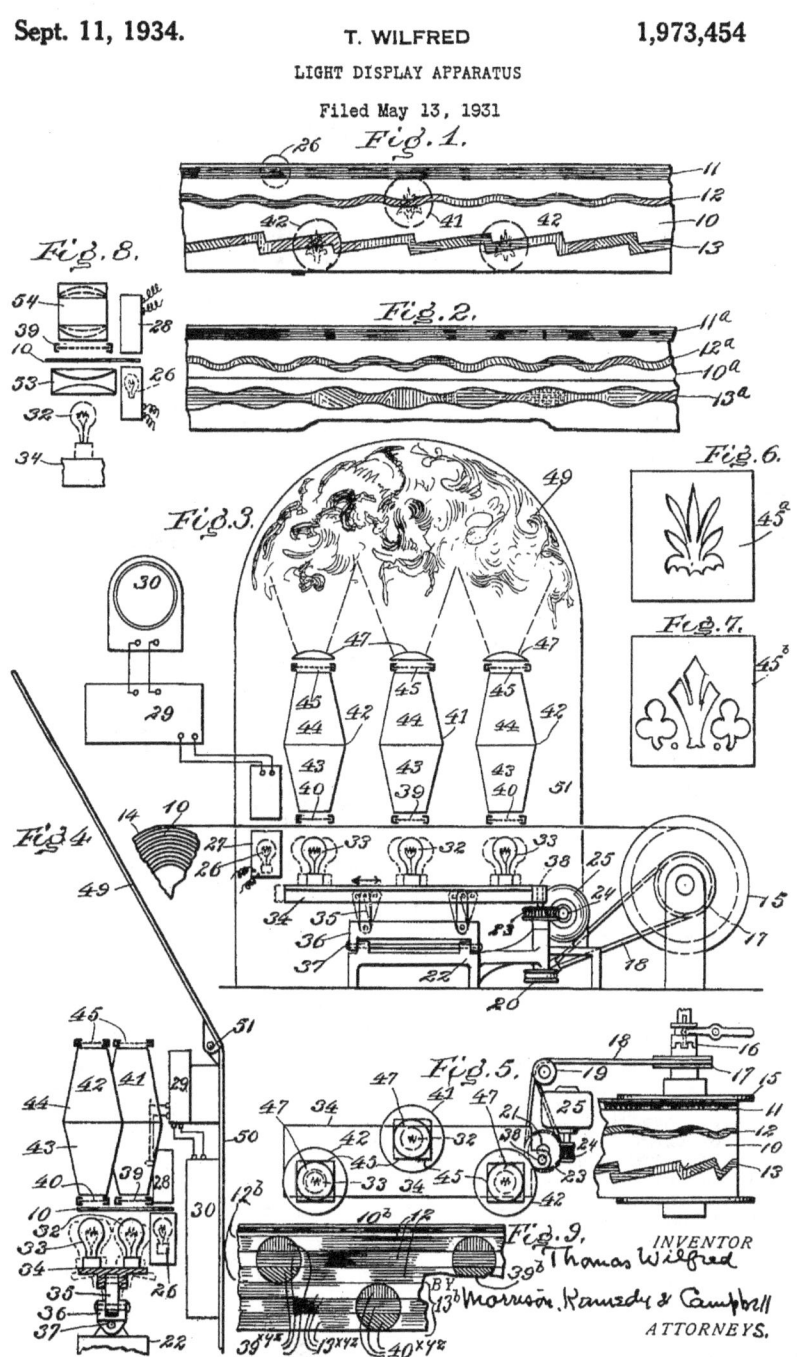

Sept. 11, 1934. T. WILFRED 1,973,454
LIGHT DISPLAY APPARATUS
Filed May 13, 1931

UNITED STATES PATENT OFFICE

1,973,454

LIGHT DISPLAY APPARATUS

Thomas Wilfred, Forest Hills, N. Y.

Application May 13, 1931, Serial No. 537,052

4 Claims. (Cl. 272—10)

This invention relates to sound and light display apparatus, and has reference to the combined production of sound or music and light or color effects, under the control of a single means or record, in a manner for example wherein each part of the performance, the sound and the light, constitutes an accompaniment for the other part, the two preferably being coordinated or arranged in synchronism. Certain parts of apparatus shown or available for use in the present invention have been disclosed in prior patents of mine, for example, No. 1,758,589 of May 13, 1930, to which reference may be had for details.

The main object of the present invention is to afford an automatic system or apparatus whereby compositions or other performances involving the simultaneous production of sound and the projection of light may be afforded. The results are not only productive of enjoyment, but are useful as interpretations, accompaniments to dancing or other performances, or the like. Other and further objects and advantages of the invention will be explained in the hereinafter following description of an illustrative embodiment, or will be apparent to those conversant with the subject.

In the accompanying drawing Figure 1 is a face view of a record member, strip or band having a plurality of tracks, paths or zones controlling the production respectively of sound and light effects. Fig. 2 is a similar view of a modified form of record strip. In these two views the light or color tracks are indicated as of changing colors, with illustrative color designations shown in accordance with the Patent Office rules of practise.

Fig. 3 is a front elevation view, largely diagrammatic, of a complete apparatus embodying the cooperative features of the present invention. Fig. 4 is an end elevation view of certain parts of Fig. 3, with certain modifications. Fig. 5 is a top plan view of certain parts of Figs. 3 and 4.

Figs. 6 and 7 are face views of different forms of mask or cut-out screens for use in the apparatus.

Fig. 8 shows a modification of a portion of the apparatus, in a view similar to Fig. 4.

Fig. 9 indicates a modified character of record strip and certain screens cooperating therewith.

Referring first to the embodiment shown in Figs. 1, 3, 4 and 5, the record or film 10 is shown as having a sound track or lane 11 and first and second light or color tracks 12 and 13. For example the color track 12 may represent and produce by its changes of form and color an accompaniment coordinated with the sound composition of track 11, while the color track 13 may produce a supplemental or solo color performance. Each of the color tracks is shown as changing in width, form and color from point to point, the selection and arrangement being in accordance with the judgment of the artist.

The sound track may be of the type which varies in density as in Figs. 1 and 2, or the type which is of uniform density but varies in width, as in Fig. 5, according to the system used.

The actuation of the strip is indicated in Figs. 3 and 5. It passes from a convenient supply spool 14 to a take-up spool 15 driven through a clutch 16 by a pulley 17 engaged by a belt 18 passing over idler pulleys 19 and driven by a pulley 20. The pulley 20 is shown mounted at the lower end of a shaft 21 turning in a bearing formed on a frame base 22. At the top end of the shaft is shown a worm wheel 23 driven by a worm 24 on the shaft of a motor 25. By this arrangement the film is steadily progressively advanced through the apparatus. Both the sound production and light projection are by or from the record, strip or film continuously controlled, and no step-by-step actuation is necessary.

The sound reproduction part of the apparatus, along lines per se already known, comprises a lamp 26 mounted in a box 27 having a top slit coordinated with the record track 11. Above the record strip is indicated a pick-up device 28 which may be of the photoelectric type, the same having electric connections to an amplifying apparatus indicated at 29, which in turn operates a loud speaker 30, conveniently located, for example concealed as in Fig. 4. The music or other sound performance represented by the track 11 of the record strip is thus delivered by the loud speaker 30 to the audience.

The light or color projecting part of the apparatus may be of various types and details, including those indicated in prior patents. Thus the projecting apparatus may comprise a system of one or more filamentary light sources or lamps projecting through suitable optical devices and eventually received upon a curtain, wall or other surface. For example, there may be a plurality of filamentary lamps projecting cooperatively upon a curtain or surface of relatively small size so that the entire apparatus may be fitted into the fire place of a room for viewing from a nearby point; although the performance might equally be projected to a distant point, ceiling or wall.

In Figs. 1, 3, 4 and 5 are indicated a plurality of filamentary lamps 32 and 33. For example the lamp 32 may be below the color track 12, while the lamps 33 are below the color track 13. All the lamps are shown mounted in proper position upon a table 34 adapted to be moved methodically, as in a horizontal manner, to give predetermined movements to the filaments during the performance. Thus the table 34 may be mounted upon links 35 affording longitudinal movement, the links being pivoted to a carriage 36 which in turn is connected for lateral shifting by a pivot shaft 37 mounted on the base 22.

The table and lamps thus can be put through longitudinal and lateral movements and have, for example, a circular movement, so that images of the filaments will undergo evolutionary shiftings. The progressive operation of the table 34 may be effected by any desired mechanism, for example by a crank pin 38 upstanding from the worm wheel 23 and engaging in a portion of the table, thus compelling the table to move circularly.

The optical means above the lamps 32 and 33, and above the tracks of the record strip, may be variously arranged, for example as follows. Above each lamp 32 is indicated a screen 39, and above each lamp 33 a color screen 40, these serving to modify if desired the colors appearing on the record strip; or instead of color screens the screens 39 and 40 might contain designs in shadow, such as quadrilles, spirals and the like.

Above each lamp 32 and screen 39 is shown a projecting tube 41 and above each lamp 33 and screen 40 is shown a projecting tube 42. Each of these projecting tubes may for example be a tubular internal reflector of double conical form, having a flared lower portion 43 and a tapered upper portion 44. In said prior patent I have described the effect produced by the projection of filamentary light through such an instrument.

Above the several projecting tubes are shown cutout screens or masks 45 which may for example resemble those shown in Figs. 6 and 7. Above the screens 45 are shown plano-convex lenses 47. These however may be omitted as indicated in Fig. 4.

From the lenses the projected effects pass to the receiving surface or curtain 49. This is indicated as an inclined surface extending down and back, and continued as a back wall 50, and if desired the two may be hinged at 51 for ease of assembly or mounting.

In the modification shown in Fig. 8 the light source or lamp 32 is shown as placed beneath a lens 53 of the double plano-convex form, this in turn being placed beneath the record member or strip 10, above which, as before may be arranged a screen 39, and thereabove, in Fig. 8, in place of the flared-tapered tubes 41 a special lens 54 of the double concavo-convex form, from which the light or color may project directly or indirectly to the receiving surface.

Referring further to the record member 10 as shown in Fig. 1, this is preferably in the form of a strip or band, adapted to be advanced as already described or otherwise; but broadly the record member may comprise other physical forms, for example, where a given performance is desired to be repeated over and over again, the record may be in the form of a transparent disk with the several tracks arranged concentrically near the periphery.

The track 11 is indicated as having portions of greater density than others, thus diagrammatically representing a known system of controlling the production of sound through an electrical pick-up and connected apparatus. The track 12 is shown as having a wavy form, in color, and the color changing periodically from red to blue or green, or otherwise. The wavy form brings about lateral shiftings or vibrations of the projected effect, and these movements, or the color changes from point to point, or both, may be predetermined in synchronism or harmony with the sound production which is to result from the sound record track 11. The second light or color track 13 is shown of arbitrary character, with changes of form, direction and color, representing an endless variety of possible effects and arrangements. Preferably the record spaces between the three tracks are opaque so that the passage of light is confined to the tracks themselves, although in some cases the intermediate spaces might be transparent or partly so to admit a certain amount of white or colored light for projection. Fig. 2 shows a variation from Fig. 1, wherein the first light track 12^a of the record 10^a is maintained in co-ordination with the sound track 11^a, whereas the light track 13^a is distinctively different in character from the track 13 in Fig. 1, but also embodies changes of form, position and color.

Records of the general character as shown in Figs. 1 and 2 may be produced for example as follows. The sound track may be produced by photoelectric means, in a manner already known in connection with talking motion picture films. During the production of the sound record, for example music, the performer may play one or more beams of light upon part of the sensitive surface, screened off from the sound track, in sympathy with the music, so as to give results which upon development will produce the light tracks 12 and 13. The development of positive films or records will leave transparent tracks 12 and 13, which may thereafter be colored, for example by spraying liquid color, changed from time to time, upon the transparent track. This may be done either by judgment, or under mechanical control, as by a perforated paper roll, for manufacture purposes.

Fig. 9 indicates an arrangement wherein the manual coloring of the light tracks may be dispensed with. In this form the record 10^b is shown as having a sound track 11^b and light tracks 12^b and 13^b. Each of the light tracks may be subdivided into color zones. For example the track 12^b is shown divided into three longitudinal zones 12^x, 12^y and 12^z, and the track 13^b similarly into three zones 13^x, 13^y and 13^z. Each of the zones of each of the light tracks may control the projection of a certain color, for example the zones 12^x and 13^x the color red, the zones 12^y and 13^y the color blue, and the zones 12^z and 13^z the color green. The coloring may then be provided by means of screens 39^b and 40^b, corresponding with the screens 39 and 40 as seen in Figs. 3 and 4. Each of these screens may be a color screen divided into three color zones, for example the screen 39 may be divided into longitudinal zones 39^x, 39^y and 39^z actually colored red, blue and green respectively, and the same with the zones 40^x, 40^y and 40^z of the screens 40^b. By this arrangement any particular color or combination of colors may be projected to a more or less degree of intensity. If at any given point the zones are opaque all color will be shut off, whereas if one zone is transparent it will pass for example blue light, and the degree of transparency may change gradually, so that the colors may be combined in various proportions, giving practically universal control of the color projection effects.

The general character of the operation of, and effects produced by, the present invention have been indicated in the above description. A more specific statement of the projected effects is not made, since the effects are infinitely changeable according to the requirements and desires of the artist. In Fig. 3 is roughly shown a possible projected effect wherein it will be understood that patterns and colors appear on the screen, and may progressively undergo changes of form, evolutions of movement, and alterations of color and intensity of light from moment to moment. A complete performance in light and color may be predetermined, and may be such as per se to give pleasure or useful effects, and in this aspect certain parts of the light and color apparatus may be useful apart from the production of sound. In the complete preferred embodiment however the music or sound performance accompanies or is accompanied by the light or color performance, giving a combined result.

There has thus been described a sound and light display apparatus embodying the principles and attaining the objects of the present invention. Various matters of combination, arrangement, operation, coordination, design and detail may be modified without departing from the principles; therefore the invention is not limited to such matters except to the extent set forth in the appended claims.

What is claimed is:

1. In a light projection display apparatus the combination of a light source, and beyond the light source the following: a traveling film adjacent the light source and comprising separate lanes each having progressive variations in density to control intensity of projection, a color screen subdivided longitudinally into two or more zones of different color whereby each color is separately controlled by the corresponding lane of the film, and beyond such screen a projection means, as a reflector or lens, adapted to control and blend the several portions of colored light traversing the film and color screen; whereby a color display projection is afforded wherein elements of design and color are in varied evolution of intensity, color and movement.

2. In a light projection display apparatus the combination of a light source, and beyond the light source the following: a traveling film adjacent the light source and comprising separate lanes each having progressive variations in density to control intensity of projection, means for imposing color effects upon the portions of light traversing the respective lanes of the traveling film, and a projection means, as a reflector or lens, adapted to control and blend the several portions of colored light traversing the film and color screens; whereby a color display projection is afforded wherein elements of design and color are in varied evolution of intensity, color and movement.

3. Apparatus as in claim 2 and wherein the light source comprises filamentary lamps, with means maintaining them in relative movement lateral to the film travel during projection.

4. In a light projection display apparatus the combination of a light source, and beyond the light source the following: a traveling film adjacent the light source and comprising a plurality of series of separate lanes each having progressive variations in density to control intensity of projection, a plurality of color screens each subdivided longitudinally into two or more zones of different color whereby each color is separately controlled by the corresponding film lane of one lane series, and there being at least one such screen in line with each such series of lanes, and beyond each such screen a projection means, as a reflector or lens, adapted to control and blend the several portions of colored light traversing the film and color screens; whereby a combination color display projection is afforded wherein overlapping elements of design and color are in varied evolution of intensity, color and movement.

THOMAS WILFRED.

RICHARD M. CRAIG

Radio Color Organ (1929)

Feb. 3, 1931 R. M. CRAIG 1,790,903
RADIO COLOR ORGAN
Filed Sept. 23, 1929

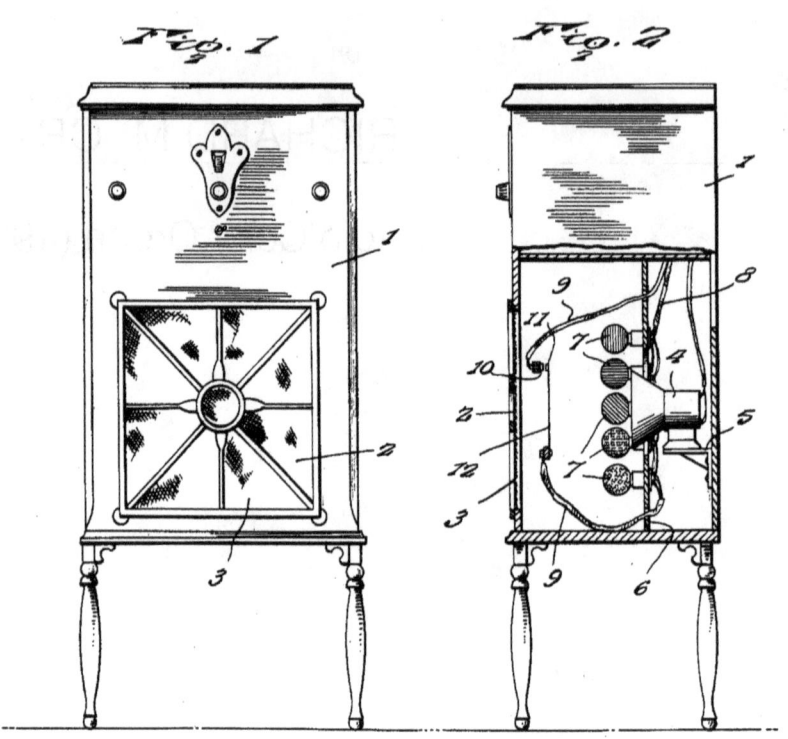

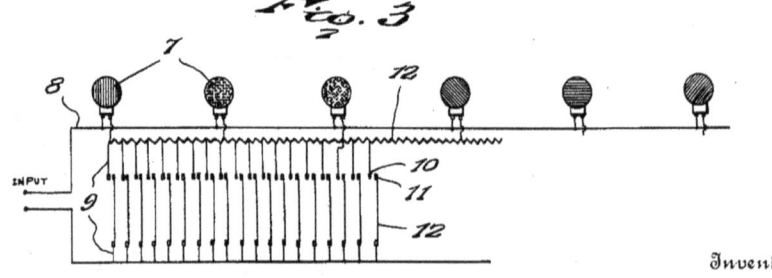

Inventor
R. M. Craig.
By Lacey & Lacey, Attorneys

Patented Feb. 3, 1931

1,790,903

UNITED STATES PATENT OFFICE

RICHARD M. CRAIG, OF SAN ANTONIO, TEXAS

RADIO COLOR ORGAN

Application filed September 23, 1929. Serial No. 394,692.

It has long been recognized that there is more or less affinity between musical tones and color, and organs and pianos have been heretofore built which linked color and sound in such a manner that when certain keys were struck and the corresponding notes sounded certain colors would be displayed so that an audience would be entertained visually as well as orally. These pianos and organs, however, were costly to build and install and could be operated only by a skilled musician. The present invention seeks to provide an inexpensive device which may be installed upon a radio receiving set and so arranged that when musical tones are emitted by the loud speaker correspondingly colored lights will be displayed to the entertainment of the listeners. One embodiment of the invention is illustrated in the accompanying drawing and will be hereinafter fully set forth and particularly defined.

In the drawing:

Figure 1 is a front elevation of a radio receiving cabinet having my invention installed therein,

Figure 2 is a side elevation, with parts broken away and in section, showing the invention, and

Figure 3 is a diagrammatic illustration of the operating mechanism.

In the illustrated form of the invention, the reference numeral 1 indicates a radio receiving cabinet having a sound outlet opening 2 in its front side which opening may be covered by a screen 3 of translucent material. A practical arrangement is a white translucent glass in front of which is a wire screen or piece of bolting cloth having a dark tapestry pattern which will not detract from the appearance of the cabinet. When the interior of the cabinet is dark, the white glass will not be seen but when a lamp behind the glass is lit, the color may be easily seen. Within the cabinet there is shown a loud speaker 4 which may be of any preferred form and is supported within the cabinet upon a bracket 5 secured to the rear wall of the cabinet. In accordance with the present invention, a partition 6 is erected within the cabinet in spaced relation to the rear wall and adjacent the front of the loud speaker, and upon this partition I mount electric lamps 7 having their globes colored, as indicated. Current for illuminating the lamps may be supplied over wires 8 in the usual manner and shunted from the said wires are other wires 9 which extend to a switch consisting of a fixed contact 10 supported in any convenient manner within the cabinet and a movable member 11 which is intended to be vibrated through sympathy with the vibrations of the sounds issuing from the loud speaker. By referring to Fig. 3 particularly, it will be noted that the switch elements are interposed between the terminals of the wires 9 and that a series of said switch elements are provided to extend across the entire front of the cabinet, the wires extending from the fixed switch elements leading into a resistance coil 12' which extends along the entire series of lamps and is connected at intervals with the several lamps. The movable switch member 11 may be of any material or constructed in any preferred manner to accomplish the desired results. In the particular form illustrated, reeds 12, such as are employed in harmonicas, were used but violin strings or piano strings may be employed successfully. The several reeds are each tuned to a different note or half note of the musical scale and when the radio is operating the several reeds will vibrate in sympathy with the vibrations of the particular note or sound to which they are respectively tuned and when so vibrated will impinge against the fixed contact member and close a circuit through one or more lamps. Upon reference to Fig. 3, it will be noted that the reed at the extreme left of the figure when in contact with its mating switch member will establish a path for the current leading directly into the corresponding lamp so that said lamp will be illuminated to its full brilliancy. The lamp next to the right also has a direct path to a reed and between the two lamps there are other reeds which connect into the resistance coil at successively greater distances from one lamp and successively lesser distances from the other lamp. Now, when a sound wave issues from the loud speaker having a wave length or wave motion half-way between the wave lengths or sounds to which the previously specifically mentioned reeds are tuned, the reed midway between the two lamps will be vibrated and the current will flow in both directions equally through the resistance coil to the lamps. Consequently, both lamps will be illuminated but only to about one-half of their full brilliancy. Likewise, if the second reed in the series be vibrated, the first lamp will be illuminated almost to full brilliancy while the second lamp will be slightly illuminated. The rays passing from the lamps will, of course, blend and will be thrown upon the screen 2 so that the observer will see a color which is a blend of the colors of the two lamps and which will more closely approach the color of the lamp closer to the reed which is vibrated.

Obviously, my color attachment can be mounted within any radio cabinet at very slight expense and will prove a highly attractive addition. The results of the installation will not only be entertaining and curiosity creating but will cultivate a fine sense of color as well as teach through indirection an association of color and sound which will be gratifying to artistic sensibilities.

While I have shown and described a plurality of lamps, if desired a single lamp or luminescent tube may be used and the color thereof changed or varied at will by varying the resistance.

Having thus described the invention, I claim:

1. A color attachment for radio receiving sets comprising colored lights, means for mounting the lights adjacent the sound-emitting element of a radio receiving set, and means whereby the lamps will be selectively energized through sympathetic vibrations.

2. A color attachment for radio receiving sets comprising a series of colored lights adapted to be arranged adjacent the sound-emitting element of the radio receiving set, and vibratory elements in circuit with the lights and arranged to be operated through sympathy with the vibrations of the sounds issuing from the receiving set.

3. A color attachment for radio receiving sets comprising a plurality of various colored lamps adapted to be arranged adjacent the sound-emitting element of the radio receiving set, and switches in circuit with the lamps and comprising a fixed member and a vibratory member each tuned to a different sound whereby to vibrate in sympathy with a corresponding sound wave issuing from the receiving set.

4. A color attachment for radio receiving sets comprising a plurality of various colored lamps, an electric circuit for illuminating the lamps, the lamps being arranged adjacent the sound-emitting element of the receiving set, a resistance coil in the lamp lighting circuit connected with one side of each lamp in the series, and a plurality of switch members each including a fixed member connected to the resistance coil, and a movable switch member connected to the opposite side of the electric circuit and consisting of a vibratory member tuned to vibrate in sympathy with a single sound wave issuing from the radio receiving set.

5. A color attachment for radio receiving sets comprising a plurality of electric lamps, means for mounting the lamps adjacent the sound-emitting element of a radio receiving set, and means whereby the lamps will be selectively energized through sympathetic vibrations, certain of said lamps being lighted brighter than others according to the tones of the sound-emitting element.

6. A color attachment for radio receiving sets comprising colored electric lamps, means for mounting the lamps adjacent the sound-emitting element of a radio receiving set, vibratory elements in circuit with the lamps and responsive to different tone variations of the sound-emitting element, certain of said vibratory elements being operated to cause some of the lamps to be brilliantly lighted, and other of the vibratory elements being operable to cause other of the lamps to be dimly lighted.

7. A color attachment for radio receiving sets comprising colored electric lamps adapted to be arranged adjacent the sound-emitting element of a radio receiving set, vibratory elements in circuit with the lamps and responsive to different tone variations of the sound-emitting element, certain of said vibratory elements being responsive to certain tones of the sound-producing element to cause some of the lamps to be brilliantly lighted, and other of the vibratory elements being responsive to other tones to cause the lighting of adjacent lamps and the blending of the colors thereof.

8. A color attachment for radio receiving sets comprising a plurality of vari-colored electric lamps adapted to be arranged adjacent the sound-emitting element of a radio receiving set, switches in circuit with the lamps and each comprising a fixed member and a vibratory member, the vibratory members being tuned to different tones of the sound-emitting element whereby to vibrate in sympathy with a corresponding sound wave issuing from the receiving set, certain of the vibratory members being actuated to cause some of the lamps to be brilliantly lighted and other of said vibratory members being actuated to cause the blending of the light of adjacent lamps.

9. The combination with a radio receiving set including a sound chamber and loud speaker, a partition disposed within the sound chamber and surrounding the loud speaker, a plurality of different colored electric lamps mounted on the partition, switches

disposed in advance of the loud speaker and included in the circuit with the lamps, each switch comprising a fixed member and a vibratory member, the vibratory members being tuned to different sounds whereby to vibrate in sympathy with a corresponding sound wave of the loud speaker.

10. The combination with a radio receiving set including a sound chamber and loud speaker, a partition disposed within the sound chamber and surrounding the loud speaker, said partition having openings formed therein, a plurality of different colored electric lamps secured to the front of the partition, a support arranged in front of the lamps, switches carried by the support and each comprising a fixed member and a vibratory member, electric conductors extending through the openings in the partition and operatively connected with the switches and lamps respectively, said vibratory elements being operable through sympathy with the vibrations of sounds issuing from the loud speaker to close the switches and light the lamps.

In testimony whereof I affix my signature.

RICHARD M. CRAIG. [L. S.]

CLINTON W. HOUGH

Projection System (1930)

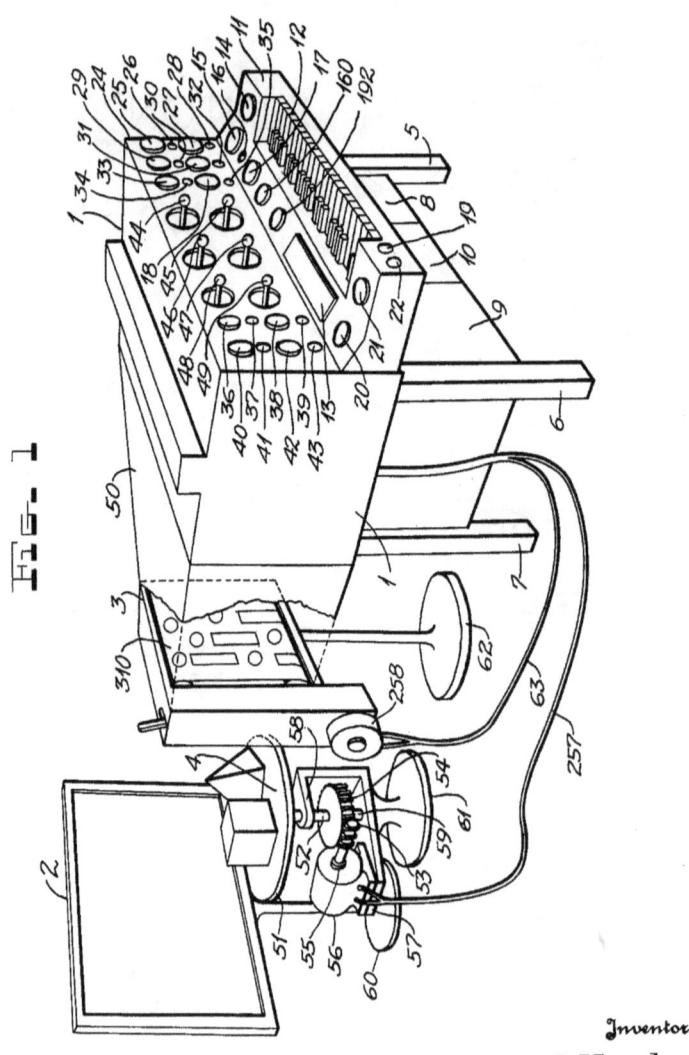

Dec. 13, 1932. C. W. HOUGH 1,891,216
SYSTEM FOR PROJECTING LIGHT IN VARIANT COLORS
Original Filed Jan. 24, 1930 9 Sheets-Sheet 2

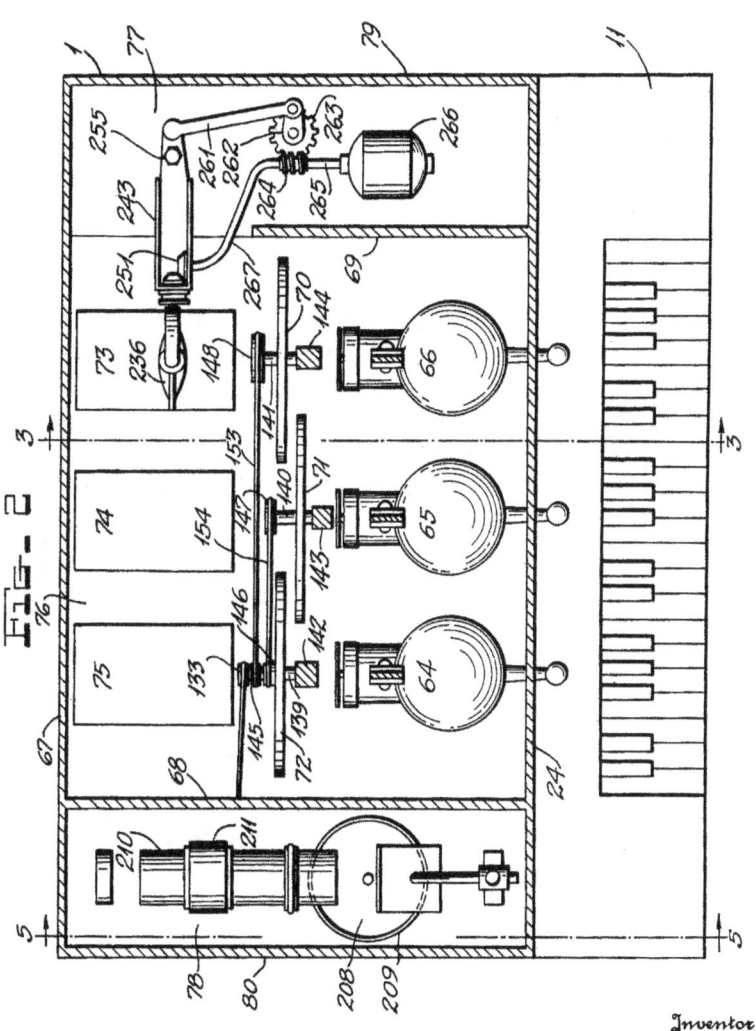

Inventor
Clinton W. Hough
By Wm. J. Herdman
Attorney

Dec. 13, 1932.   C. W. HOUGH   1,891,216
SYSTEM FOR PROJECTING LIGHT IN VARIANT COLORS
Original Filed Jan. 24, 1930   9 Sheets-Sheet 3

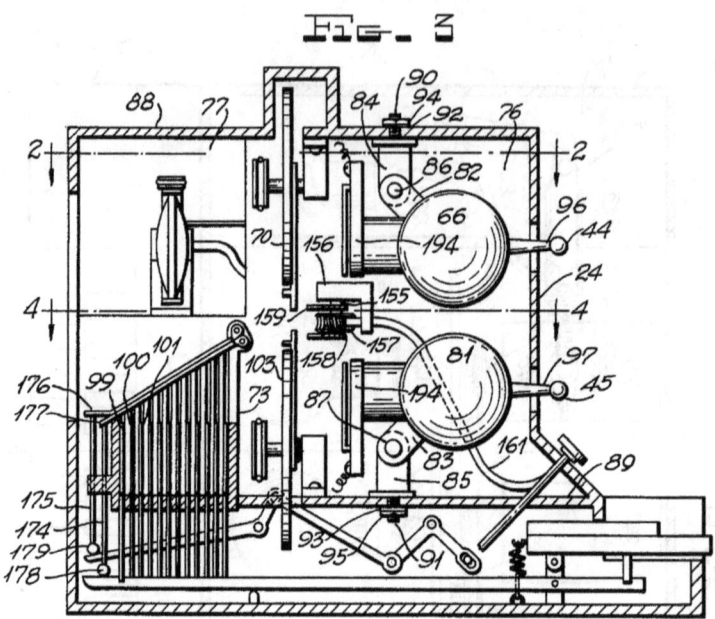

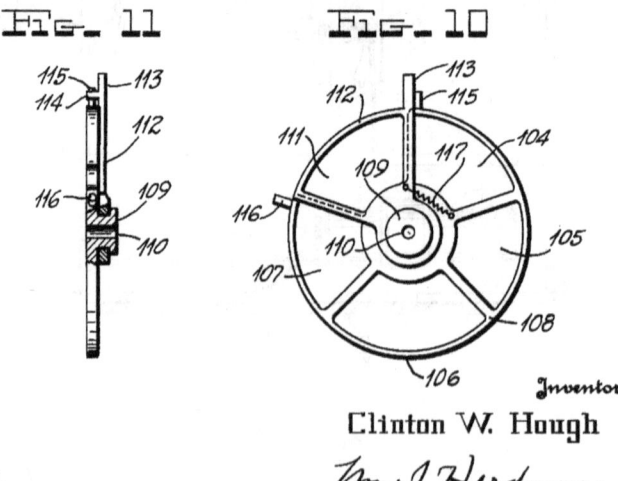

Inventor
Clinton W. Hough
By Wm. J. Herdman
Attorney

Dec. 13, 1932.   C. W. HOUGH   1,891,216
SYSTEM FOR PROJECTING LIGHT IN VARIANT COLORS
Original Filed Jan. 24, 1930   9 Sheets-Sheet 4

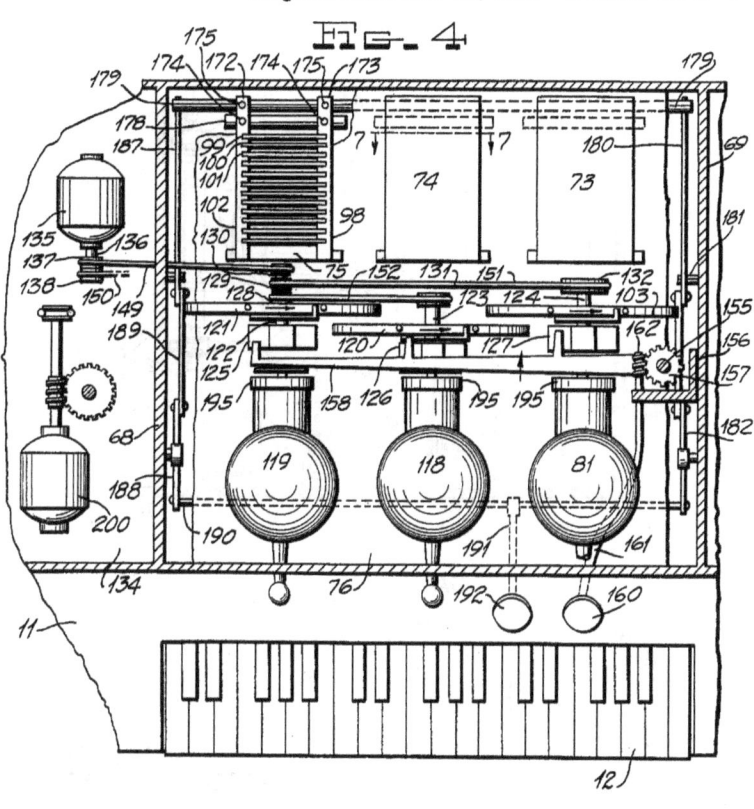

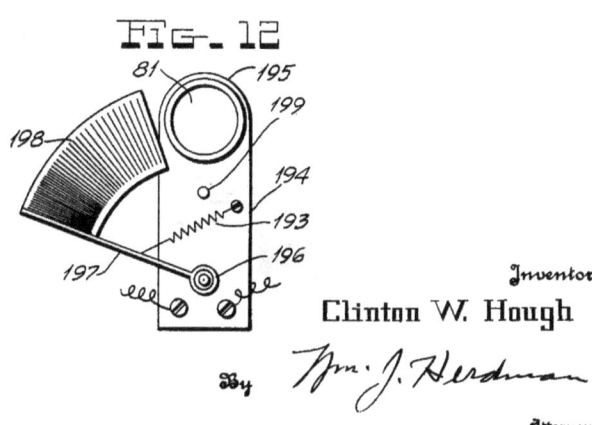

Inventor
Clinton W. Hough
By Wm. J. Herdman
Attorney

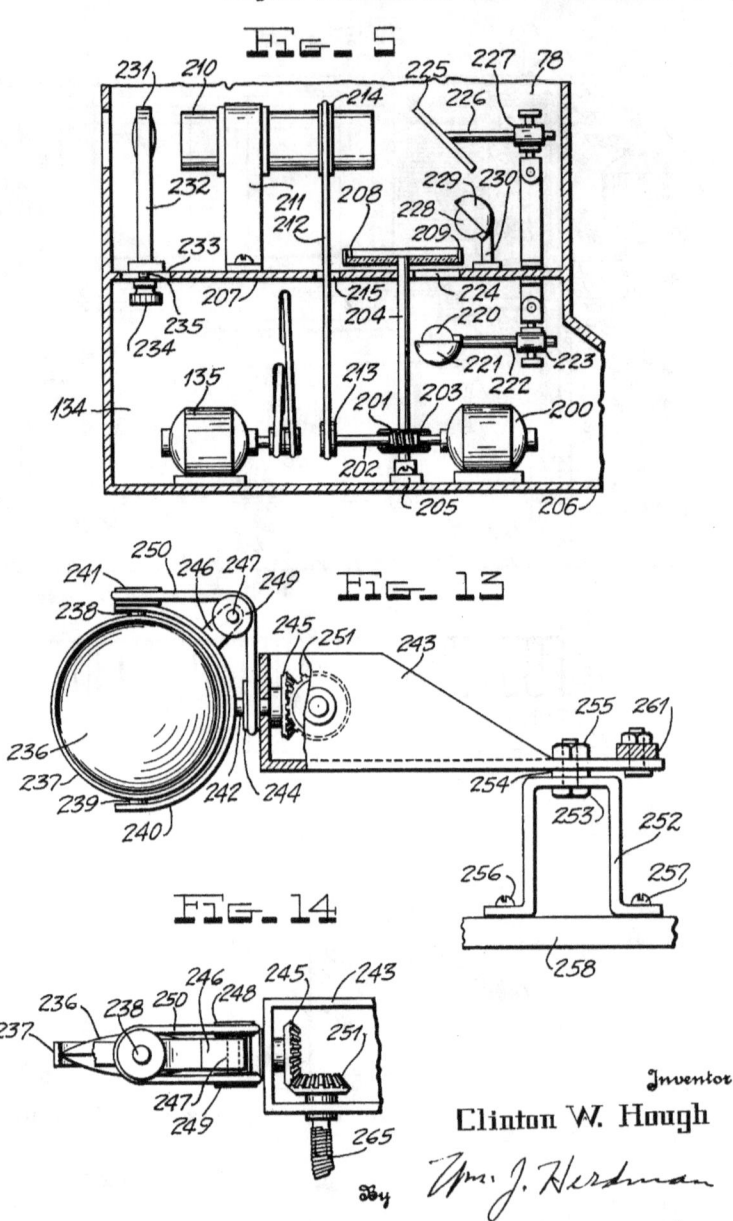

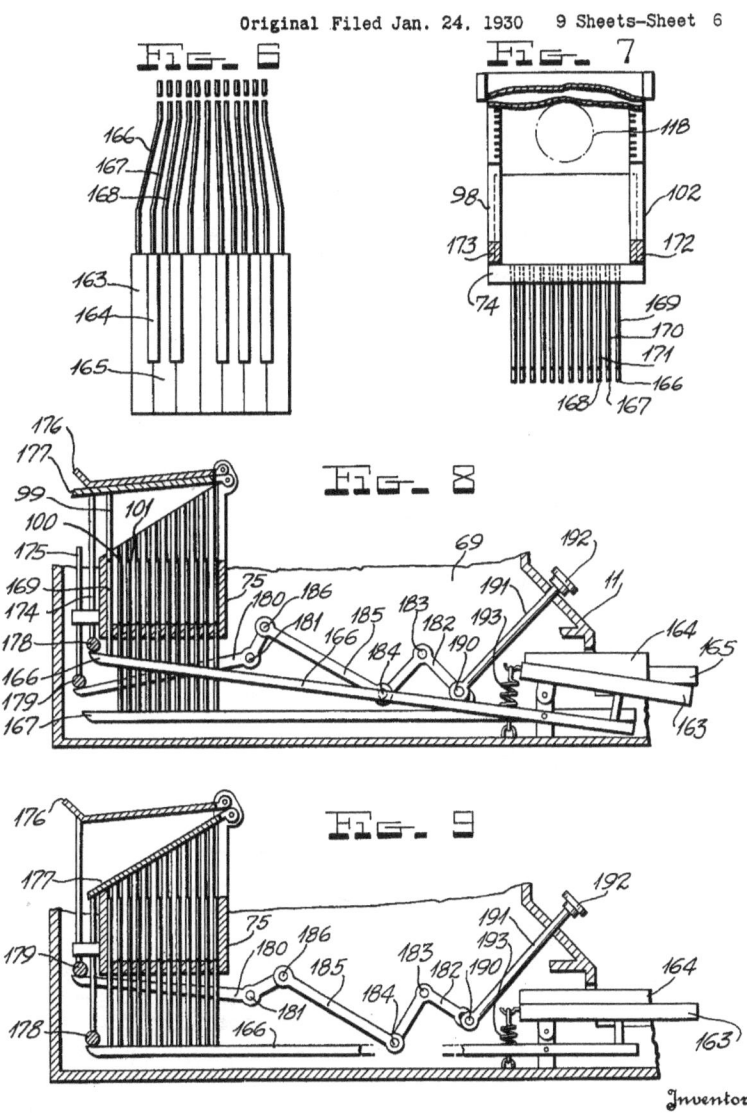

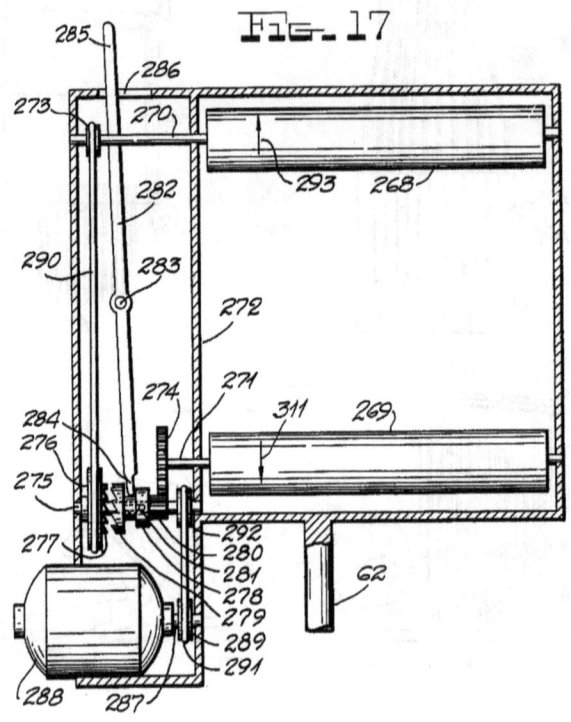
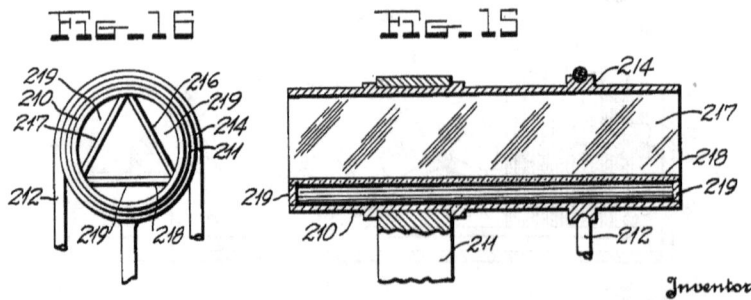

VISUAL MUSIC INSTRUMENT PATENTS (I) 181

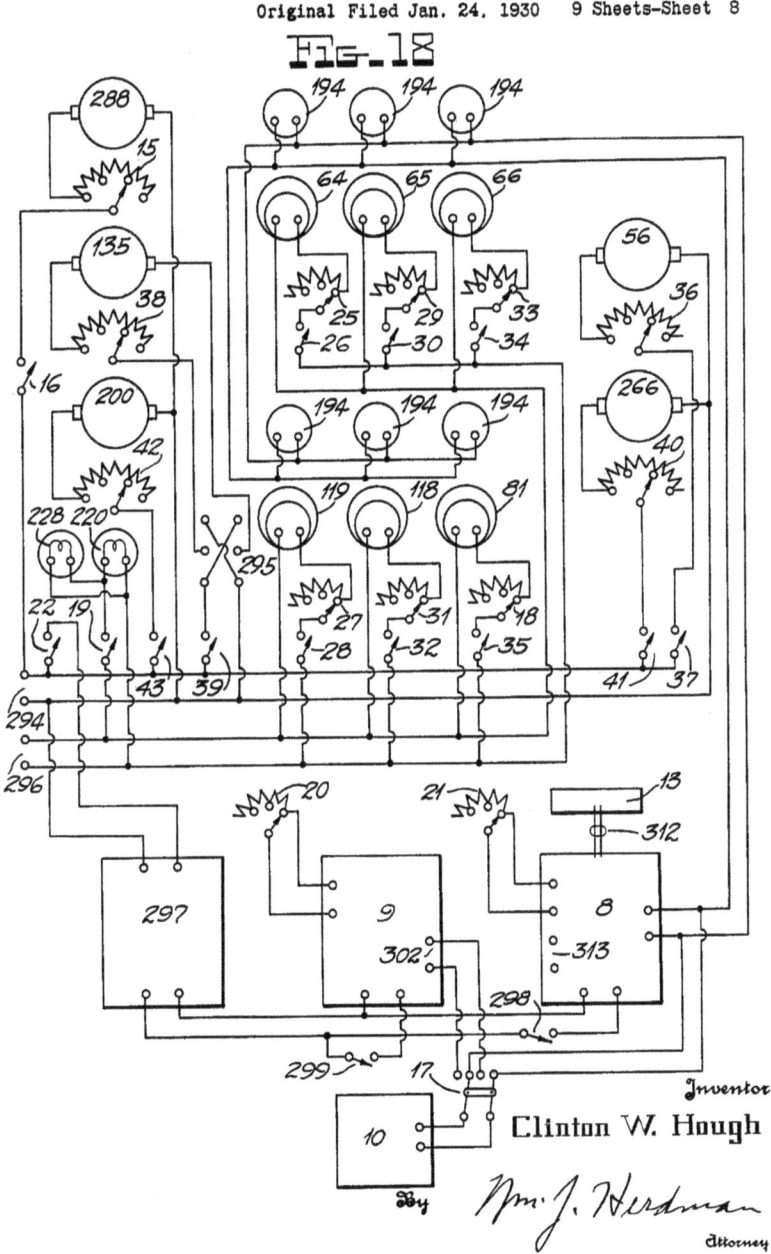

Dec. 13, 1932.   C. W. HOUGH   1,891,216
SYSTEM FOR PROJECTING LIGHT IN VARIANT COLORS
Original Filed Jan. 24, 1930   9 Sheets-Sheet 8

Inventor
Clinton W. Hough
By Wm. J. Herdman
Attorney

Dec. 13, 1932. C. W. HOUGH 1,891,216
SYSTEM FOR PROJECTING LIGHT IN VARIANT COLORS
Original Filed Jan. 24, 1930 9 Sheets—Sheet 9

Fig. 19

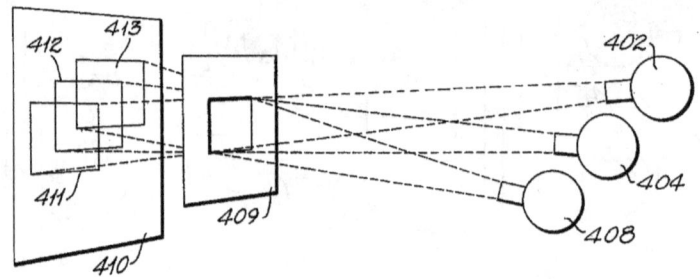

Fig. 20

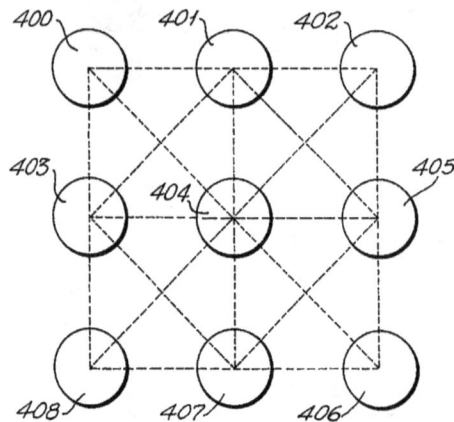

Inventor
Clinton W. Hough
By Wm. J. Herdman
Attorney

Patented Dec. 13, 1932   1,891,216

UNITED STATES PATENT OFFICE

CLINTON W. HOUGH, OF NEW YORK, N. Y., ASSIGNOR TO WIRED RADIO, INC., OF NEW YORK, N. Y., A CORPORATION OF DELAWARE

SYSTEM FOR PROJECTING LIGHT IN VARIANT COLORS

Original application filed January 24, 1930, Serial No. 423,004. Divided and this application filed April 30, 1931. Serial No. 533,940.

This is a division of my application Serial Number 423,004, filed January 24, 1930, entitled System for projecting light in variant colors, and specifically relates to a system for projecting light in variant colors under control of electrical energy at audio frequencies.

One of the objects of my invention consists in providing a projector system adapted to be manually controlled to project overlapping beams of light of variant colors upon a screen or upon stationary or moving objects to produce color and form combinations for educational and entertainment purposes.

Another object comprises, producing a projector system in which the colors of a plurality of overlapping beams of light are automatically varied to produce upon a screen or objects either stationary or moving a great variety of color combinations.

Another object contemplated by my invention consists in providing a projector system which may be both manually and automatically controlled to project overlapping beams of light of variant colors to produce through manual and automatic control a very great variety of color combinations.

Another object consists in providing a projector system in which overlapping beams of light of variant colors are transmitted through one or more pattern screens in motion or stationary to produce colored patterns of an infinite variety of color, form, and relative intensities, which may serve as designs for fabrics, wall paper, and the like.

A further object comprises producing a projector system wherein the intensities of a plurality of overlapping beams of light of variant colors are controlled in accordance with the tempo and volume of music or electrical currents of audio frequency.

I accomplish the above desirable features and effects by a novel projector system in which a plurality of light projectors are individually controlled, either manually or automatically, or in combination, to control the colors and intensity of the light projected by each of such projectors in such manner as to produce beams of variant colored light overlapping in one of a plurality, or in a plurality of planes to produce an infinite variety of color and form combinations and effects, and to give the effect of motion to the multicolored shadows of pattern screens or objects interposed between the projectors and a screen upon which the light is projected.

In the drawings accompanying and forming a part of the specification and in which like reference numerals designate corresponding parts throughout:

Fig. 1 is a perspective view of the general arrangement of the apparatus employed in an embodiment of my invention, comprising, a projection machine, a pattern machine, an object supporting turntable, and a screen.

Fig. 2 is a horizontal sectional view along the line 2—2 of Fig. 3 of the said projection machine.

Fig. 3 is a vertical sectional view along the line 3—3 of Fig. 2.

Fig. 4 is a partial horizontal sectional view along line 4—4 of Fig. 3.

Fig. 5 is a partial vertical sectional view along the line 5—5 of Fig. 2.

Fig. 6 is a top plan view of an arrangement of keys and key levers employed in the said projection machine.

Fig. 7 is a longitudinal sectional view along the line 7—7 of Fig. 4.

Fig. 8 is a vertical sectional view of an arrangement of certain mechanical elements of the said projection machine.

Fig. 9 is a vertical sectional view corresponding to the view shown in Fig. 8 but illustrating the same mechanical elements in different relative positions.

Fig. 10 is a front elevation of a rotary color screen employed in the before mentioned projection machine.

Fig. 11 is a side elevation and partial sectional view of the rotary color screen shown in Fig. 10.

Fig. 12 is a front elevation of a light intercepting device employed in the said projection machine.

Fig. 13 is an elevation of a distorting lens also employed in the said projecting machine.

Fig. 14 is a partial top plan view of the distorting lens shown in Fig. 13.

Fig. 15 is a longitudinal sectional view of a

kaleidoscopic tube employed in the said projection machine.

Fig. 16 is an end elevation of the kaleidoscopic tube shown in Fig. 15.

Fig. 17 is a sectional view of the pattern machine before mentioned and shown in Fig. 1.

Fig. 18 is a diagrammatic representation of the electrical circuits and electrical apparatus as used in the embodiment of my invention described herewith.

Fig. 19 is a schematic representation of a method of light projection employed in my invention.

Fig. 20 is a schematic representation of an arrangement of projectors which is a part of my invention.

Referring to the drawings in detail, and particularly to Fig. 1, in the housing 1, which is a part of the projection machine, means are disposed for projecting a plurality of variant colored beams of light on a screen 2. Interposed in the path of these beams there is provided a pattern machine 3, and an object supporting turntable 4, either, or both, of which may be used, at the option of the operator, to define and affect the variant colored light beams in a way such as to cause a great variety of different shapes and shadows to be cast upon the screen 2.

The housing 1 is mounted upon supporting members, there being four in all, one at each corner of the housing, three of these supporting members 5, 6, and 7 being shown in Fig. 1. Centrally disposed between these supporting members, and beneath the housing 1, are three compartments 8, 9, and 10, which form a component part of the projection machine, and which contain, respectively, a complete radio receiving set with auxiliary stages of audio frequency amplification, a complete reproducing phonograph of the type which employs an electrical pick-up device for reproducing sound recordings through the agency of a loud speaker, and a loud speaker which is common to both of the foregoing. These sound reproducing devices are provided for the purpose of furnishing sound effects, principally music, to accompany sympathetic visual effects which are cast upon the screen 2, and also for the purpose of altering these visual effects in accordance with the rhythm and intensity of the sound effects in a manner hereinafter described.

An extended part 11 of the housing 1 is provided on that side of the housing 1 which normally faces the operator. Positioned in this extended part 11 of the housing 1 is a keyboard 12 outwardly similar in construction to the keyboard to be found in an ordinary pianoforte. Positioned on the extended part 11 of the housing 1, and above the keyboard 12, is a remote control panel 13 for operating and controlling the radio broadcast receiver contained in the compartment 8. Also positioned upon the extended part 11 of the housing 1 are knobs 14, 15, 16, 17, 18, 19, 20, 21, 160 and 192 for operating controlling elements more fully described later. Additional knobs 25, 26, 27, 28, 29, 30, 31, 32, 33, 34, 35, 36, 37, 38, 39, 40, 41, 42, and 43 for operating controlling elements are positioned upon the panel 24. Extending through apertures in the panel 24 are knobs 44, 45, 46, 47, 48 and 49 which are associated with light beam projectors to be described later.

A shielding 50 is provided between the housing 1 and the pattern machine 3 and is constructed so as to completely enclose the path of the variant colored light beams and prevent extraneous light from being reflected from the pattern machine 3. Such extraneous reflected light has a tendency to dilate the irises of the observer's eye and is therefore undesirable.

The object supporting turntable 4 essentially comprises a platform 51, a shaft 52, a worm 53, a worm gear 54, a shaft 55, a driving motor 56, and a mounting structure 57. The platform 51 is rigidly secured to one end of the shaft 52 as shown. The shaft 52 is mounted in a bearing member 58 of the mounting structure 57, and also in a depression 59 in the mounting structure 57 so that the shaft 52 is free to rotate therein. The worm gear 54 is rigidly secured to the shaft 52 in a position to engage with the worm 53 which is rigidly mounted upon the shaft 55 extending from the driving motor 56. The driving motor 56 is secured to the mounting structure 57. Rotation of the shaft 55 will cause the worm 53 to rotate the shaft 52 by means of the worm gear 54, whereby the platform 51 will be caused to rotate. Objects placed upon the platform 51, in the path of the variant colored light beams, will revolve with the said platform and will therefore intercept the light beams at variant angles and cause corresponding changes in the visual effects which are cast upon the screen 2.

The screen 2 is substantially a plane surface suitable for showing light projections to best advantage, and is similar to screens employed in cinematographic projection. Supporting standards 60, 61, and 62 are provided for the screen 2, the object supporting turntable 4, and the pattern machine 3, respectively. Cables 63 and 257 are provided between the housing 1 and a driving motor 258 in the pattern machine 3, and between the housing 1 and the driving motor 56 in the object supporting turntable 4, respectively, so that the electrical circuits of the same may be controlled from the housing 1.

In Fig. 2, disposed within a compartment 76 enclosed by four panels 67, 68, 69, and 24, of the housing 1, are three rows of projectors positioned in parallel planes; projectors 66,

65, and 64 being the top projectors of each row, respectively, there being six projectors in all. However, it is intended in my invention that at least nine projectors be provided and arranged as hereinafter described, three of the projectors being here omitted for simplicity of description. These projectors are substantially devices for providing a source of relatively strong white light, from an electric current, and projecting the same in directed beams to points distant from the source. Positioned in front of projectors 66, 65, and 64 are rotary color screens 70, 71, and 72, respectively, which revolve in the path of the light beam from each projector. Also disposed within the compartment 76 are three housings 73, 74, and 75 associated with manually operated color screens.

In compartment 77, enclosed by the panels 67, 69, 24, and 79, are positioned means for actuating a distorting lens, more fully described later.

In compartment 78, enclosed by the panels 67, 68, 24, and 80, are positioned members associated with a kaleidoscopic projection arrangement more fully described later.

In Fig. 3, disposed within the compartment 76 are two projectors 66 and 81 which are the end projectors, respectively, of two rows of projectors in parallel planes. The members 82 and 83, which are extended parts of projectors 66 and 81, respectively, are forked and pivotally mounted upon members 84 and 85 by means of rivets 86 and 87, in a manner such that there will always be sufficient tension between the members 82 and 84, and the members 83 and 85, to hold the same, by friction, in any relative position in which they may be set. (See Fig. 2.) The members 84 and 85 are also pivotally secured to the panels 88 and 89, by means of studs 90 and 91, washers 92 and 93, and nuts 94 and 95, respectively, so that the members 84 and 85 may be partially rotated in parallel planes perpendicular to the plane of movement of the members 82 and 83. Such an arrangement, permitting adjustment of the projectors and corresponding adjustment of the direction of the light beams, is provided for each projector. Adjusting rods 96 and 97 are rigidly secured to the projectors 66 and 81, respectively, and have knobs 44 and 45 secured to their outward extremities. These adjusting rods 96 and 97 extend through apertures in the panel 24 so that the projectors may be adjusted, for direction of beam projection, from without the housing 1. Similar adjusting rods are provided for each projector.

Positioned in front of projector 81, in Fig. 3, and intercepting the path of the light beam projected from the same, is a housing 73 shown in section, which is one of three similar housings 73, 74, and 75, and which contains an arrangement of manually controlled color screens. The housing 73 is mounted in an aperture in the panel 89, so that the bottom of the housing 73 is open to mechanical elements beneath the panel 89. Viewed from the top in Fig. 4, it will be seen that the housing 73 has two side members 98 and 102 which are slotted, as shown, to accommodate a series of color screens 99, 100, and 101, similar mechanical elements being associated with each of the three housings 73, 74, and 75, more fully described later.

In Fig. 3, positioned in front of projectors 66 and 81, are rotary color screens 70 and 103, respectively. These rotary color screens are substantially disks comprising sectors of transparent material, such as glass, which have been variantly colored to act as filters which will, in effect, pass only light of the same color as the filter. When a beam of white light is projected through one of the colored sectors of the rotary color screen, and the rotary color screen is rotated in a manner such that successive colored sectors will intercept the light beam, the light beam, upon passing through the colored sectors, will be substantially of a series of colors corresponding to those in the rotary color screen. In Fig. 10, the variantly colored sectors 104, 105, 106, and 107, of the rotary color screen 103, are radially positioned about the hub 109 of a circular mounting frame 108. A hole 110 is provided in the center of the hub 109 for mounting upon a shaft. An additional colored sector 111 is positioned in a mounting sector 112 which is adapted to be rotated about an annular channel in the periphery of the hub 109 as shown in Fig. 11. An arm 114 is provided to one side of the member 113 which is an extension of the mounting sector 112, and will describe, in rotation upon the hub 109, a circular path concentric with the hub 109. However, the mounting sector 112 is restricted in its movement by two pins 115 and 116 which are positioned upon the periphery of the mounting frame 108, on either side of the arm 114, and engage therewith. A small helical tension spring 117 is provided between the mounting sector 112 and the mounting frame 108 and normally holds the mounting sector 112 in a position such that the arm 114 is in engagement with stop pin 115. If the mounting frame 108 is rotated clockwise, the mounting sector 112, will also be rotated in the same direction. A stopping member, if moved into the path of the projection 113 so that it comes into engagement therewith as the same is rotated, will stop mounting sector 112, but, due to the construction of the mounting sector 112 with reference to the hub 109, will permit the mounting frame 108 to continue to rotate until the arm 114 comes into engagement with the stop pin 116 when the mounting frame 108 will also come to a stop. However, the mounting sector 112 will now be in a position over the colored sector 107, and will be superimposed thereon, whereas there will be an opening in the mounting frame 108, indicated by the dotted lines in Fig. 10, and consequently, a beam of white light which is directed through this opening will not be intercepted by a color sector and will show white. All of the rotary color screens employed are of the same construction.

In Fig. 4, disposed within the compartment 76 are three projectors 81, 118, and 119, which are the bottom projectors of three rows of projectors in parallel planes, respectively, of which the projectors 66, 65, and 64, in Fig. 2, are the top projectors. Positioned in front of projectors 119, 118, and 81, are rotary color screens 121, 120, and 103, respectively. Shafts 122, 123, and 124, upon which the rotary color screens 121, 120, and 103, are rigidly mounted, are positioned in bearing members 125, 126, and 127, respectively, and are free to rotate therein. Rigidly mounted upon the shaft 122 are three pulley wheels 128, 129, 130, of the same size. A pulley wheel 131, which is somewhat larger in diameter than pulley wheels 128, 129, and 130, is rigidly mounted upon the shaft 123. Another pulley wheel 132, somewhat larger in diameter than pulley wheel 131, is rigidly mounted upon shaft 124. The rotary color screens 72, 71, and 70, shown in Fig. 2, have shafts 139, 140, 141, bearing mountings 142, 143, 144, and pulleys 145 and 146, 147, and 148, respectively, similarly associated therewith; pulley wheel 133, in Fig. 2, corresponding to pulley wheel 130 in Fig. 4. Positioned in compartment 134, which is disposed directly beneath compartment 78, shown in Fig. 4, is a driving motor 135. Rigidly mounted upon the shaft 136 extending from the driving motor 135, are two pulley wheels 137 and 138. Belts 149, 150, 151, 152, 153, 154 are provided between the pulleys 137 and 130, 138 and 133, 129 and 132, 128 and 131, 145 and 148, 146 and 147, respectively. These belts are preferably composed of helically wound wire which, in transmitting power from one pulley to another, will frictionally engage the peripheral channel of the pulley only when the coefficient of friction of the belt is greater than the inertia of the pulley. Rotation of pulley wheels 137 and 138 by the driving motor 135 will cause a corresponding rotation of the pulley wheels 130 and 133, respectively, by means of the belts 149 and 150. Pulley wheels 129 and 128, and pulley wheels 145 and 146, being rigidly mounted on the same shafts which carry pulley wheels 130 and 133, respectively, will also rotate so as to cause pulley wheels 132 and 131, and pulley wheels 148 and 147, to rotate by means of the belts 151 and 152, and 153 and 154, respectively. Such rotation of the pulley wheels mounted upon the shafts 122, 123, 124, 139, 140, and 141 will cause a corresponding rotation of their respective rotary color screens, so that the color sectors of the same will intercept the light beams from their associated projectors and cause a sequence of variant colored light beams to be projected. However, difference in the size of the pulley wheels associated with the rotary color screens will cause a variation in the speed at which they will rotate, and a corresponding variation in the time which each rotary color screen will require for one rotation in the path of the light beams.

A shaft 155, in Fig. 3, is mounted in the bearing member 156 and is free to rotate therein. Rigidly secured to the shaft 155 is a worm gear 157 (see Fig. 4). Two stopping arms 158 and 159 are rigidly secured to the shaft 155 on either side of the worm gear 157 and positioned so that partial rotation of the shaft 155 will bring the stopping arms 158 and 159 into engagement with the member 113 of the mounting sector 112 associated with each of the rotary color screens 70, 71, 72, 103, 120, and 121 as the same are rotated. However, the stopping arms 158 and 159 are so shaped that upon being partially rotated by the shaft 155, they will come into engagement first, with members 113 associated with rotary color screens 71 and 120, second, with members 113 associated with rotary color screens 70 and 103, and third, with members 113 associated with rotary color screens 72 and 121. A knob 160, in Fig. 4, mounted in the extended part 11 of the housing 1 so that it is free to rotate therein, is coupled to a flexible shaft 161 which is in turn coupled to an extended part of a worm 162 which is mounted in the bearing member 156 so that it is free to rotate therein. Rotation of the knob 160 will cause the worm 162 to rotate, by means of the flexible shaft 161, and the worm 162, being in engagement with the worm gear 157, will cause the same to move the stopping arms 158 and 159 in or out of engagement with the members 113 associated with the rotary color screens as the same are rotated.

Inasmuch as the stopping arm 158 is positioned so that it is accessible to the top of rotary color screens 103, 120 and 121, and the stopping arm 159 is positioned so that it is accessible to the bottom of rotary color screen 70, 71, and 72, it is evident that the members 113 (see Fig. 10) associated with the said rotary color screens will be accessible for engagement with the stopping members 158 and 159 in the same relative positions.

If, while the rotary color screens are being normally rotated in a clock-wise direction by the driving motor 135 and periodically changing the color of light beams from their respective projectors, it is desired to project beams of substantially white light, the knob

160 is rotated. Such rotation of the knob 160 will cause the stopping arms 158 and 159 to be slowly moved so that they will come into engagement with first, the members 113 associated with the rotary color screens 70 and 103, second, with members 113 associated with the rotary color screens 71 and 120, and third, with the members 113 associated with the rotary color screens 72 and 121, as the same are rotated. Such engagement of the members 113 associated with the said rotary color screens will cause the mounting sectors 112, associated with each of the said rotary color screens, and upon which the members 113 are positioned, to stop rotating. As these sector mountings 112 are stopped, the rotary color screens will also be stopped, in the order before mentioned, as the stop pins 116 associated with each rotary color screen are rotated into engagement with the arms 114 associated with the now stationary mounting sectors 112, and an opening in each color screen, shown in Fig. 10, by dotted lines, will be presented before each projector, while light beams originating from each projector will pass through without being intercepted by a color sector. When the rotary color screens are stopped, the belts, which normally frictionally engage with the pulleys associated with the color screens, will slip, but, due to the order in which the rotary color screens are stopped, the shafts 139 and 122 and associated pulleys, which intermediately drive the rotary color screens 70, 71, 103, and 120, will be the last to be stopped and will consequently serve as driving means for the rotary color screens 70, 71, 103, and 120, until they are stopped. When, as the stopping arms 158 and 159 finally stop the rotation of the rotary color screens 72 and 121 as above described, the shafts 139 and 122 and associated pulleys will be brought to rest and the belts 149 and 150 will slip thereon as they are driven by the driving motor 135. The driving motor 135 may then be shut down, if desired, as hereinafter provided for. Starting the motor 135, and bringing the arms 158 and 159 out of engagement with the members 113 associated with the rotary color screens, by rotating the knob 160, will cause the rotary color screens to resume their normal rotation in the path of the projectors.

In Fig. 6, the keys 163, 164, and 165, of a group which forms a part of the keyboard 12, are shown as they are positioned with reference to their respective key levers 166, 167, and 168. The entire keyboard 12, which is of the commonly used pianoforte type, is arranged into three groups of twelve keys corresponding to the twelve keys comprising an octave on the pianoforte, each group being arranged similarly to Fig. 6 so that the twelve keys of each group have twelve corresponding key levers for actuating, respectively, mechanical elements, hereinafter described, associated with each of the color screen housings 73, 74, and 75.

In Fig. 7, a series of push rods 169, 170, and 171, are slidably positioned in the bottom of the housing 75, which is similar in construction to housing 73 in Fig. 3, so that they transmit motion from the key levers 166, 167, and 168 to corresponding color screens slidably positioned in slots in the side members 98 and 102 of the housing 75. These color screens are substantially flat rectangular shaped pieces of transparent material, such as glass, which have been variantly colored to act as filters which will, in effect, pass only light of the same color as the filter.

In Fig. 8, it will be seen that the color screens 99, 100, and 101, are part of a series of color screens in the housing 75. These color screens are slidably positioned in the housing 75 in a manner such that, when actuated by their respective key levers by means of their corresponding push rods, they will be raised into a position intercepting the path of the light beam from their associated projector, as illustrated in Fig. 8, by color screen 99 which is shown in such raised position. The push rod 169, the key lever 166, and the key 163, which are associated with the color screen 99, are shown in their actuated position. When any one of the group of keys of the keyboard 12 which are associated with the housing 75, is depressed, a corresponding color screen will be raised so as to intercept the light beam from its associated projector and affect the color of the said beam. The housings 73, 74, and 75 are all similar in construction, each housing containing twelve color screens and associated mechanical elements to be operated by the three groups, or octaves, of keys of the keyboard 12, in a manner such as to intercept the light beams from the three projectors 119, 118, and 81, respectively. It is evident, then, that the light beams projected from the projectors 119, 118, and 81 will be intercepted by their respective rotary color screens and, at the option of the operator, by one or more of the series of manually operated color screens disposed in front of each of the said projectors.

In Fig. 3, a shutter 176 and a color screen 177, which are associated with each color screen housing, are shown pivotally mounted to the top of the housing 73 between the side members 98 and 102, which are a part of each color screen housing. The shutter 176 is substantially a flat rectangular shaped piece of an opaque material, such as sheet metal, while the color screen 177 is a flat rectangular shaped piece of transparent material, such as glass, which has been colored to act as a filter, which will, in effect, pass only light of the same color as the filter. (See Fig. 4.) The shutter 176 and the color screen 177 are mounted in a manner such that in a normal position at rest upon the top surface of the housing 73, they will intercept the path of the light beam from the associated projector.

In Fig. 4, positioned in front of the housing 75, and on the side members 98 and 102, are two bearing members 172 and 173, respectively. Slidably positioned in the bearing members 172 and 173 are push rods 174 and 175, respectively. Referring to Fig. 3, it will be seen that the push rods 175 and 174 are positioned adjacent to the projecting ends of the shutter 176 and the color screen 177, respectively. Similar bearing members and push rods are associated with each of the three color screen housings 73, 74, and 75. Referring to Fig. 8, it will be seen that the push rod 174, which is positioned adjacent to the color screen 177, when actuated so as to be moved into an upward position, as shown, will correspondingly move the color screen 177 and the shutter 176 which is pivotally mounted superimposed upon the color screen 177, so that they will be in a position such that they will not intercept the path of the light beam from the associated projector. Rigidly secured to the lower extremity of the push rods 174 associated with each of the color screen housings, and beneath the bearing members 172 and 173 are the transverse lift rods 178, which, upon being moved upwardly, will correspondingly move the two push rods 174 associated with each of the color screen housings 73, 74, and 75. Extending beneath the transverse lift rods 178, and adjacent thereto, are the projecting ends of the key levers, of which the key levers 166 and 167 form a part of a group of key levers associated with the housing 75 in Fig. 8. As a transverse lift rod 178 is similarly associated with each of the housings 73, 74, and 75, it is evident then, that if any one, or more, of the keys of the keyboard 12, which are associated in groups of twelve keys with their respective color screen housings, be depressed, the transverse lift rod corresponding to the color screen housing with which the key depressed is associated will be moved upwardly with a corresponding movement of the shutter 176 and the color screen 177 associated therewith. It is evident then, that when a color screen disposed within any particular housing, such as color screen 99 in Fig. 8, be raised upwardly by a key lever, such as key lever 166, by means of the depressing of a key, such as key 163, that the shutter 176 and the color screen 177 will also be simultaneously raised into an upward position so that the same will not interfere with the movement of the said color screen 99, and will not intercept the path of the light beam from the associated projector.

Rigidly secured to the lower extremity of the push rods 175, associated with each of the housings 73, 74, and 75, is a transverse lift rod 179 which extends across the front of the compartment 76, as shown in Fig. 4, and will, upon being moved upwardly, correspondingly move all of the push rods 175 simultaneously. In Fig. 8, extending beneath the transverse lift rod 179, and adjacent thereto, is the projecting end of an arm 180 pivotally mounted upon the panel 69, by means of the pivot member 181, so that, upon being moved, it will raise the transverse lift rod 179. Another arm 182 is pivotally mounted upon the panel 69, by means of the pivot members 183, as shown. One side of the arm 182 is pivotally secured, by means of a coupling pin 184, to a coupling link 185, which is pivotally secured to one part of the arm 180 by means of the coupling pin 186. A similar arrangement of mechanical elements is positioned on panel 68, in Fig. 4; arm 187, arm 188, and coupling link 189 corresponding to arm 180, arm 182, and coupling link 185, respectively. Disposed between the arm 182 and the arm 188, and pivotally secured to both, is a coupling rod 190 which, when moved, will cause the arms 182 and 188 to move accordingly. Rigidly secured to the coupling rod 190, at a point between the projectors 118 and 81, is a rod 191 which extends through the extended part 11 of the housing 1, in which it is slidably positioned, and terminates in a knob 192. In Fig. 8, these mechanical elements are shown in a normal unactuated position. When the knob 192 and the rod 191 are pulled into an extended position, the coupling rod 190 will be correspondingly moved so as to make the intermediate mechanical elements move the transverse lift rod 179 into an upward position thereby raising the shutters 176 associated with each of the color screen housings as shown in Fig. 9. It is therefore evident that when the transverse lift rod 179 has raised all of the shutters 176, the color screens 177 will remain in a normal position upon the top of the color screen housings, as shown, and intercept the path of the light beams from the associated projectors. However, when any of the colors screens 99, 100, 101, which are disposed within the housings 73, 74, and 75 are raised by their respective key levers, the associated color screens 177 will also be simultaneously raised by the transverse lift rods 178, which are adjacent to the said key levers, so that the said color screens 177 will not interfere with the movement of the color screens 99, 100, and 101. The rod 191 and associated mechanical elements are arranged so that when the knob 192 is extended, the said mechanical elements will remain in the position in which they are set, it being necessary to manually depress the knob 192 to return them to a normal position and lower the shutters 176. The manual key-levers 166, 167, and 168, and associated members will return to their normal positions by gravity, and the keys 163, 164, and 165 will return to their normal positions through tensions of associated helical springs indicated by the spring 193 in Fig. 8 and Fig. 9.

It will now be evident that, in addition to the color changes obtainable by rotating the rotary color screens 103, 120, and 121 in the path of the light beams from the projectors 81, 118, and 119, other color changes are to be obtained by using the keyboard 12 to manipulate the manually controlled color screens contained in the housings 73, 74, and 75. While the rotary color screens 103, 120, and 121, in Fig. 4, are rotating in the path of the light beams from the said projectors and producing a sequence of color changes, it will usually be desirable to have the knob 192 in an extended position so that the intermediate mechanical elements will cause the transverse lift rod 179 to raise the shutters 176 (see Fig. 9) associated with the manually operated color screen housings, so that the light beams may pass through the color screen housings. The color screens 177, still being in a position to intercept the light beams, will filter the said beams in accordance with the colors of the said screens. The three color screens 177, associated with the three color screen housings 73, 74, and 75, are colored, respectively, light red, green, and blue-violet, which, being the three primary colors, will change the light beams accordingly, and, when the said light beams are originally white, will change them in a manner such that, upon convergence after leaving the said color screens, they will again produce white light. The manually operated color screens 99, 100, and 101 may be arranged, with reference to colors, in spectrum sequence, or any other colors or order of colors which may be desired.

Adjustment of rheostats controlling the electric current supply to the respective projectors, more fully described later, will cause a corresponding change in the intensities of the respective component primary colors of the said converged white light. Consequently, such adjustment can be utilized to bring the said component primary colors to proper intensities to produce the converging white light, or can be utilized to disproportion the intensities of the component primary colors, so that effects other than pure white light will be produced.

However, it is evident that when the rotary color screens are revolving in the path of the light beams between the said projectors and the manual color screens, the beams of light reaching the manually operated color screens will not be white, due to the filtering effect of the colored sectors of the rotary color screens. The light beams will therefore be additionally filtered, and of a great variety and complexity of colors, which is desirable for certain purposes. However, for certain other purposes, to project white light through the manually operated color screen housings it will be necessary to stop the rotation of the associated rotary color screens and open the movable mounting sectors 112, associated with the same, so that the white light beams can pass through the said rotary color screens without being intercepted thereby. The rotary color screens are stopped and their associated mounting sectors 112 opened by rotating the knob 160, in Fig. 4, as before described.

At any time while light beams are being projected through the manually operated color screen housings, whether intercepted by rotary color screens or not, the keyboard 12 may be used to manipulate the manually operated color screens so that they intercept the said light beams thereby producing other and additional color effects which are entirely manually controlled by the operator.

It is intended in my invention that similar manually controlled color screens, and associated housings and mechanical elements, be provided for all of the projectors, the same being here omitted for simplicity of description.

Referring to Fig. 12, a housing 194 is suspended to a projector by means of an encircling band 195. Mounted upon a shaft 196 extending from the housing 194, is an arm 197. Mounted upon the arm 197 is a sector 198 composed of a transparent material, such as glass, upon which opaque radial lines, of varying spacing, have been ruled. Positioned between the housing 194 and the arm 197, and connecting the same, is a small helically wound tension spring 193 which normally holds the arm 197 against the pin 199 in the housing 194 so that the part of the sector 198 whereon the opaque lines are ruled closest will intercept the path of the light beam from the projector 81. Disposed within the housing 194 are means, such as a moving coil ammeter or measuring instrument, for exerting a torque upon the shaft 196 in accordance with the intensity and rhythm of an alternating electric current at audio frequencies. Relative high intensities of the current will move the arm 197 in a manner such that the sector 198 will be entirely out of the path of the projected light beam, or will intercept it only at that end of the sector where the opaque lines are more widely spaced; whereas, relatively low intensities will only slightly move the arm 197, and the sector 198 will intercept the projector light beam where the opaque lines are closely spaced. Inasmuch as the opaque lines on the sector 198 cut off the light which they intercept, it is evident that the most light will be cut off where the opaque lines are more closely spaced. Consequently, the intensity of the light beam will vary in proportion to the intensity of the current controlling the movement of the sector 198. Rhythmic modulations of the said current will produce corresponding oscillations of the sector 198. A device similar to the foregoing is mounted upon each projector, so that all of the light beams will be affected in the manner described. (See Fig. 3).

In Fig. 5, disposed within compartments 78 and 134 is apparatus comprising a kaleidoscopic projection arrangement. A driving motor 200, in the compartment 134, is positioned so that a worm 201, rigidly mounted on the shaft 202 extending from the driving motor 200, engages a worm gear 203. The worm gear 203 is rigidly mounted upon a shaft 204. The shaft 204 is mounted in a bearing 205 situated on the bottom panel 206 of the compartment 134, and extends through the bottom panel 207 of the compartment 78, and is free to rotate therein. A turntable, comprising, a platform 208 composed of a transparent material, such as glass, and a peripheral retaining ring 209, is rigidly mounted upon the shaft 204. (See Fig. 2.) Positioned above the platform 208, in the compartment 78, is a kaleidoscopic tube 210 mounted in the supporting member 211 and free to rotate therein. A belt 212 extends from a pulley 213 rigidly mounted upon the shaft 202, through an aperture 215 in the panel 207 to a pulley 214 integral with the kaleidoscopic tube 210. Rotation of the shaft 202 by the driving motor 200 will cause a corresponding rotation of the transparent platform 208 and the kaleidoscopic tube 210.

In Fig. 15 and Fig. 16, the said kaleidoscopic tube is shown in more detail. Disposed within the tube 210 are three rectangular shaped reflecting mirrors 216, 217, and 218 arranged in the form of an elongated hollow prism, and mounted upon members 219, as shown, with their reflecting surfaces turned towards the center of the tube 210. Both ends of the prism shaped arrangement of mirrors are open so that light reflected from variant shaped objects and directed through the tube will be reflected from more than one side and give an effect of geometrical patterns. Such an arrangement is commonly used in ordinary kaleidoscopes.

Referring again to Fig. 5, an electric lamp 220 and reflector 221 are rigidly secured to a rod 222 which is mounted in a universal mounting 223 which can be adjusted in several planes. The said electric lamp 220 and reflector 221 are positioned so that light rays from the electric lamp 220 will be directed through an aperture 224 in the panel 207, and through the transparent platform 208. A reflecting mirror 225 is rigidly secured to a rod 226 mounted in a universal mounting 227 which can be adjusted in several planes. The reflecting mirror 225, intercepting the path of the light directed through the transparent platform 208 at an angle of approximately forty-five degrees, will reflect the same through the kaleidoscopic tube 210 which is positioned approximately ninety degrees from the axis of the path of the light directed through the transparent platform 208. An auxiliary electric lamp 228 and reflector 229 are mounted upon the mounting 230 and positioned so that the surface of the transparent platform 208 will be illuminated. It is evident, then, that if small objects, such as fragments of colored glass, or colored beads, be placed upon the transparent platform 208, their illuminated images will be reflected through the kaleidoscopic tube 210, and, when the transparent platform 208 and the kaleidoscopic tube 210 are rotated by the driving motor 200, will form a great variety of variant shaped and variant colored moving geometric patterns. A bi-convex lens 231 is mounted in the member 232, which is positioned in front of the kaleidoscopic tube 210 so that the images reflected through the same can be projected upon the screen 2 situated some distance away. A stud 235, which is integral with the member 232, extends through an elongated hole 233 in the panel 207. A hand nut 234 is provided for the stud 235 so that the member 232 can be secured in any position in the elongated hole 233, and the lens 231 correspondingly focused with reference to the kaleidoscopic tube 210 and the screen 2.

In Fig. 13 and Fig. 14, a bi-convex lens 236 is positioned in a mounting ring 237. The mounting ring is pivotally mounted, by means of the pivot members 238 and 239, in a semi-circular yoke 240, the pivot member 238 extending through the yoke 240 and terminating in a pulley wheel 241 to which it is rigidly secured. Rotation of the pulley wheel 241 will cause a corresponding rotation of the mounting ring 237 and lens 236 with reference to the yoke 240. The yoke 240 is rigidly secured to a spindle 242 which extends through a pulley wheel 244 and a frame 243, and is free to rotate therein. The pulley wheel 244 is rigidly secured to the frame 243. Rigidly secured to the spindle 242 is a miter gear 245, positioned as shown. Mounted upon the yoke 240, midway between the pulley wheels 241 and 244 is a bearing block 246 in which a spindle 247 is rigidly secured. Mounted upon the spindle 247, and free to independently rotate thereon, are two idler pulley wheels 248 and 249. A belt 250 is provided between the pulley wheels 241 and 244 over the idler pulley wheels 248 and 249. When the yoke 240 is turned upon the axes of the spindle 242, the pulley wheel 244, being secured to the frame 243, will remain stationary and hold the belt 250 in frictional engagement therewith, whereby the pulley wheel 241 will be made to revolve once for every revolution of the spindle 240. Consequently, the lens 236 will be simultaneously rotated about two axes which intersect at right angles. A miter gear 251 is mounted in the frame 243, so that it is free to rotate therein, and engages the corresponding miter gear 245.

The frame 243 is pivotally mounted upon the support 252 by means of a bolt 253, washer 254, and nut 255. The support 252 is secured, by means of screws 256 and 257, to the panel 258 which is the bottom panel of compartment 77. Referring to Fig. 2, it will be seen that the frame 243 is positioned in the compartment 77 and extends through an aperture in the panel 69 so that the lens 236 intercepts the path of the light beam from the projector 66. (See Fig. 3). A coupling link 261 is pivotally secured to the frame 243 and to an arm 262 which is rigidly secured to the worm gear 263. The worm gear is mounted so that it rotates in engagement with a worm 264 which is mounted upon a shaft 265 extending from a driving motor 266. A flexible shaft 267 is connected between the shaft 265 and the miter gear 251 in the frame 243 so that rotation of the shaft 265 will cause a corresponding rotation of the gear 251. When the driving motor 266 rotates the worm gear 263 and the arm 262 by means of the worm 264, the coupling link 261, in following the rotation of the arm 262, will oscillate the frame 243 in a manner such that the lens 236 will move back and forth in the path of the light beam from the projector 66. Simultaneous with such oscillating movement, the lens 236 will be rotated, as before described, in two planes by the miter gears 245 and 251, which are mechanically connected to the shaft 265 by means of the flexible shaft 267. It is evident, then, that the lens 236 will intercept the light beam from the projector 66 at a great variety of angles at varying positions with reference to the projector 66. Consequently, the said light beam will be, in effect, continually distorted, and will produce a great variety of unusual effects. A similar distorting lens arrangement may be provided for each of the other projectors so that similar distorted effects can be produced with all of the variant colored light beams, when so desired.

In Fig. 17, which is a construction detail of the pattern machine 3, two rollers 268 and 269 are rigidly mounted upon spindles 270 and 271, respectively, which are mounted in a housing 272, as shown, and are free to rotate therein. A pulley wheel 273 is rigidly mounted upon the spindle 270, and a spur gear 274 is rigidly mounted upon the spindle 271. A shaft 275 is positioned below the spindle 271 in the housing 272 and is free to rotate therein. Rigidly mounted upon the shaft 275 is a pulley wheel 276, somewhat larger in diameter than pulley wheel 273, to one face of which there is rigidly secured the driven member 277 of a ratchet tooth clutch. Slidably positioned on the shaft 275 is a collar 278 to one face of which there is rigidly secured the driving member 279 of a ratchet tooth clutch, positioned for engagement with the driven member 277. A spur gear 280, considerably smaller than the spur gear 274, is rigidly secured to the opposite face of the collar 278. A pin 281, rigidly secured to the collar 278, extends through an elongated hole in the shaft 275 so that the collar 278, the spur gear 280 and the clutch member 279, associated therewith, may be moved lengthwise on the shaft 275 and yet remain in engagement with the same with respect to rotation. A pulley wheel 292 is rigidly mounted upon the end of the shaft 275 opposite from the pulley wheel 276. A lever 282, pivotally mounted upon the housing 272 by means of a pivot member 283, is positioned so that one end 284 of the lever 282 will engage in a peripheral channel in the collar 278. When the other end 285 of the lever 282, which extends through an aperture 286 in the housing 272, is moved, the collar 278 will be slid lengthwise on the shaft 275 and the spur gear 280 associated therewith, will be disengaged from the spur gear 274, and the clutch member 279 will engage with the clutch member 277, or vice versa according to the direction of the movement of the lever 282. A shaft 287, extending from a driving motor 288 positioned in the lower part of the housing 272, is mounted in the housing 272, as shown, and is free to rotate therein. Rigidly secured to the shaft 287 is a pulley wheel 289. Belts 290 and 291 are provided between the pulley wheels 273 and 276, and 289 and 292.

It is intended that patterns, such as pattern 310 in Fig. 1, be secured to the rollers 268 and 269 so that the same may be wound from one roller to the other. These patterns are substantially long pieces of flexible opaque material, which has been cut out in variant shapes, or long pieces of flexible transparent material upon which variant opaque shapes have been secured.

In starting position, the major part of the pattern will be reeled upon the roller 268, and the mechanical elements of the pattern machine will be in the same relative position as shown in Fig. 17. The motor 288, then, when started, will rotate the shaft 275 by means of the belt 291 and the pulleys 289 and 292, so that the spur gear 280, being in engagement with the spur gear 274, will rotate the roller 269 in the direction indicated by the arrow 311, winding the pattern thereon from the roller 268 across the intervening space and intercepting the path of the variant colored light beams so as to form corresponding shapes and patterns.

When the pattern has been wound as far as possible on the roller 269, the lever 282 may then be shifted so that the spur gears 274 and 280 will be disengaged, and the clutch members 277 and 279 engaged, thereby rotating roller 268 in the direction indicated by the arrow 293, by means of the pulleys 273 and 276, and belt 290 associated therewith, while the roller 269 idles. The pattern, then, will be wound back on to roller 268. When the pattern has been wound as far as possible on the roller 268, the lever 282 can again be shifted, and the entire winding process repeated as before. However, due to differences in size of the rotating driving elements, it is evident that the pattern will be slowly wound upon the roller 269, whereas it will be comparatively quickly wound upon the roller 268. Inasmuch as it is generally desirable, in projecting light beams through the pattern machine, to have the pattern always moving slowly in one direction this difference in speed of winding directions makes it possible to quickly re-wind the pattern after it has slowly run through in one direction.

In Fig. 18, the driving motors 56, 266, 135, 200, and 288 are connected in parallel to a suitable source of current supply having an input at the terminals 294. The motors 56, 266, 135, 200, and 288, are controlled by switches 37, 41, 39, 43, and 16, and by the rheostats 36, 40, 38, 42, and 15, respectively, so that the said motors can be selectively stopped and started and regulated as to speed. A reversing switch 295 is shunted across the current supply line of the motor 135 so that the direction of rotation of the said motor can be reversed. The projectors 64, 65. 66, 119, 118, and 81, are connected in parallel to a suitable source of current supply having an input at the terminals 296. The projectors 64, 65, 66, 119, 118, and 81 are controlled by switches 26, 30, 34, 28, 32, and 35, and by the rheostats 25, 29, 33, 27, 31, and 18, respectively, so that the light source in each projector may be selectively turned off and on. and regulated as to intensity. The kaleidoscopic lamps 220 and 228 are connected in parallel to the source of current supply having an input at the terminals 296, and controlled by the switch 19 so that the said lamps can be turned on and off.

A motor generator set 297, provided as a source of electrical supply for operation of the radio receiving set 8 and electric phonograph 9, is connected in parallel, on the input side, to the source of current supply having an input at the terminals 294, and is controlled by the switch 22 so that the motor generator set may be stopped and started. The radio receiving set 8 and the electric phonograph 9 are connected in parallel to the output current supply of the motor generator set 297. Switches 298 and 299 are provided for selectively opening and closing the said current supply circuit to the radio receiving set 8 and the electric phonograph 9. The radio receiving set 8 comprises a selective tuning arrangement, several stages of radio frequency amplification, a detector, and several auxiliary stages of audio frequency amplification. The remote control panel 13 is electrically connected to the radio receiving set 8 by the remote control cable 312, so that the selective tuning arrangement in the radio receiving set can be operated from the housing 1 of the projection machine. (See Fig. 1.) A wired radio carrier line, a space radio antennæ system, or other source of radio frequency signals, is connected to the input terminals 313 of the radio receiving set. The light intercepting devices 194 associated with the projectors 64, 65, 66, 119, 118, and 81, and which are actuated by audio frequency currents, are connected in parallel to the audio frequency output terminals 301 of the radio receiving set 8. A loud speaker 10 is connected to a double pole switch 17 which is, in turn, connected to the output terminals 302 of the electrical phonograph 9, and to the audio frequency output of the radio receiving set 8, so that the loud speaker 10 can be alternately used for the reproduction of sound from either source. Rheostats 20 and 21 are provided for controlling the output volume of the electric phonograph 9 and the radio receiving set 8, respectively.

The operation of the embodiment of my invention, further than has been described in the foregoing, is given in what follows:

The person who operates the projection machine positions himself in front of the housing 1, so that he has access to the keyboard 12 and the controlling elements adjacent thereto.

Referring to Fig. 1, the projectors 64, 65, 66, 119, 118, and 81 in the housing 1 are adjusted with reference to direction, by means of the knobs 48, 46, 44, 49, 47, and 45, respectively so that overlapping light beams are projected upon the screen 2. The rotary color screens, then, intercepting the path of these light beams at different rotating speeds, will cause these beams to be of variant colors which change at a rate which is not uniform, the overlapping portions of the beams being of colors which are resultants of the superimposed colors. The projectors may be individually turned on and off, and regulated as to intensity of light beam projection, by the associated rheostats. To project these beams upon the screen 2, it is necessary to raise the shutters 176 associated with each of the manual color screen housings, by means of the knob 192, so that the light beams can be projected through the same. In addition to the variant colors obtainable by intercepting the light beams with the rotary color screens, further effects can be obtained by manipulating the manual color screens by means of the keyboard 12 so as to selectively choose any one or more of the said color screens and intercept the light beams therewith.

To project, upon the screen 2, light beams the colors of which are entirely determined by manual operation, it is necessary to stop the rotation of the rotary color screens, by turning the knob 160, and open the movable color sector in each of the same so that white light can pass through without being filtered. At the same time, the shutters 176 associated with each of the manual color screen housings should be lowered, by means of the knob 192. The shutters 176 will then prevent light from passing through the color screen housings except when a manual color screen is raised to intercept the light. The operator can then control the color effects entirely by manipulation of the keyboard 12.

Inasmuch as more than one color screen may simultaneously intercept the light beam from one projector, it is thereby possible to obtain other superimposed color combinations, in addition to those produced by the overlapping colored light beams.

When white light beams are being projected through the manual color screen housings, the shutters 176 may be raised, by means of the knob 192, and special color effects obtained, without employing either the rotary color screens or manual color screens, by regulating the rheostats associated with each projector so as to vary the intensity of the light beams projected through the color screens 177. (See Fig. 8.) Inasmuch as the color screens 177 associated with the several manual color screen housings are primary colors which are intended to filter the white light beams in a manner such that upon convergence they will again form white light, it is evident that if the intensities of these white light beams be varied, the component primary colors will be unbalanced so as to decrease or increase one or more of the colors to produce delicate tints and fine gradations and variations of color shading.

To produce unusual and extremely varied color shapes upon the screen 2, the distorting lens, in compartment 77 in Fig. 2, may be set in motion by starting the associated driving motor. The variant colored light beams intercepted thereby will then be continually distorted.

The kaleidoscopic projection arrangement in compartment 78 may also be brought into use by closing the circuits to the associated lamps and driving motor. A great variety of moving geometric patterns, corresponding in shape and color to the objects placed upon the kaleidoscopic transparent platform, will be projected upon the screen 2.

The pattern machine 3 and the associated shielding 50, in Fig. 1, are adapted to be readily positioned for operation when desired by the operator. The pattern may then be used in a stationary position, or the associated driving motor may be started so as to move the pattern across the path of the variant colored light beams, intercepting the same in accordance with the design of the pattern. It is obvious that two or more of these pattern machines can be used simultaneously to intercept and define the variant colored light beams, the patterns running in the same direction, or in opposite directions, at the same time, or different relative speeds.

The object supporting turntable 4 is also adapted to be readily positioned for operation when desired by the operator. Objects of any shape or form may then be placed upon the said turntable and used in a stationary position, or rotated by the associated driving motor, to intercept the variant colored light beams, at variant angles, to form a great variety of shapes and shadows upon the screen 2.

All of the driving motors are selectively controlled so that they may be started and stopped at will and varied as to speed of rotation. Consequently, any of the elements which are driven by motors may be individually and selectively controlled as to relative speed, or used stationary. In the event that an especially desirable color or pattern is cast upon the screen, the driving motors can be immediately stopped so as to retain that particular color or pattern. The driving motor which revolves the rotary color screens is provided with a reversing switch, and the driving mechanism of the pattern machine 3 is provided with a direction reversing clutch, by means of which it is possible to reverse the order of formation of colors and patterns, thereby making it possible to cause the immediate return of any especially desirable color or pattern which has been replaced by other formations before it has been possible to stop the driving motors.

Simultaneous with the formation of color effects and patterns on the screen 2, it is possible to produce accompanying sound effects, which may be of a nature sympathetic to the color effects, through the agency of the loud speaker 10 which can be selectively connected to either the electrical phonograph 9, or the radio receiving set 8. At the same time, the variant colored light beams will be rhythmically affected as to intensity by light intercepting devices, positioned upon each projector, which are actuated in accordance with the modulated audio frequency currents from the radio receiving set.

Permanent records of the color effects and patterns may be made by the employment of any of the commonly used methods of color photography. For recording occasional color formations, the moving elements may be stopped, as hereinbefore provided, and a color photograph made of the screen 2, whereas, if a continuous record of all of the effects presented to the eye is desired, a color motion picture may be made of the same.

In Fig. 19, a diagonal row of projectors

402, 404, 408, of a group of nine projectors 400, 401, 402, 403, 404, 405, 406, 407, 408, in Fig. 20, which is the normal arrangement of the projectors in a preferred embodiment of my invention, are shown, schematically, in their relation to light beams projected through a pattern 409 upon a screen 410. The light beams are directed upon the screen 410 in a manner such that they overlap at an angle corresponding to the angle of the diagonal row of projectors. The light beams are defined by the pattern 409 so as to project these variant colored overlapping light beams in the form of squares 411, 412, 413, upon the screen 410. The squares 411, 412, and 413 are projected by the projectors 402, 404, and 408, respectively.

The pattern 409 is substantially any means for defining light, and corresponds to pattern 310, in Fig. 1, or to the objects on the object supporting turntable 4. It is evident, now, that any pattern or object which intercepts the paths of the variant colored light beams will cause corresponding shapes and shadows of variant colors, overlapping in variant planes, to be cast upon the screen 410. Inasmuch as the projectors are selectively controlled, it is evident that any one projector, any row of projectors, or any group of projectors, such as are defined by the dotted lines in Fig. 20, may be used, as desired, with varying intensities of light, and with variant light defining and intercepting devices, to produce by beams of light overlapping in one or selected planes an almost infinite variety of different colored shapes, forms and patterns.

While in the description of my invention I have referred to certain details of mechanical construction and arrangement of parts as well as to electrical circuits, I do not limit myself thereto except as may be pointed out in the appended claims.

What I claim as new and desire to secure by Letters Patent of the United States is as follows:

1. A projector system comprising, a plurality of projectors, a plurality of color screens adjacent each of said projectors, means for controlling said projectors and color screens to project overlapping beams of light of variant colors to produce a composite pattern, and means for utilizing electric currents of audio frequencies to control the intensity of light from each of said projectors in accordance with the rhythm and intensity of said currents.

2. A projector system comprising, a plurality of projectors, a plurality of color screens adjacent each of said projectors, means controlling said projectors and said color screens to produce overlapping beams of light of variant colors to form a composite pattern, means for utilizing electric currents of audio frequencies to control the intensity of the light from each of said projectors in accordance with the rhythm and intensity of said currents, and means for selectively receiving said audio currents from any one of several broadcast sources.

3. A projector system comprising, a plurality of projectors, means controlling said projectors to produce a composite pattern of overlapping beams of light in variant colors, a radio receiving system and means under control of said receiving system for controlling said beams of light to vary the aspects of said composite pattern.

4. A projector system comprising, a plurality of projectors for producing a composite pattern of overlapping beams of light of variant colors, a source of music translated electrical energy, and means under control of said electrical energy for individually affecting said light beams in accordance with the rhythm of said music.

5. A projector system comprising, means for producing a plurality of overlapping beams of colored light, and means under control of music translated electrical energy for controlling said light beams.

6. A projector system comprising, light projection means, a source of music translated electrical energy, and shutter means under control of said electrical energy for controlling said light in accordance with said music.

7. A projector system comprising, a plurality of projectors for producing overlapping beams of light, a plurality of color screens adjacent each of said projectors, means for moving said color screens to alter the color of said overlapping beams of light, a source of audio frequency currents, and a plurality of electrically actuated shutters each of which is mounted upon one of said projectors for controlling the light beam emergent therefrom, said shutters being under control of said audio frequency currents.

CLINTON W. HOUGH.

ERNEST NANFELDT

Projection System (1934)

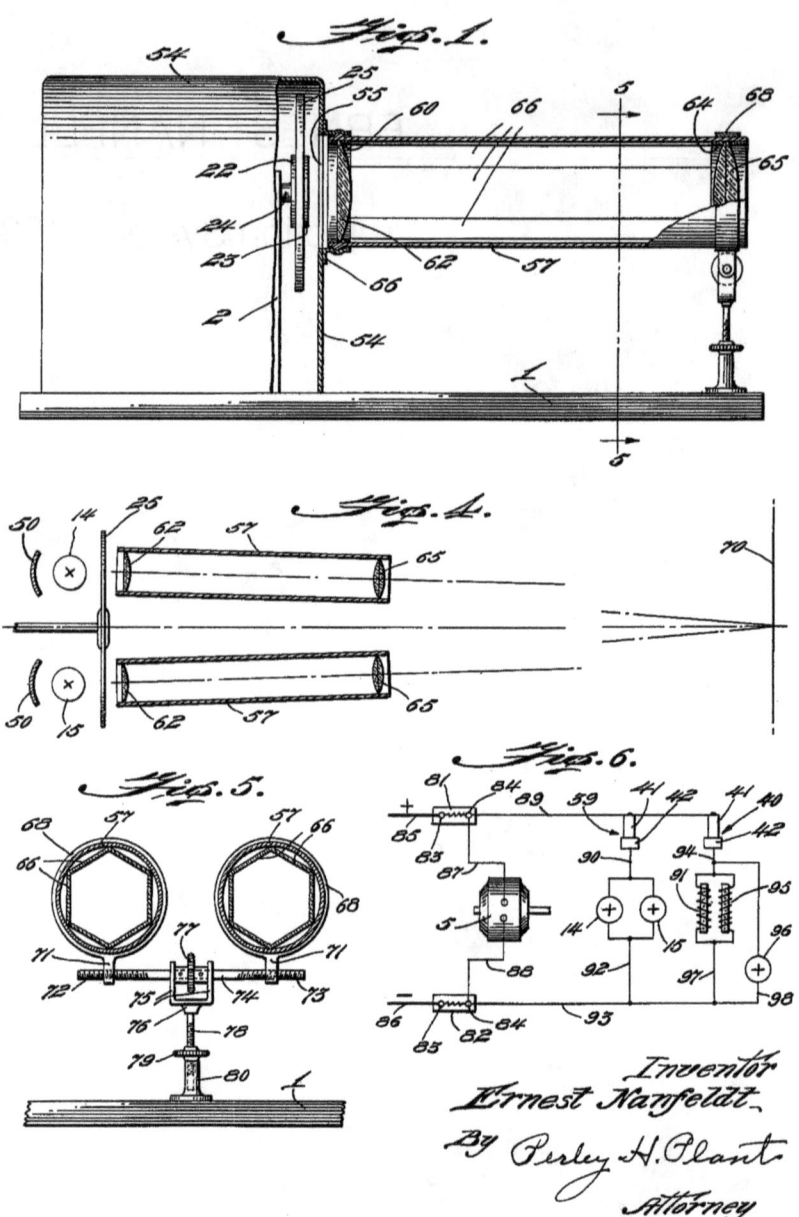

VISUAL MUSIC INSTRUMENT PATENTS (I)

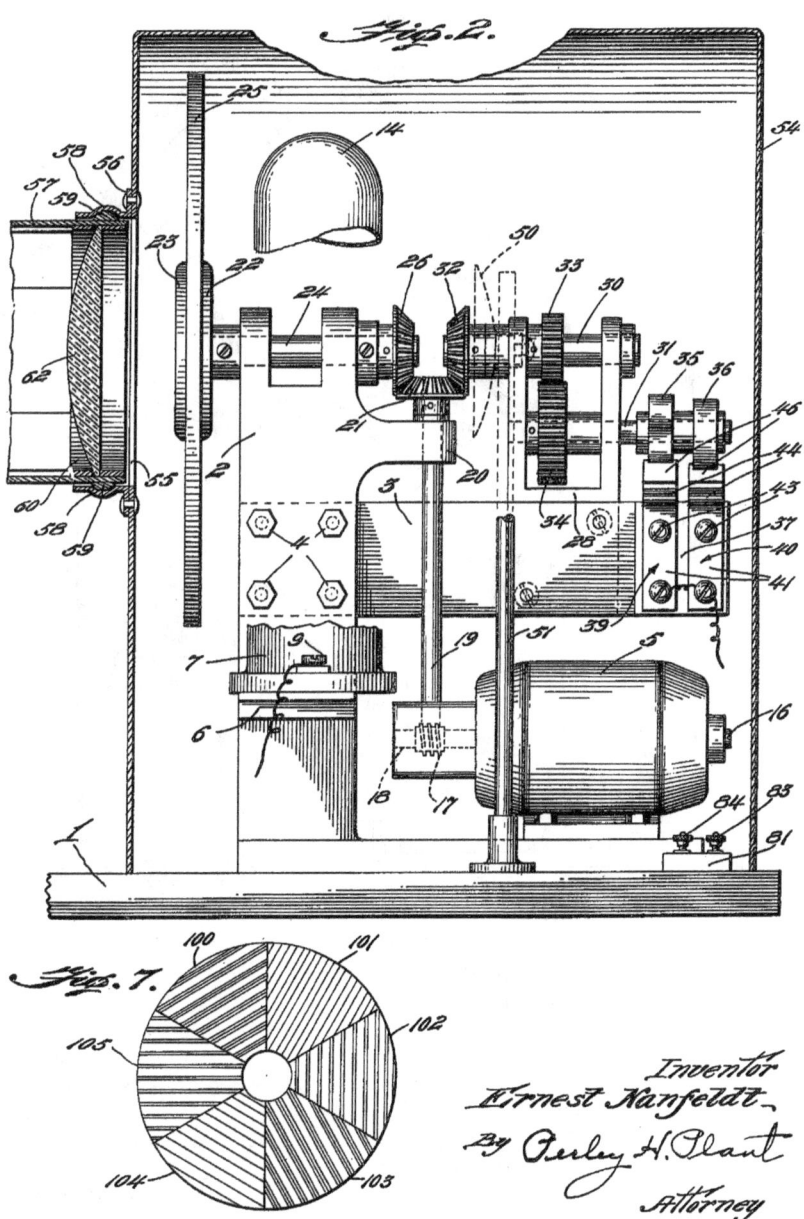

May 24, 1938. E. NANFELDT 2,118,264
LIGHT PROJECTION DISPLAY MEANS
Filed July 12, 1934 — 3 Sheets-Sheet 2

Inventor
Ernest Nanfeldt
By Perley H. Plant
Attorney

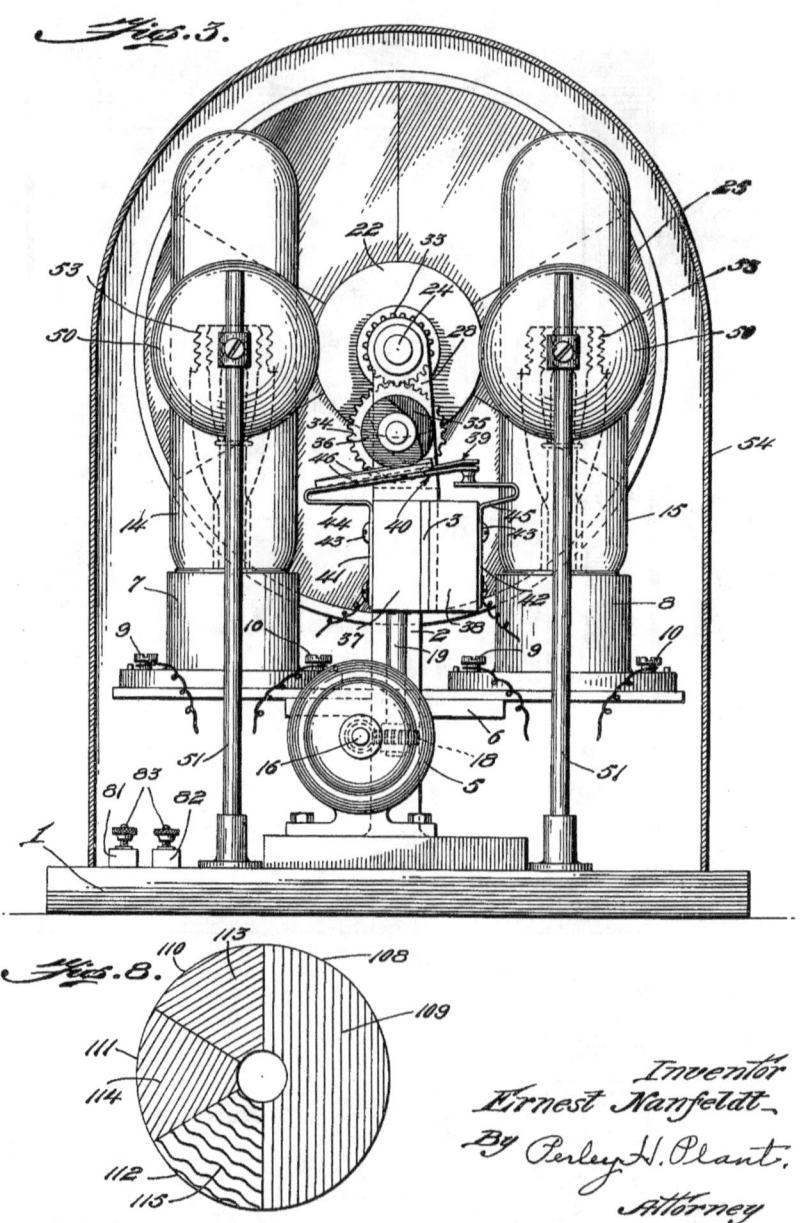

UNITED STATES PATENT OFFICE

2,118,264

LIGHT PROJECTION DISPLAY MEANS

Ernest Nanfeldt, New Haven, Conn., assignor to Respro, Inc., Cranston, R. I., a corporation of Rhode Island

Application July 12, 1934, Serial No. 734,727

4 Claims. (Cl. 272—10)

This invention relates to the art of light projection display, such as, in the projection of novel effects in light or color upon a screen or other receiving surface to provide novel and changeable light and/or color effects for the purpose of entertainment, advertising or the like involving the use of novel means and combinations of means for effecting the display.

One object of the invention is the provision of means producing superposed light or color and image effects simultaneously whereby each effect is modified by the other to obtain a composite display of a novel and pleasing character.

Another object of the invention is the provision of means for modifying color and image effects before their projection upon the receiving surface.

Another object of the invention is the provision of a color or image or combined color and image forming means having corresponding portions arranged in position for the substantially simultaneous passage of projected light rays to form a display, and having similar but contrasting portions arranged for the substantially simultaneous passage of projecting light rays to produce two or more varying displays alternately or in sequence.

A further object of the invention is the provision of a plurality of light reflecting surfaces located substantially parallel with the projected light rays to further modify and produce changeable variations in the display.

Another object of the invention is the provision of a novel combination of operating means including mechanism whereby novel light effects may be produced upon a receiving surface in a predetermined order or the display effects alternated with others to vary or modify the display.

A further object of the invention is the provision of means for projecting dissimilar but correlated images of a changing character from different light sources upon a receiving surface simultaneously to produce a combined color and/or image effect.

Another object of the invention is the provision of spaced light sources with means for passing reflected light from each light source through a common light modifying member formed of sections, in such a manner that corresponding sections may modify the reflected light rays simultaneously, and projecting the modified light rays from different sections upon a light receiving surface simultaneously.

A further object of the invention is the provision of a movable light modifying member provided with different light modifying sections adapted to be traversed by reflected light rays from different light sources simultaneously and means operable from the movement of the light modifying member for lighting or extinguishing one or another of said light sources in accordance with a prearranged plan of operation.

Other objects and advantages of the invention relate to various novel parts and arrangements and combinations of parts as well as new and improved methods of combining and operating the same as will be more fully set forth in the detailed description to follow.

Referring to the drawings:—

Fig. 1 is a side elevational view of the light projection display means showing one of the projection tubes in partial section and with a portion of the main casing broken away,

Fig. 2 is a sectional view through the main portion of the casing showing the operating parts in side elevation, and illustrating the manner of connecting one of the projection tubes with the casing,

Fig. 3 is a transverse sectional view through the casing showing the operating parts in rear elevation,

Fig. 4 is a diagrammatic top plan view illustrating the relative positions of the light sources, reflector members, light transmitting member and projection tubes with respect to each other and a light receiving surface,

Fig. 5 is a transverse sectional view through a portion of the light projection tubes, taken substantially along the line 5—5 of Fig. 1, and showing the tube adjusting means in elevation,

Fig. 6 is a diagrammatic view of one arrangement of electric circuits such as may be employed in connecting the motor, filamentary lamps, auxiliary light and control means, and the operating means therefor with a source of electric power,

Fig. 7 is a plan view of one form of light transmitting member such as may be employed in connection with the light display projection means, and,

Fig. 8 is a plan view of a modified form of light transmitting member.

In the form of the invention illustrated herein, 1 designates a supporting base which may support such operating parts as the motor, sources of light, light transmitting means, reflector members and the operating parts generally through any suitable or desired arrangement of means for maintaining these parts in proper operative relation with each other.

In the present instance, a suitable upright supporting frame member 2 is carried by the base 1 and provided with a horizontally extending arm 3, which may be formed integral with the frame 2 or secured thereto in any desired manner. A motor 5 of suitable character and design is also carried by the base 1 for actuating certain of the operating mechanisms such as may be supported by the upright frame 2.

The supporting frame 2 may be provided with laterally extending shelves 6 for supporting lamp sockets 7 and 8, each of which is provided with suitable terminal connections 9 and 10, and in which may be mounted any suitable light emitting means, such as filamentary lamps 14 and 15 respectively. The lamps may be of any ordinary or special character such as are adapted for use in the emission of light rays of the desired intensity.

The motor 5 is provided with a shaft 16, carrying a worm pinion 17 meshing with a spiral gear 18 carried by a vertical shaft 19, which is in turn rotatably supported by a bearing 20 carried by the frame 2 and is provided with a beveled gear 21 for driving certain operating mechanisms supported by the upright frame 2. The main portion of the upright frame 2 is provided with aligned bearings for rotatably supporting a shaft 24 which has a suitable light transmission member 25 secured thereto, as by collars 22 and 23, and carries a beveled gear 26 mounted for meshing engagement with the beveled gear 21 carried by the shaft 19.

A suitable frame 28 may be formed integral with or secured to the horizontal arm 3 by any suitable means, the frame 28 being provided with aligned bearings for rotatably supporting shafts 30 and 31. The shaft 30 is provided with a beveled gear 32 secured thereto and mounted for meshing engagement with the beveled gear 21 carried by the vertical shaft 19. A second gear 33 is fixed to the shaft 30 and operatively engages a gear 34 secured to the shaft 31. The shaft 31 extends materially beyond the frame 28 and carries cams 35 and 36 secured thereto for rotation therewith. Blocks 37 and 38 of any suitable insulating material, such as rubber, Bakelite, or the like, are carried by the horizontal arm 3 and spaced from the frame 28. Current interrupters 39 and 40 are carried by the blocks 37 and 38 and located in operative relation with the cams 35 and 36 respectively.

Each of the current interrupters 39 and 40 may be formed of two parts 41 and 42, each part having a portion adapted for attachment to one of the insulating blocks 37 or 38, as by screws 43. Each of the parts 41 and 42 is provided with a resilient contact carrying portion 44 and 45 respectively, of which the portion 44 may be provided with an insulating plate 46 mounted for operative engagement by one of the cams 35 or 36.

A reflector member 50 of any desired construction and design may be adjustably mounted upon a standard 51 carried by the base 1, and suitably located relative to the luminous portion or filament 53 of each lamp for reflecting light rays of maximum intensity through portions of the light transmitting member 25.

A casing 54 is provided for enclosing the operating parts of the mechanism and supported in any suitable manner from the base 1. The casing 54 may be provided with shaped openings 55 formed therein and located upon opposite sides of the vertical plane of the shaft 24, each opening being located substantially within the path of light rays as reflected from one light source by the reflector member 50.

Any suitable means, such as a collar 56, may be secured to or carried by the casing 54 for mounting one end of a projection tube 57 in substantial axial alignment with each opening 55 formed in the casing, or in such operative relation with the opening as will result in the passage of the major portion of the reflected light rays passed through the light transmission member 25 from one light source through one of the light projection tubes 57. Each collar 56 and projection tube 57 may be provided with suitable means for supporting the end of a light projection tube 57 so as to permit a certain degree of adjustment of the outer ends of the projection tubes 57, whereby the projected light rays from the tubes may be brought into superposed relation and into the desired position upon a light receiving surface. Such supporting means may comprise a curved recess 58 formed in the collar for receiving a rounded rib 59 carried by the end of the projection tube, as shown in Fig. 2 of the drawings.

Each light projection tube 57 may be provided at the end adjacent to the casing 54 with an internal collar 60 or other suitable means for supporting a condensing lens 62, which may be planoconvex, as shown in Figs. 1 and 4 of the drawings. A similar internal collar 64 located adjacent to the outer end of each light projection tube 57 is adapted to support a magnifying lens 65, as shown in Figs. 1 and 4, of the drawings. Each projection tube may be provided with a plurality of plane mirrors 66, located within the tube and extending longitudinally thereof, and which may be held in position therein by the internal collars 60 and 64. In the present case each tube is provided with six plane mirrors of substantially equal widths, after the manner shown, to form a substantially hexagonal light passage extending therethrough although a greater or less number may be employed as desired.

An external collar 68 may be provided for each light projection tube 57 and firmly secured thereto adjacent to the outer end thereof to provide means for adjustably supporting the outer ends of the tubes 57 in various positions towards or from each other so that the reflected light rays from the light sources 14 and 15 may be thrown into superposed relation upon a light receiving surface 70. Each collar 68 is provided with an internally threaded lug 71, the lugs being adapted to receive reversely threaded end portions 72 and 73 of an adjusting bar 74 which may be rotatably supported by the arms 75 of a vertically adjustable supporting member 76. The adjusting bar 74, as shown, is provided with an angular portion 77 for adjusting the outer ends of the projection tubes towards and from each other. The supporting member 76 is provided with an externally threaded portion 78, adapted to be threaded within an adjusting nut 79 carried by a post 80 for securing the desired vertical adjustment of the outer ends of the projection tubes.

The operation of the motor 5, as well as the provision of means for effecting continued or intermittent illumination by the light sources 14 and 15 may be effected from any suitable electric current source by means of a system of wiring similar to that shown in Fig. 6 of the drawings wherein terminal supporting blocks 81 and 82 may be carried by the base 1 and each provided with electrically connected binding posts 83 and 84 for connection respectively with line conductors 85 and 86 and conductors completing circuits through the motor 5, lamps 14 and 15 and other electrically operated devices. Conductor wires 87 and 88 connect the binding posts 84 with the terminals of the electric motor 5, while a conductor wire 89 connects the binding post 84 of the block 81 with the parts 41 of each interrupter. A conductor 90 connects the part 42 of the interrupter 39 with one terminal each of the lamps 14 and 15, while a conductor 92 connects the other terminals of the lamps 14 and 15 with a conductor 93 which connects with the terminal 84 carried by the block 82. A branched conductor 94 connects the part 42 of the interrupter 40 with one terminal each of solenoids 91 and 95 and a lamp 96, which are in turn connected to the conductor 93 by conductor wires 97 and 98.

The solenoids 91 and 95 and lamp 96, operated through the interrupter 40, may constitute part of an auxiliary light projection mechanism, such for example, as may be adapted for use in connection with the present structure, as in the following manner;—for operating the display mechanism and displaying one or more films or light images simultaneously or alternately with the display of variable light images by the means herein described. One form of auxiliary projection mechanism such as may be adapted for use in connection with the present structure and capable of being controlled by the arrangement of solenoids 91, 95 and lamp 96 as above set forth is shown and described in my copending application Serial No. 734,728, filed July 12, 1934.

In the operation of the structure herein described the electric motor 5 may be continually operated by current from the line source 85, 86, to drive the upright shaft 19 and thus impart rotation to the shafts 24 and 30, whereby the light transmission member 25 is caused to rotate across the path of reflected light rays from the light sources 14 and 15. The countershaft 31 is driven from the shaft 30, through gears 33 and 34 to rotate the cams 35 and 36 for alternately making and breaking the circuits through the lamps 14 and 15 and solenoids 91 and 95 and lamp 96. The effective cam surfaces 35 and 36 may each extend slightly more than 180 degrees whereby there is no interruption in the display, but one display image may merge into the other as the change is effected. If desired, the effective cam surfaces 35 and 36 may be so proportioned as to render either one or the other of the display mechanism effective for a longer or shorter period as will be readily understood. When the lamps 14 and 15 are lighted, reflected light rays therefrom will be passed through the moving light transmission member 25 and projection tubes 57 to be thrown into superposed relation upon a receiving surface 70 after the manner indicated above.

That part of the mechanism designated generally as a light transmission member may consist of various parts or sections, maintained in position relative to each other by the collars 22 and 23, each of said sections being formed of a light transmitting medium and said sections each possessing light transmitting qualities or characteristics similar to or differing from those possessed by other parts or sections thereof, whereby various changing designs or colors may be imparted to light images formed upon the receiving surface by the movement of portions of the light transmitting media across the paths of reflected light rays in such a manner as to cause the formation of a composite light image through superposing the reflected light rays from different light transmitting media upon a light receiving surface.

According to one form of my invention, as shown in Fig. 7, the light transmitting member 25 may consist of a plurality of diametrically opposed sectors 100, 101, 102, 103, 104 and 105 secured in position by means of the collars 22 and 23. Diametrically opposed sectors may be formed of any suitable light transmitting media and provided with any suitable form of contrasting design and/or color characteristics so that a composite image formed by superposing reflected light rays passed through such opposed sections will present a composite image or design upon the light receiving surface which may change with movement of either set of the opposed sectors, such as 102 and 105, and be further changed by the use of other and different contrasting design and color characteristics carried by the other sets of diametrically opposed sectors, such as 100, 103 and 101, 104. The different color and/or design characteristics of the light transmitting media of any two diametrically opposed sectors, such as 102 and 105, when the light rays pass therethrough are superposed upon the light receiving surface, as 70, to present a composite color or design image or combined color and design image possessing characteristics imparted to the reflected light rays by the light transmitting media of the opposed sectors, whereby different design or color effects may be merged to form a colored or uncolored design which is a composite of the designs formed upon the separate sectors. Since a similar arrangement of contrasting designs may be carried by the sectors 100, 103 and 101, 104, which may also vary from those carried by 102—105, the continued rotation of the light transmitting member 25 across the path of light rays will result in the presentation of constantly changing images caused by the superposing of light rays passed through various different light transmitting media containing or embodying different design and/or color characteristics, and different from each other throughout the extent of the light transmitting member 25.

It will be understood that any desired number of opposed sectors may be employed to make up the light transmitting member 25 and the design and/or color characteristics of the opposed and successive sectors may differ from or correspond with each other in accordance with a predetermined plan for obtaining any desired arrangement of blending or contrasting design and/or color characteristics.

In another form which my invention may assume in practice, as shown in Fig. 8 of the drawings, substantially one-half of the light transmitting member 25 constitutes a sector 108 which is made up of a light transmitting medium possessing uniform design and/or color characteristics throughout its extent as indicated by the design 109. The sectors 110, 111 and 112 located in opposition to the sector 108 may be provided with designs 113, 114 and 115 respectively, differing from the design carried by the sector 108, whereby the composite image produced by the superposing of reflected light rays passed through the sector 108 in combination with reflected light rays alternately passed through sectors 110, 111, 112 will provide a composite image which combines the color and/or design characteristics 113, 114 and 115 with the design and/or color characteristics 109 of the sector 108. By means of such an arrangement of light transmitting media a single basic color or design characteristic may be employed with and modified by its combination with two or more secondary design or color characteristics to produce constantly changing images upon light reflecting surfaces each of which may possess a basic characteristic modified by two or more secondary characteristics to form a constantly changing design.

In employing the plane mirrors 66 within the projection tubes 57 the transmitted design characteristics may be further modified by reason of the multiple reflections of image effects constantly produced by the mirror 66.

While I have shown two forms of light transmitting members having sectors made up of light transmitting media which may possess different light and/or color characteristics, that is, capable of transmitting light rays to form images of different color or design on a light receiving surface, various other arrangements of parts may be employed for the purpose, and the light transmitting means may differ as desired in shape and arrangement of parts from that shown to provide light transmitting media of corresponding or contrasting color and/or design characteristics movable across the paths of reflected light rays from each light source without departing from the spirit and scope of my invention. In any case, the modification of transmitted light rays with respect to their color, design and/or light characteristics produce changing design, light and/or color characteristics in the formed image which may be caused to merge to produce a composite image of substantially regular character or a constantly changing effect, and the employment of different light media successively may produce a continually changing effect in the display. The light transmitting media employed in connection with the different light sources at one time may differ from each other either in color or in design, or in both, which differences may combine to produce a regularly or irregularly changing image when light rays pass therethrough are superposed upon a light receiving surface.

While I have shown and described solenoids 91 and 95 and lamp 96 as controlled through the cam 36 by the interrupter 40 for controlling the operating parts of an auxiliary projection device directly from the shaft 31, such auxiliary projection device may be dispensed with if desired, or incorporated into the present structure, or controlled by independent means, as may be found desirable in practice.

What I claim is:—

1. A light projection display means comprising spaced light sources, means for reflecting light rays from each light source, means for variably modifying the reflected light rays from one light source in accordance with a predetermined plan, means for uniformly modifying the reflected light rays from the other light source during the period of variable modification of the light rays from the first light source, means for reversing the manner of modifying the reflected light rays from the said light sources at intervals and means for projecting the reflected light rays from said light sources into superposed relation upon a light receiving surface.

2. In a light projection display mechanism, spaced light sources, means for reflecting light rays from said spaced light sources along separate paths, combined color and design modifying light transmitting means having portions differing from each other in color and design effect but each of uniform color and design effect throughout its extent movable simultaneously across the paths of the light rays from said light sources, and means for projecting the modified light rays from said separate light sources after passage through said light transmitting means into superposed relation upon a light receiving surface.

3. In a light projection display mechanism, spaced light sources, means for reflecting light rays from said spaced light sources along separate paths, design modifying light transmitting means discontinuously variable throughout for imparting periodically changing design characteristics to transmitted light rays passed therethrough independently of the light density due to color variations in said transmitting means, said transmitting means being movable across the path of the light rays from said light sources continuously, and means for projecting the modified light rays from said separate light sources after passage through said light transmitting means into superposed relation upon a light receiving surface.

4. A device for producing a superposed light effect comprising in combination a pair of lights, a reflector for each light, a single rotatable color and design producer, said producer consisting of pairs of diametrically opposed differently colored transparent sectors having upon them the desired designs, one of each pair of sectors in its rotation transmitting alternately one of the reflected beams, and means bringing to a common point upon a screen the separately transmitted beams.

ERNEST NANFELDT.

CECIL STOKES

Auroratone (1940)

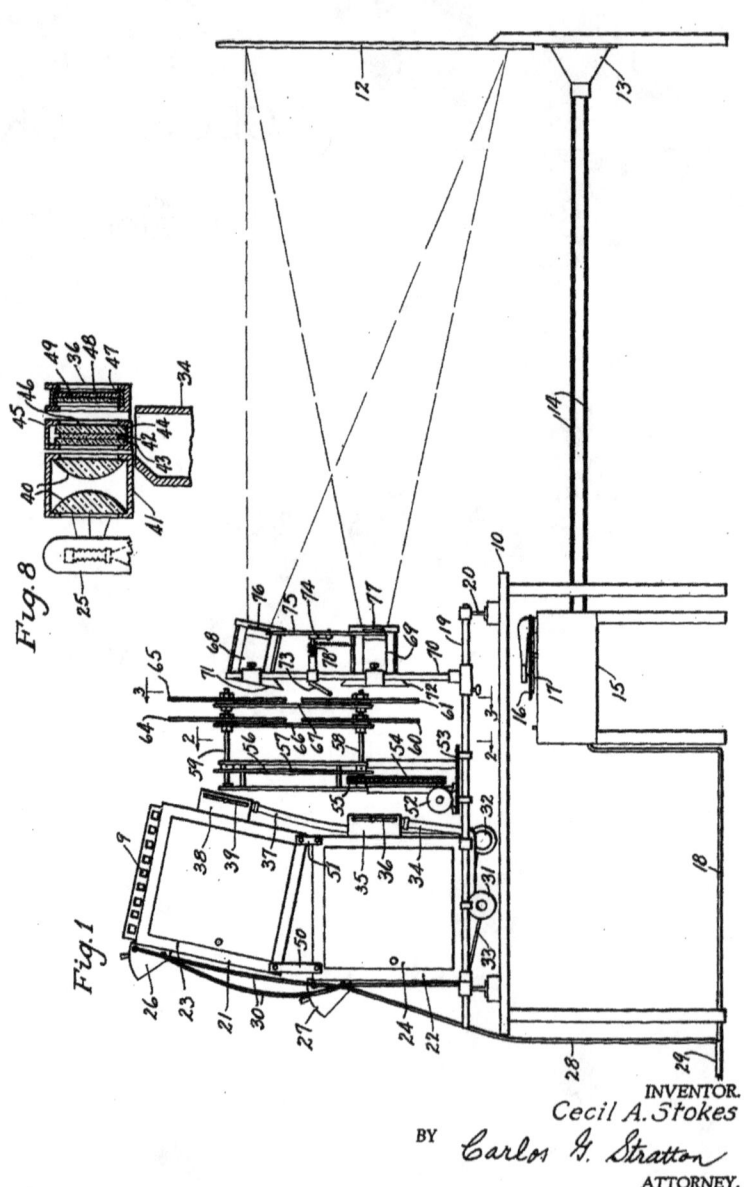

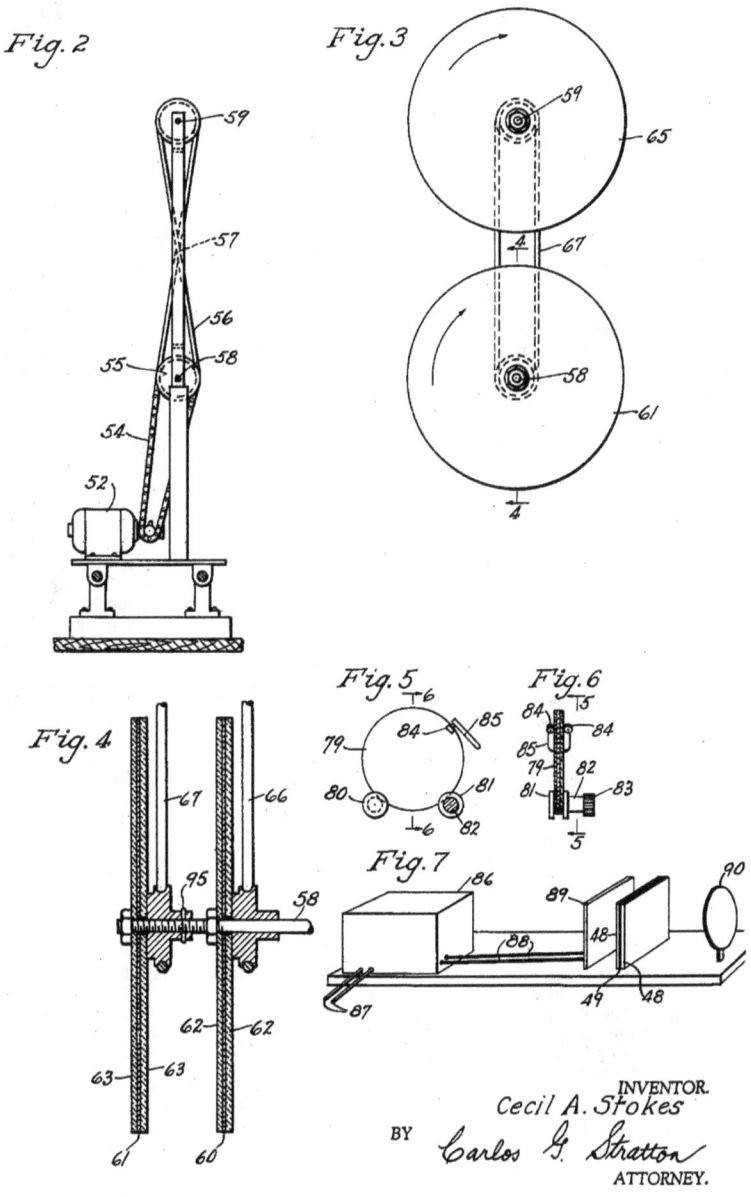

UNITED STATES PATENT OFFICE

2,292,172

PROCESS AND APPARATUS FOR PRODUCING MUSICAL RHYTHM IN COLOR

Cecil A. Stokes, West Los Angeles, Calif.

Application May 24, 1940, Serial No. 336,955

2 Claims. (Cl. 88—26)

My invention relates to a process and apparatus for producing musical rhythm in color. The principal object is to provide such a process and apparatus by which the effects of musical rhythm may be reproduced in visible colors.

Another object is to produce a flowing rhythm of color synchronized with the rhythm of the music that produced the color medium.

Still another object is to produce light in motion that is synchronized with rhythm of music.

The invention also comprises novel details of construction and novel combinations and arrangements of parts, which will more fully appear in the course of the following description. However, the drawings merely show and the following description merely describes an embodiment of the present invention, which is given by way of illustration or example only.

In the drawings, like reference characters designate similar parts in the several views:

Figure 1 is an elevation of an embodiment of the invention.

Figure 2 is an enlarged section taken on the line 2—2 of Figure 1.

Figure 3 is an enlarged elevation looking in the direction of the arrows 3—3 of Figure 1.

Figure 4 is a still further enlarged section taken on the line 4—4 of Figure 3.

Figure 5 is a detail, partly in section, of rotating mechanism comprised in the embodiment, taken on the line 5—5 of Figure 6.

Figure 6 is the section taken on the line 6—6 of Figure 5.

Figure 7 is a perspective view of plate-producing mechanism, for use in connection with the mechanism shown in Figure 1.

Figure 8 is an enlarged vertical section of mechanism comprised in the embodiment.

It is to be understood that changes may be made in the details of the construction and arrangement of said embodiment, without departing from the spirit and scope of my invention.

Referring more in detail to the drawings, the reference numeral 10 generally designates a support upon which the embodiment in Figure 1 is mounted. A screen is shown at 12 upon which the color patterns may be projected. A loud speaker 13, shown adjacent the screen 12, is connected by means of wires 14 with a suitable phonograph 15. A record is shown at 16 on the phonograph turntable 17. Details of the phonograph mechanism and of the loud speaker are well known to those skilled in the art. Suffice to state that an electrical cable 18 provides power for motor mechanism to drive the phonograph 15.

Rods 19, mounted on beams 20, support various elements of the projection mechanism shown in Figure 1. Housings 21 and 22 are arranged with doors 23 and 24 respectively. These housings respectively contain strong sources of light. Strong electric lamps, such as shown at 25, or conventional carbon arc lights, or other suitable means may provide the sources of light. Cooling outlets are shown at 9.

Switches 26 and 27 respectively control the lights in the housings 21 and 22. Branch cable 28 connects a main cable 29 with the switch 27, and cables 30 connect the two switches together in parallel in the main electric circuit 29.

Suitable motor means (not shown) may be used to operate centrifugal pumps 31 and 32. Wiring 33 is shown for connecting the motor that operates the pump 31, with the main circuit. Suitable wiring may also be employed for the motor that drives the pump 32. A pipe 34 conveys air pressure from the pump 31 to a box 35, in which may be reciprocated a slide holder 36.

A pipe 37 conveys air pressure from the pump 32 to a box 38, in which is reciprocated a slide holder 39. Between the source 25 of light and the holder 36 are condensers or condenser lenses 40 that are plano-convex in section, with their convex surfaces facing each other. A housing 41 supports the lenses in position.

Disposed between the condenser lenses and the slide holder 36 is a relatively stationary polarizing element 42, arranged between heat resisting glass plates 43 and 44. The polarizing element may be Polaroid or any other suitable polarizing medium. The polarizing element and its protecting glass plates are mounted in a container 45 having openings 46 for the transmission of light through the polarizing element.

A slide in the holder 36 comprises a frame 47 in which are arranged transparent glass plates 48, between which is disposed a crystallized medium 49. The air pressure pipes 34 and 37 are arranged to project streams of air upon the polarizing elements 42 (one in each box 35 and 38) to cool such elements.

It is to be understood that the arrangement shown in Figure 8 is duplicated for each of the two projection machines 21 and 22. Braces 50 and 51 maintain the projection machine 21 at an angle with respect to the machine 22, in order that their beams of light may coincide on the screen 12.

A motor 52, supported on a platform 53 on the rods 19, drives a chain 54 engaging a pulley 55,

A driving belt 56, which is crossed as shown at 57, connects a shaft 58, driven by the pulley 55, with a counter-shaft 59.

A rotary, disc, tint plate 60 is mounted on the shaft 58 between the pulley 55 and a rotary polarizing plate 61. As shown in Figure 4, the tint plate and rotary polarizing plate may be maintained flat and in position by means of glass plates 62 and 63 respectively.

A similar tint plate 64 and a similar rotary polarizing plate 65 are mounted on the counter-shaft 59. The tint plates 60 and 64 may be of Cellophane, translucent plastic, mica, or other suitable material. A belt 66 is connected to drive the tint plates synchronously, while belt 67 is connected to drive the rotary polarizing discs synchronously.

The tint plate 64 is keyed or pinned to the shaft 59, while the polarizing plate 65 is loose upon the shaft 59. Tint plate 60 is loose upon the shaft 58, while the polarizing plate 61 is pinned or keyed to the shaft 58, as shown at 95. By reason of the crossing of the belt 56, the shafts 58 and 59 rotate in opposite directions. Both tint plates follow the rotation of the shaft 59, since the belt 66 causes them to rotate together and since the tint plate 64 is fastened to the shaft 59. Both polarizing plates 61 and 65 follow the rotation of the shaft 58 since the plate 61 is fastened to the shaft 58 and since the belt 67 causes the rotary polarizing discs to rotate together.

The discs shown in Figures 1, 3 and 4 are arranged for the beam of light from the source 25 to shine through the discs at the side of the shafts and belts, in order that such driving means may not interfere with the beam of light.

Suitable projection lenses 68 and 69 are mounted on a standard 70. Shields 71 and 72 respectively protect the lenses 68 and 69 from extraneous light. A crank 73 controls a crank arm 74, which in turn operates a rod 75 that is connected at its ends to shutters 76 and 77, opposite the projection lenses 68 and 69 respectively. Spring means 78 is arranged to provide tension upon the crank arm 74, in order to maintain the shutters in adjusted positions. The rod 75 is arranged to simultaneously open one shutter as the other is being closed, in order to blend beams from the respective projection machines.

In the modification shown in Figures 5 and 6, a rotary disc 79 (which represents a modified form of both the tint plate and the rotary polarizing plate) is rotatably supported on flanged wheels 80 and 81 and driven by a shaft 82, which is connected to the flanged wheel 81. Suitable gear means 83 may be connected to the motor 52 by any skilled mechanic. Guide rollers 84 on a bracket 85 prevent tipping of the disc 79.

When this modification, shown in Figures 5 and 6, is used, the light may shine through any portion of the disc 79 that is not obstructed. This is the reason for driving the disc from the periphery thereof. A different effect is produced by shining the beam through different portions of the disc. A swirling effect is produced when the beam is projected through the center of the disc, and upward and downward effects are produced by projecting the beam through downward moving and upward moving portions of the disc.

In Figure 7 a short wave broadcasting set is suggested at 86. Audio input wires 87 transmit the sound to the set 86. Audio output wires 88 connect the set 86 with a copper plate antenna 89. Spaced from the antenna 89 is a conductive disc 90 of relatively smaller diameter than the width of the antenna plate 89.

In between the antenna 89 and the disc are the glass plates 48. Disposed between these plates is a crystallizing material 49.

In the carrying out of the present process and in the operation of the present apparatus, material that is adapted to crystallize upon hardening is disposed between the plates 48. Rhythmic or other sounds, either produced by a record or by the original instrument or artist, is received by the broadcasting set 86 through the wires 87. Mechanism for transmitting to the set 86 is well known to those skilled in the art.

During the crystallization of the material between the plates 48, the sound is projected from the antenna 89 to the plate 90, the radio frequency waves passing through the plates 48 and producing a definite pattern in the plastic material 49 that is crystallizing. As soon as the crystallization is complete, the pattern is set.

In practice, different time periods of broadcasting are used upon successive plates or slides. Thus, for instance, when the input into the broadcasting set 86 is by means of a record, a certain period of time is used to make each of a series of slides, so that each slide will represent a portion of the record.

In the use of the embodiment shown in Figure 1, the records are played back by means of the phonograph 15 and simultaneously therewith polarized light is passed through the slides and projected upon the screen 12. The slides that respectively represent portions of the records are shown on the screen simultaneously with the playing of the respective portion of the record. Thus, the audience is seeing the pattern produced by the portion of the phonograph record that is being heard. The slides are manually inserted in the holders 36 and 39.

The relatively stationary polarizing medium 42 and the relatively rotary polarizing medium 61 polarize the light beams from the respective projecting machines. The rotating tint discs 60 and 64 color the polarized beams of light, and together with the other mechanism described, project rhythmic, ever-changing color patterns upon the screen, in a kaleidoscopic effect.

Due to the connections of the tint plates and rotary polarizing plates, with the shafts 58 and 59, the tint plates rotate in opposite directions from the rotary polarizing plates 61 and 65.

The slides are alternately projected by the upper and lower projection machines and the blending from one to another is effected by means of the shutters 76 and 77, which are actuated by the crank 73. Thus, there is no break in the continuity of the color designs, but they progress synchronously with the playing of the music that produced the patterns that are shown upon the screen.

In the hereunto appended claims, the word "configuration" is to be interpreted as meaning a form, design, pattern, photograph of a scene, of one or more persons, or a series of such configurations, or any other representation, pattern, form, design, or picture of any nature whatsoever.

While I have illustrated and described what I now regard as the preferred embodiment of my invention, the construction is, of course, subject to modifications without departing from the spirit and scope of my invention. I, therefore, do not wish to restrict myself to the particular form of construction illustrated and described, but desire to avail myself of all modifications which may fall within the scope of the appended claims.

Having thus described my invention, what I claim and desire to secure by Letters Patent is:

1. In a projection means, the combination of a screen, two sources of light, lens means arranged to project light from the sources in beams upon the screen, translucent elements disposed in said beams and containing configurations to be projected on the screen the configurations on said plate conforming to the radio frequency waves of a broadcast, shafts connected to be rotated in opposite directions, rotary light-polarizing elements and rotary tint plates arranged in said beams, the polarizing elements being arranged to be rotated by one of the shafts in one direction and the tint plates being arranged to be rotated by the other shaft in the other direction, and shutter means to blend one beam into another.

2. In a projection means, the combination of a screen, two sources of light, lens means arranged to project light from the sources in beams upon the screen, translucent elements disposed in said beams and containing configurations to be projected on the screen the configurations on said plate conforming to the radio frequency waves of a broadcast, rotary light-polarizing elements and rotary tint plates arranged in said beams, means to rotate the polarizing elements and the tint plates in opposite directions, and shutter means to blend one beam into another.

CECIL A. STOKES.

OSKAR FISCHINGER

Lumigraph (1950)

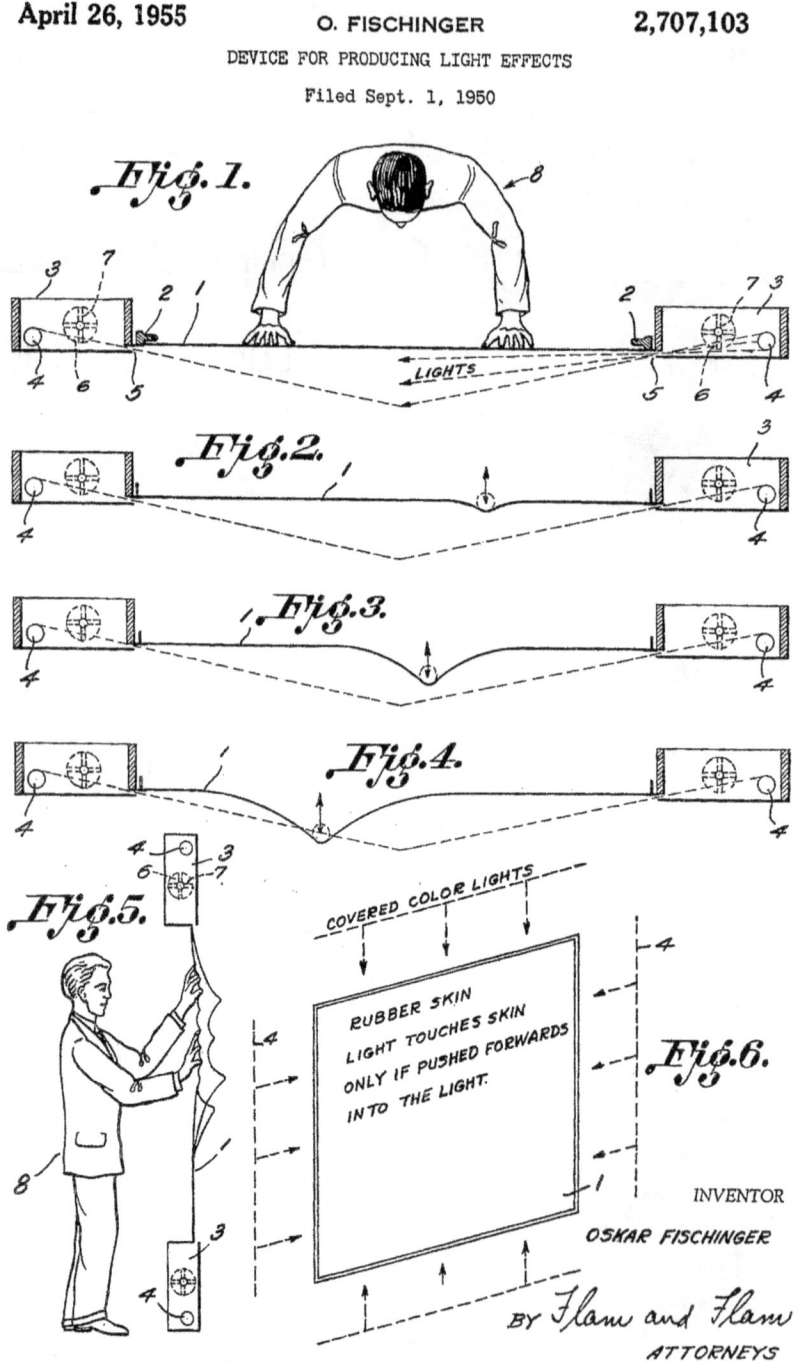

United States Patent Office

2,707,103
Patented Apr. 26, 1955

2,707,103

DEVICE FOR PRODUCING LIGHT EFFECTS

Oskar Fischinger, Los Angeles, Calif.

Application September 1, 1950, Serial No. 182,669

8 Claims. (Cl. 272—10)

This invention relates to an instrument that utilizes light for producing artistic effects. Such instruments may be used, for example, for public performances, as in theatres, or for reproduction by the aid of television, or motion pictures.

It is one of the objects of this invention to provide an instrument that is capable of expressing artistic ideas by the aid of light, either colored or otherwise.

It is another object of this invention to make it possible for a performer to produce, in proper succession and in accordance with his desires, a succession of luminous effects caused by the casting of light on a continually changing succession of prominences or protuberances. In order to produce the desired effects, the protuberances are made to project from a substantially plane surface; and one or more sources of light are directed to produce rays substantially parallel with the plane from which the protuberances rise, or at a slight angle thereto.

It is still another object of this invention to provide an instrument of the character described that permits the performer great latitude in expressing artistic ideas or impressions by the aid of light and shadow, such as may be produced by contrast between colors.

It is still another object of this device to combine the effects of light and sound, and to produce both effects by the same instrumentality.

Referring to the drawings:

Figure 1 is a horizontal, sectional view of an apparatus illustrating one form of the invention;

Figs. 2, 3, and 4 are diagrammatic views, similar to Fig. 1, illustrating the manner in which protuberances may be produced;

Fig. 5 is a vertical section of the apparatus shown in Fig. 1; and

Fig. 6 is a diagram illustrating the principles of the invention.

The important feature of the invention is the use of a taut, flexible element 1 that is preferably of rubber or other elastic material. However, thin fabric of non-elastic material could also be used. For example, a multiplicity of layers of fabric could be utilized. Furthermore, the visible surface of element 1 may be painted in a single color or a multitude of colors; and the paint may be either fluorescent or may include fine reflecting crystals. Alternatively, infra-red or ultra-violet light may be used to stimulate the fluorescent paint. Furthermore, the element may be either wholly or partially transparent.

The element or membrane 1 can be held in the stretched condition by the aid of an appropriate frame structure 2 provided adjacent the edges of the membrane 1. The membrane 1 can, of course, take any desired form. In the present instance, a rectangular form is illustrated, but the invention is not confined to that shape.

Adjacent each of the edges of the frame structure 2 is an enclosure 3. Thus, four such enclosures may be utilized, corresponding to the four sides of the rectangle. In each of these enclosures, a source of light 4 is provided, adapted to project rays through a narrow slit 5. Accordingly, the light emanating from the slits 5 projects in a direction substantially parallel with the plane of the membrane 1, or only at a slight angle thereto. The sources of light may be movable, and may be artificial or natural. They are capable of being controlled as desired, as by switches or shutters. One way to control the color or character of the light is by the aid of adjustable or movable filters.

For this purpose, there is interposed in the beam of light a color wheel 6. Such a color wheel is located in each of the enclosures 3, for intercepting the light from the source 4. It may include a series of filter arms 7, each having areas of different colors. Thus, when the light passes through any one of the filters 7, the filter 7 may produce a plurality of colors. The filter areas may be arranged at different radial distances from the axis of the wheel to produce thin, superposed layers of light of different colors close to the plane surface of element 1.

In order to utilize the instrument, protuberances may be formed in the membrane 1, as by a performer 8. Thus, as shown in Figs. 2, 3, and 4, protuberances are formed of various heights and in various locations on the membrane 1. There are usually a multiplicity of such protuberances. These protuberances may be produced by any appropriate part of the human body, such as the elbows, feet, hands, or fingers; or the performer may project his entire body into the membrane 1. Likewise, he may utilize especially formed implements for producing specific types of protuberances. As the membrane is struck, sounds due to the vibration, therefore, are also produced.

As the wheels 6 rotate, the lights cast upon the protuberances change. Furthermore, since the filter 7 can be arranged to produce a series of different layers of light substantially parallel to the membrane 1, the heights of the protuberances determine the variety and number of colors cast upon them by these sources of light. Furthermore, the performer 8 can operate switches for the control of the light sources 4; and any desired projection of images or light can be cast upon the membrane 1 by an appropriate film projector.

It is obvious that, by the aid of this instrument, a performer can produce startling effects capable of utilization for many purposes, such as advertising, or the like. Great freedom of expression is permitted, since the rubber or elastic medium 1 can be made as large as possible, making it practicable for a plurality of performers to utilize the same instrument. Of course, any arrangement of a plurality of these instruments may be utilized in different angular relations to each other; and mirrors can also be provided, if desired, for permitting the performer to view his performance, or for multiplying the effects of a single member 1.

The production of the protuberances may be achieved mechanically; in fact, instead of protuberances, hollows or recesses may be formed, as by air pressure, or by magnetic means. The protuberances form cone-like reflecting surfaces. The performer may also be accompanied by music. A recording of the unusual and striking light effects may be obtained by photographing the element from the side and, in fact, the contour of these protuberances, viewed from the side or front, may be recorded on a sound track to provide a new form of synthetic music.

Ordinarily, the audience or viewers would be located on one side of the membrane or element 1, and the performer 8 would be on the other side of the membrane or element 1. However, the audience may, of course, be located in such position as to view the protuberances at an angle, instead of directly from the front.

By the term "coating capable of fluorescing," it is meant any material that can be excited to luminescence by light radiations.

The inventor claims:

1. In combination: a normally plane, flexible member capable of distortion out of said plane; a frame upon which the member is stretched; and means for casting light radiations from one or more edges of the member, said light radiations from the edge or edges forming a beam or beams making a small angle with the plane of the member, and adjacent the surface of said member, the light beam or beams being so positioned as to be intercepted by the flexible member when distorted out of its normal plane.

2. In combination: a normally plane, flexible member capable of distortion out of said plane; a frame upon which the member is stretched; means for casting light raditions from one or more edges of the member, said light radiations from the edge or edges forming a beam or beams making a small angle with the plane of the

member. and adjacent the surface of said member, the light beam or beams being so positioned as to be intercepted by the flexible member when distorted out of its normal plane; and means for varying the character of the light radiations.

3. In combination: a frame; a flexible normally plane member stretched by the frame; sources of light adjacent at least some of the edges of said member; and an enclosure for each source providing a slit near the surface of the member, said slit casting a beam adjacent the plane of said member, and so positioned as to be intercepted by the flexible member when the flexible member is distorted out of said plane.

4. In combination: a frame; a flexible normally plane member stretched by the frame; sources of light adjacent at least some of the edges of said member; an enclosure for each source providing a slit near the surface of the member, said slit casting a beam adjacent the plane of said member; and so positioned as to be intercepted by the flexible member when the flexible member is distorted out of said plane, and a changeable color filter interposed between the source and the slit.

5. The combination as set forth in claim 3, with the addition of a fluorescent layer on the member.

6. The combination as set forth in claim 4, with the addition of a fluorescent layer on the member.

7. In combination: a normally plane, flexible member capable of distortion out of the plane of the member; a frame upon which the member is stretched; and means for casting beams of light from the edges of the frame and close to, but not received on, said normally plane surface, and so positioned as to be intercepted by the flexible member when said flexible member is distorted out of the normal plane of said flexible member.

8. In combination: a normally plane, flexible member capable of distortion out of the plane of the member; a frame upon which the member is stretched; and means for casting a plurality of layers of light beams of different colors close to, but spaced from, the normally plane surface, and so positioned as to be intercepted by the flexible member when said flexible member is distorted out of the normal plane of said flexible member.

References Cited in the file of this patent

UNITED STATES PATENTS

613,703	Mellinger	Nov. 8, 1898
830,834	Hudson	Sept. 11, 1906
1,140,418	Talke	May 25, 1915
1,164,816	Huston	Dec. 21, 1915
1,480,375	Cristadoro	Jan. 8, 1924
1,698,178	Van Deventer	Jan. 8, 1929
2,196,423	Musaphia	Apr. 9, 1940
2,212,642	Jackson	Aug. 27, 1940

FOREIGN PATENTS

217,158	Great Britain	1924

PATENT NUMBER CHRONOLOGY

patent no.	filed/issued	inventor	page
000186298	1876/1877	Bainbridge	10
000547359	1894/1895	Rimington	16
000667541	1900/1901	Loring	28
001308512	1917/1919	Taylor	48
001323943	1916/1919	Wilcox	34
001385944	1919/1921	Hallock-Greenewalt	92
001388706	1917/1921	Hector	58
001432552	1917/1922	Hector	64
001432553	1927/1929*	Hector	72
001460264	1919/1923	Miles	108
001481132	1918/1924	Hallock-Greenewalt	99
re016825	1924/1927		
001484795	1923/1924	Munsell	133
001577854	1921/1926	Vinageras	114
001578373	1924/1926	Schmeer	138
001651860	1923/1927	Adler	110
001728860	1927/1929	Hector	80
001749011	1924/1930	Wilfred	142
001758589	1927/1930	Wilfred	152
001783789	1928/1930	Hector	87
001790903	1929/1931	Craig	168
001891216	1930/1932	Hough	174
001908203	1930/1933	Wilfred	159
001973454	1931/1934	Wilfred	163
002118264	1934/1938	Nanfeldt	196
002292172	1940/1942	Stokes	204
002707103	1950/1955	Fischinger	210

* indices a renewed date, but without revision.